THEN & NOW®

FLUSHING

OPPOSITE: Main Street, seen here in one of the earliest photographs taken of Flushing in 1870, was just a narrow dirt-covered lane that ended at Jamaica Avenue (Kissena Boulevard). Looking north toward Amity Street (Roosevelt Avenue), the tracks of the Flushing and North Shore Railroad visibly cross the middle of the scene. On the west side of the street is a small row of stores. The largest establishment, on the corner of Grove Street (Fortieth Road), belonged to John Titus Van De Water—dealer in choice groceries, provisions, foreign and domestic fruits, hardware, woodenware, and crockery.

THEN & NOW®

FLUSHING

Jason D. Antos

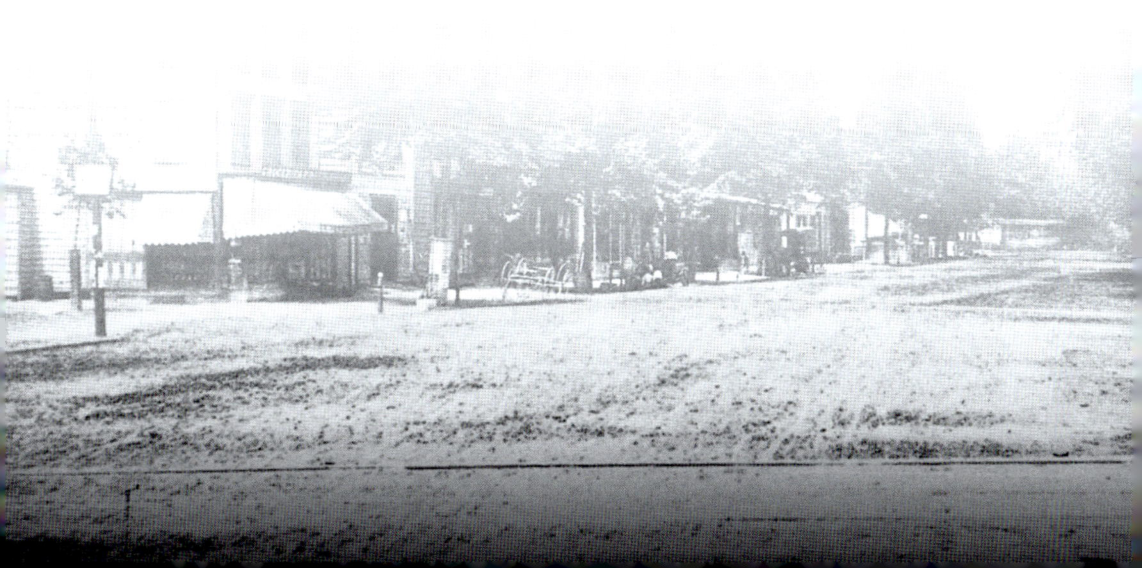

for Vincent F. Seyfried

ISBN 978-0-7385-7257-4

Library of Congress Control Number: 2009936162

Published by Arcadia Publishing
Charleston, South Carolina

Printed in the United States of America

Then and Now is a registered trademark and is used under license from Salamander Books Limited

For all general information contact Arcadia Publishing at:
Telephone 843-853-2070
Fax 843-853-0044
E-mail sales@arcadiapublishing.com
For customer service and orders:
Toll-Free 1-888-313-2665

Visit us on the Internet at www.arcadiapublishing.com

On the Front Cover: Shown is a view of a brick and cobblestoned Main Street looking north in the year 1920. Trolley tracks of the New York and Queens County Railway and New York and North Shore Traction Company lead the way to Broadway (Northern Boulevard) where E. B. Simmons's Flushing Hotel stood at the head of Main Street. Originally built on top of a lake, the hotel was demolished in 1927 so that Benjamin Franklin Keith and Edward F. Albee could construct a palatial Vaudeville theatre in its footprints. Today that theatre, the former RKO Keith's, stands as an abandoned relic and symbol of Flushing's struggle to preserve its fleeting historical past. (Courtesy of the Queens Borough Public Library, Long Island Division, Frederick J. Weber Photographs.)

On the Back Cover: Flushing was nothing more than a country village when this photograph was taken on October 24, 1902. A lone pedestrian gets ready to walk into town across the one-lane bridge, (the fourth version to be built since 1801), which also accommodated a trolley. The bridge's instability is confirmed by a sign hanging overhead that reads, "Driving Over This Bridge Faster Than A Walk is Forbidden Under Penalty of Law—Trolley Cars Must Go Slow!" In 1906, the span was replaced yet again. (Courtesy Brian Merlis/Brooklynpix.com.)

Contents

Foreword

Tell outsiders you're from Queens, and they will probably envision something linked to Flushing. Perhaps they associate the borough with the Unisphere or the Mets. Maybe they know it as a birthplace of religious freedom, home to the U.S. Open, or host of two World's Fairs. Amazingly, each connects to the same neighborhood, historically left shivering in Manhattan's shadow.

Tourists who skip Flushing miss many of the city's truest treasures. Take, for example, the Anglo-Dutch home of John Bowne, recognized among the earliest champions for the right to pray freely in colonial America. Nearby stands the Quaker Meeting House, one of the nation's oldest places of worship. Film buffs may recognize the RKO Keith's facade from its 1920s heyday, or the towering New York State Pavilion from its *Men in Black* cameo.

For the many structures that survived the decades, however, Flushing also boasts a past that can no longer be witnessed on its blocks. Instead, we turn to the types of photographs that grace these pages, preserving for posterity the long lost backdrops of prior generations. Author Jason Antos has compiled a wide-ranging array of streetscapes to document how the area has transformed so remarkably with time. Those accustomed to the modern version will no doubt be awed by its development. After browsing these images, their next Main Street trip may stir nostalgia for stagecoaches, trolley cars, and brick roads.

Anyone wishing to learn about Flushing, though, is advised not to cap his or her research with this book. Like any locale steeped in antiquity, the area begs for eyewitness exploration—a jog through Flushing Meadows-Corona Park or stroll through the Queens Botanical Garden. Journey where millions before you enjoyed field trips to the Hall of Science, concerts in Flushing Town Hall, and banquets at Terrace on the Park. These are hallmarks of a place that has remained culturally vibrant through several incarnations.

Remember, too, that failing to appreciate history will foster its disappearance. When a generation neglects its ancestors' legacy, allowing great monuments of yesteryear to crumble, we forever lose the perspective of our predecessors. Conversely, visiting these sites adds to our understanding of the past and encourages our leaders to save them from the wrecking ball. Your actions today could eliminate future needs to update *Flushing: Then & Now*—because the best of "then" will remain "now," just a No. 7 train ride away.

—Nicholas Hirshon

Acknowledgments

Many contributed their time, knowledge, and patience to this work on the history of Flushing. I am grateful to John Hyslop, Judith Todman, and everyone of the Long Island Division at the Central Branch of the Queens Borough Public Library. Brian Merlis and Ron Marzlock supplied information from their colossal historical archives of Brooklyn and Queens materials and were always available to answer questions and provide assistance. Thank you to Erin Vosgien at Arcadia. Thanks to James Driscoll and Richard J. Hourahan of the Queens Historical Society and Alison McKay of the Bayside Historical Society for their support and enthusiasm. I am indebted to Nicholas Hirshon of the *New York Daily News* and also to the late Julian Wager who spent his valuable time proofreading my work. Lastly to my family and friends, and of course, to the people of Queens for their support; they make efforts like this book worthwhile. All "now" photographs were taken by the author, and most of the "then" images, unless otherwise credited, are part of his private collection.

The following sources were helpful in preparing this book and can be utilized for further reading and study: *Queens, N.Y. in Early Photographs* by Vincent F. Seyfried and William Asadorian; *The Lawrence Family Letters of Willow Bank, Flushing, New York 1846 to 1896* by John Hooper Tennent IV and Marjorie Beverly Tennent; and *Flushing: Postcards of America* by James Driscoll (Arcadia Publishing). These next three titles are out of print but can be found at the Central Library of the Queens Borough Public Library in Jamaica. They are the earliest historical works compiled on Flushing Village. *Flushing, Past and Present: A Historical Sketch* by Rev. Giles Henry Mandeville (1860); *History of the Town of Flushing* by Rev. Harvey D. Waller (1899); and finally *Olde Flushing* by Harriet Dondero Lawson (1952). All were indispensable and should be read by all those interested in local history.

Introduction

There is always difficulty when researching the exact origins of any historic person or place; the town of Flushing is no exception to that rule.

Her name was Nelly, a black slave under the ownership of Capt. Daniel Braine, who was hired to work as a household servant in the home of Jeremiah Vanderbilt, clerk of the Town of Flushing. One day, Nelly fell in love with a half–African American, half–Native American man who wanted to marry her. Vanderbilt, fearing that he would become deprived of Nelly's services if she and her lover ran away from Flushing, offered to hire him as a laborer on his estate so that they could be together. Vanderbilt even arranged to give them a piece of land on which they could build a home and raise a family. Fearing that he too would become enslaved, the young Native American, most likely a Matinecock, abandoned Flushing and Nelly, never to return. Feeling betrayed, Nelly blamed Vanderbilt for the destroyed romance. She took her revenge on October 22, 1789, just 12 days after Pres. George Washington's tour of Flushing. Nelly waited for the Vanderbilt family to leave before she, with the help of another slave girl named Sarah, set fire to the attic filled with hay. Nelly and Sarah ran away, and within minutes, the home, containing every single vital historical record of Flushing and its first settlers, was incinerated and lost forever. The following year, Attorney General Aaron Burr prosecuted Nelly and her young accomplice. Sarah was released because she was very young. Nelly was, however, sentenced to death and hung soon after.

And so, the first property owners and dates of the area's discovery are uncertain and still debated 221 years later. From what has been gathered, we know the following to be certain: Adriaen Block, a Dutch private trader, first observed the area on his ship, the *Onrust,* in 1614 as he made his way past Flushing Bay heading to the Long Island Sound. The Dutch also were the first to chart the area in 1628. Legend has it that a cartographer aboard an exploration ship sent to map out the land by the Dutch West India Company saw a familiar resemblance between the area and his hometown of Vlissingen located in Holland. As a result, he labeled the area as such.

The word *Vlissingen* means "Salt Meadow," in Dutch. In the early 1640s, the Dutch took control of the northeastern territory of the New World and renamed it New Netherlands. Their main seat of power became New Amsterdam, now known as Manhattan.

The English first arrived in the area around 1644, and by 1645, the first settlers Thomas Farrington, John Townsend, Thomas Stiles, Thomas Saull, and John Lawrence obtained a patent for land "at the mouth of the creek now commonly called and known by the name of Vlissingen Creek and to begin at ye westward part thereof and so to run eastward as far as Matthew Garretson's Bay."

The town of Flushing was first incorporated on October 10, 1645, by order of New Netherlands governor William Kieft.

It also declared that the settlers were entitled to "have and enjoy liberty of conscience according to the customs of Holland, without molestation or disturbance."

This declaration would soon change. On December 27, 1657, a total of 30 members of the community led by town clerk Edward Hart signed the *Flushing Remonstrance*. It denounced Gov. Peter Stuyvesant's law, which prohibited Quakers the right to practice their religion. Tobias Feake, sheriff of Flushing, brought the document before Stuyvesant who angrily banged his wooden leg and ordered the sheriff arrested. The *Flushing Remonstrance* would become the first document to defend freedom of religion in American history.

New Amsterdam was renamed New York after the English conquered the Dutch in 1683. It was the Duke of York who organized New York into shires and ridings. The charter, in which the name Flushing is used for the first time, was renewed on March 24, 1685, stating, "All that contain within the Town in North Riding of Yorkshire, upon the Island of Nassau (Long Island) be called by the name of Flushing."

At the start of the 19th century, roads like Main Street were nothing but rugged, hilly paths with a handful of houses scattered along their lengths. What is now Northern Boulevard was so narrow that two stagecoaches could only pass one another with great difficulty. No roads crossed over the swamps near Little Neck to the east, and it was difficult to cross the marshy land to the south and west of the village. This made Flushing a virtual island. A traveler attempting to go west along the north shore of Long Island to Manhattan would find the way blocked and would have to take the road south to Alley Pond, pick up the road to Jamaica, then pass through Brooklyn to the East River to board a ferry bound for Manhattan. Since no bridge spanned Flushing Creek until 1801, small ferries transported people across. Two African Americans, James Rantus and Thomas Smith, operated the first ferry service for many years. Born into slavery, Rantus was the servant of John Aspinwall and would live until 111 years old. He became the first unofficial historian of Flushing, and it is to him that we owe the preservation of many interesting moments in the town's history. The one that everyone enjoyed hearing was the day that Pres. George Washington visited on October 10, 1789, along with Vice Pres. John Adams. They visited the Prince Nurseries, which despite their worldwide fame failed to impress the commander in chief. A huge celebration was held at the intersection of Main Street and Northern Boulevard underneath a tent where a sumptuous meal was prepared. "The locals tried their best to be respectful with the use of a single cannon salute," Washington wrote in his diary.

There are many secrets in Flushing now covered over by the decades of progress and building in the forever-expanding borough of Queens. North of the village was Farrington's Neck, an open meadow with several small rivers and lakes including a natural spring. Today the spring, which was rich in iron, now lays buried beneath asphalt, body shops, and the Whitestone Expressway.

The Flushing of old is gone now. Names like Bowne, Prince, Lawrence, Parsons, Garretson, and Bloodgood have long since parted. The old streets of Lincoln, Grove, Locust, and Washington were replaced in 1916, when the city adopted the Philadelphia numbering system. The palatial riverside estates with their multi-acre lawns have been torn down and gutted to make way for factories and the smell of asphalt plants.

A poem written by Mortimer Cheshire Sr. in the early 1930s titled *The Flushing That Used to Be* captured the essence of the changing times:

> Remember the days before the trolley cars came, and you stayed in old Flushing at night? Say didn't Broadway look fine, old Pal, Lit up by the corner light? And between you and I there's a tender spot left, in the heart of both you and me. When we think of the good old times we had, In the Flushing that used to be.

—Jason D. Antos
Whitestone, New York
2010

CHAPTER 1

Flushing in Olden Times

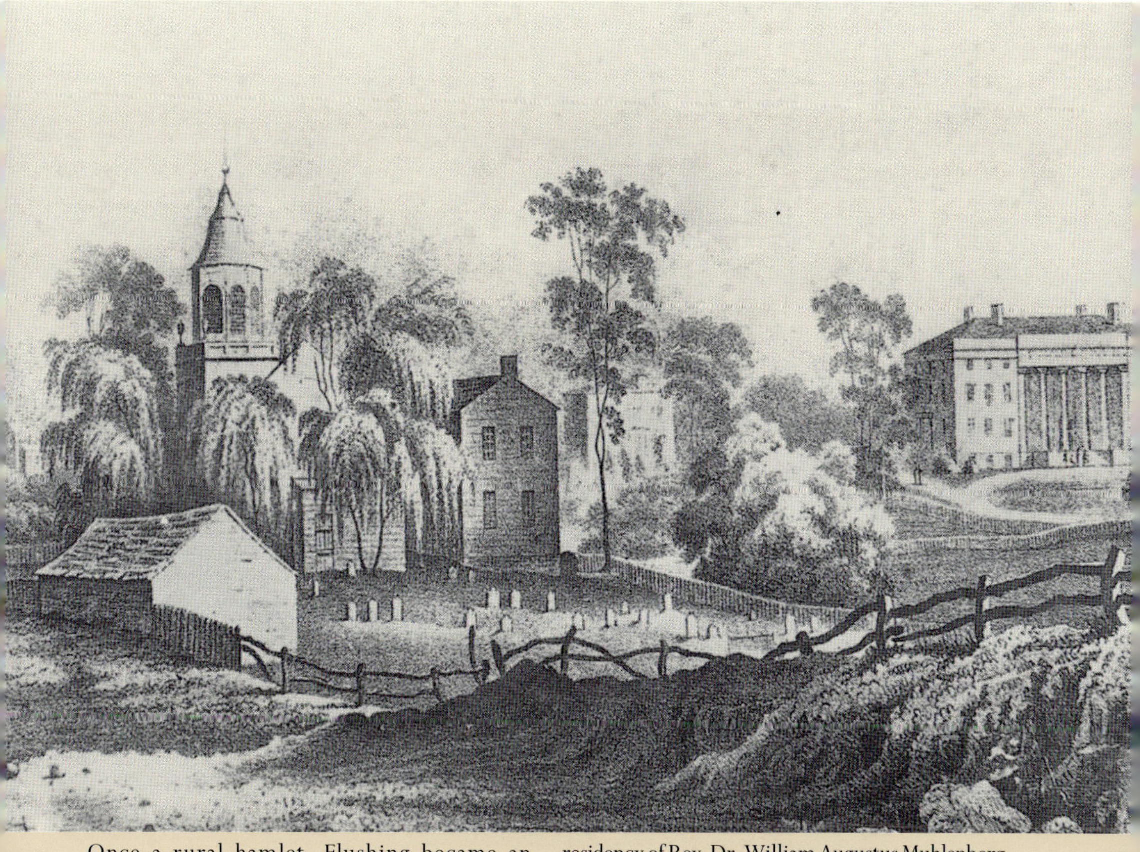

Once a rural hamlet, Flushing became an incorporated village on April 15, 1837. This lithograph created around 1840 looks east from Lawrence Street (College Point Boulevard) up Locust Street (Thirty-ninth Avenue) to Main Street. On the left is St. George's Episcopal Church, the residency of Rev. Dr. William Augustus Muhlenberg and Reverend Thorne is at center, and the Flushing Institute is on the right. At this time there were no sidewalks, paved roads, or public street lighting at night. Gaslights would not appear until 1856.

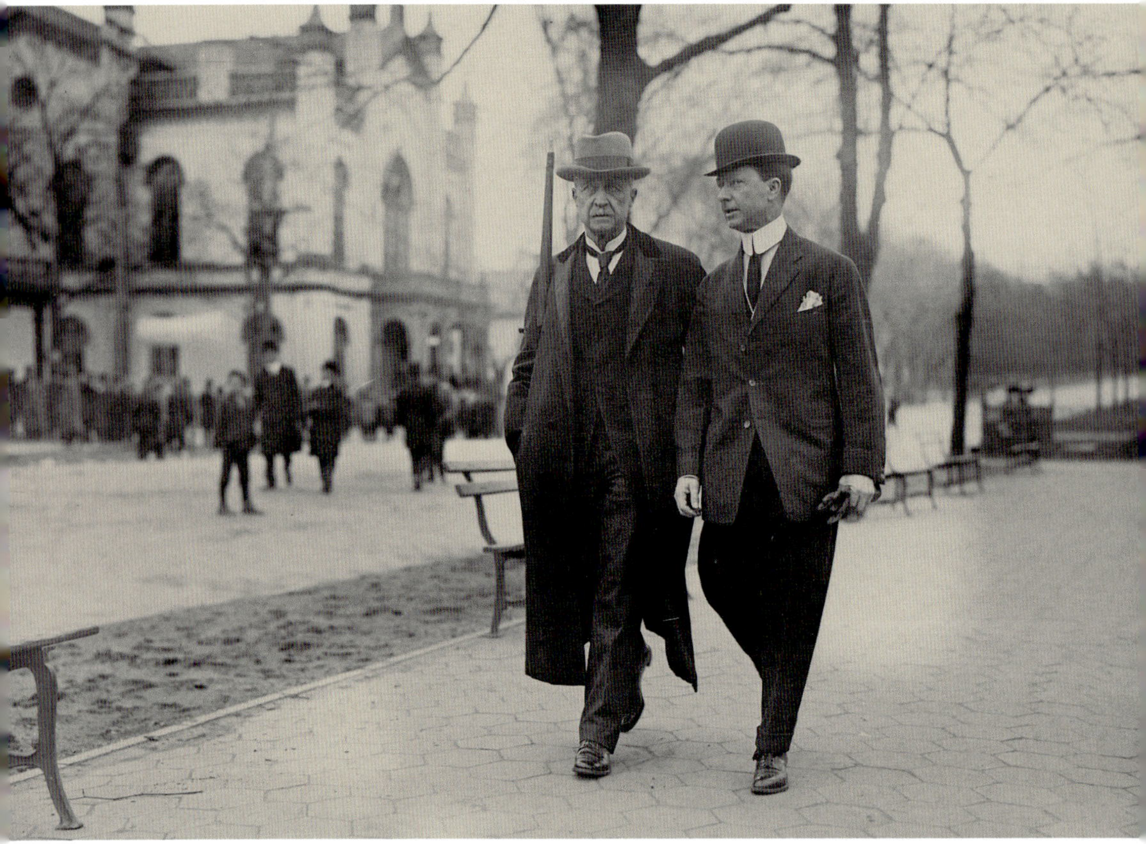

In December 1909, the trial of the century was held at the Flushing Courthouse. Thorton Jenkins Hains and his brother Peter Hains Jr. were arrested for the cold-blooded shooting of William E. Annis, a high-profile magazine editor and Flushing native, after he was caught having an alleged affair with Peter's wife, Claudia Libbey. Their father, a powerful engineer named Gen. Peter Conover Hains, at left, is seen here walking with Thorton, right, after his son's acquittal. Peter, however, was not so lucky, he received eight years for manslaughter. (Courtesy of the Library of Congress/George Grantham Baines Collection.)

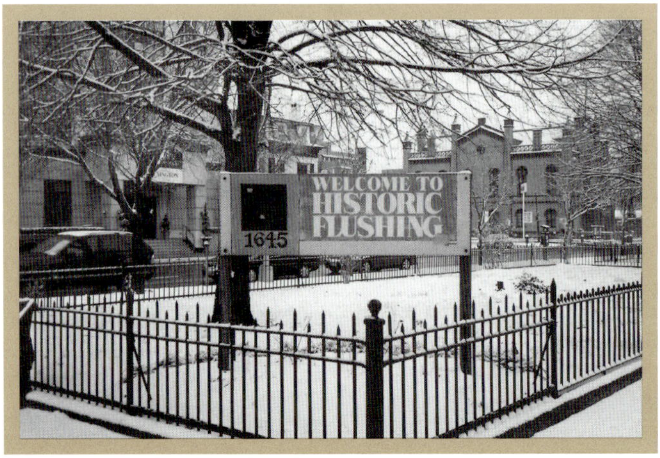

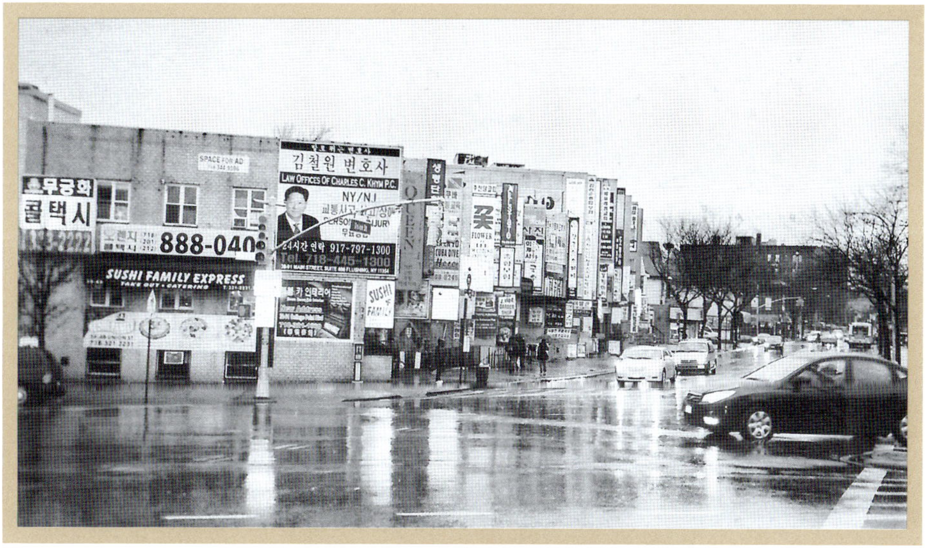

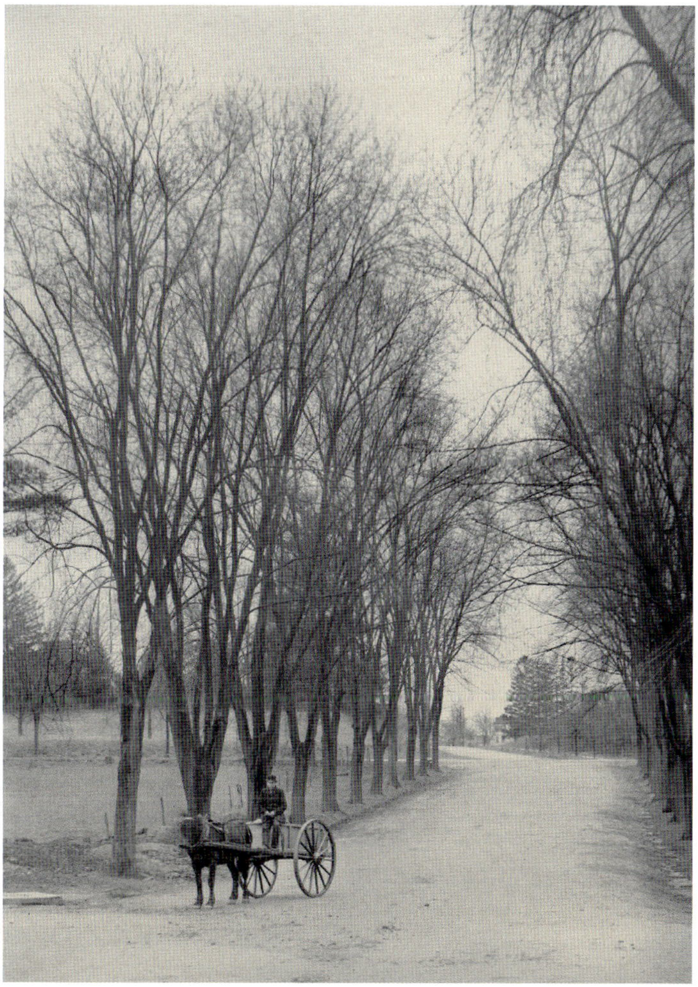

Union Street looking north toward what was called Whitestone Avenue in 1900 is a perfect example of how rural Flushing was at the turn of the century. The same view today shows a stark contrast with rows of Korean, Japanese, and Chinese-owned businesses offering everything from travel agencies, bookstores, law firms, karaoke bars, sushi restaurants, and doctor offices. The neighborhood saw a massive influx of immigrants from Asia in the early 1980s.

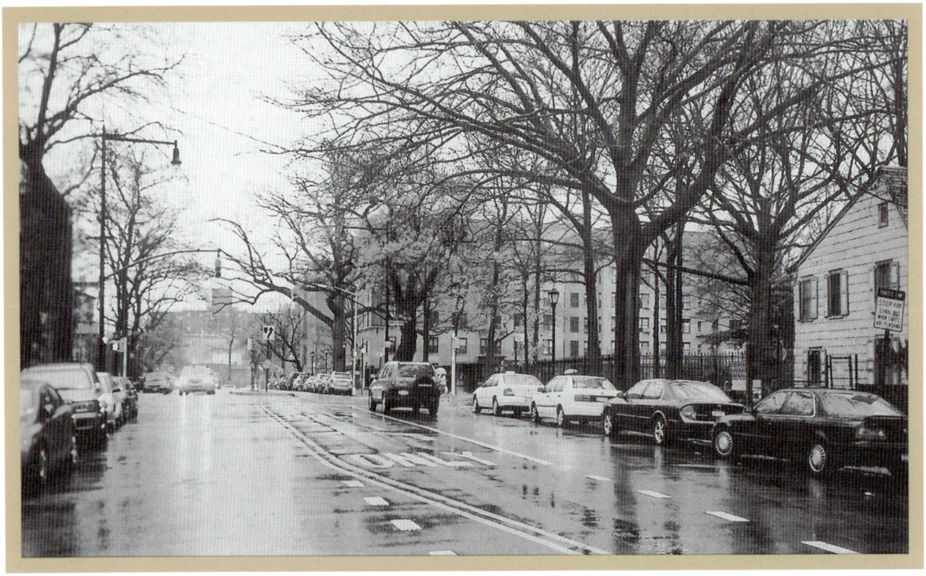

Bowne Avenue (Bowne Street) was a narrow dirt road cutting through a wooded area occupied by the residency of John Bowne, on the right, and the two large trees—under which George Fox, founder of the Society of Friends, preached to the masses over 250 years ago—on the left. Known as the "Fox Oaks," they were destroyed by lighting in 1841 and 1861. Today a stone marker and an apartment building sit in the place of the once-mighty white oaks. (Courtesy of the Nassau County Department of Parks, Recreation, and Museums, Photograph Archives Center.)

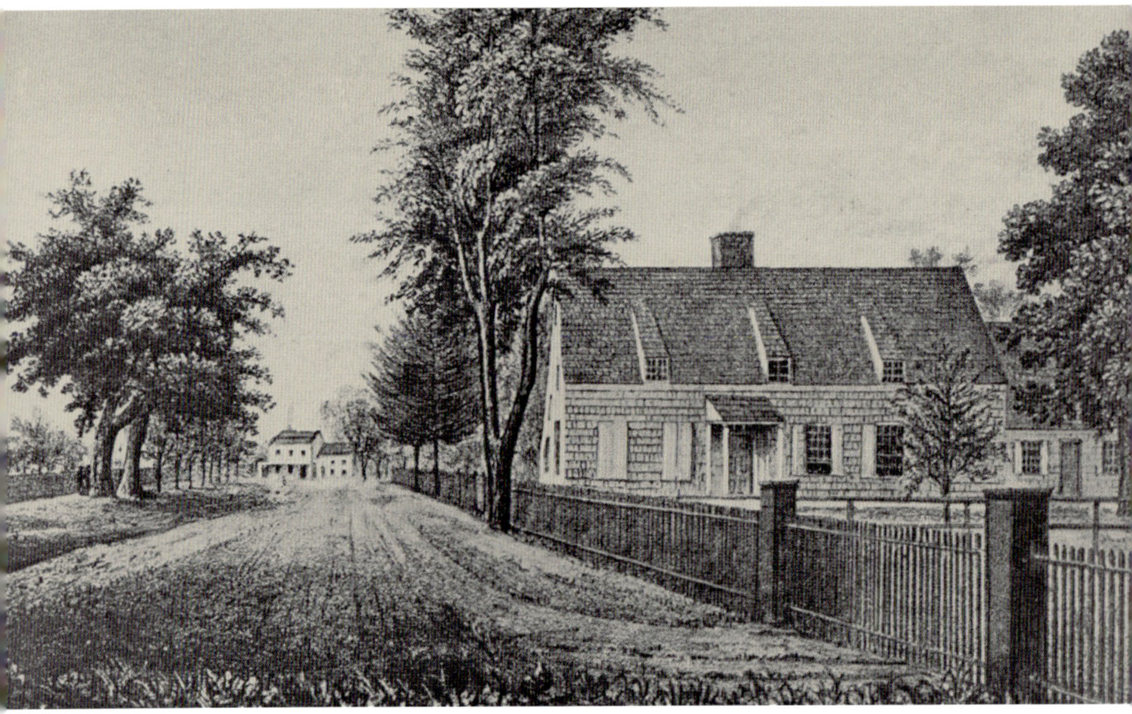

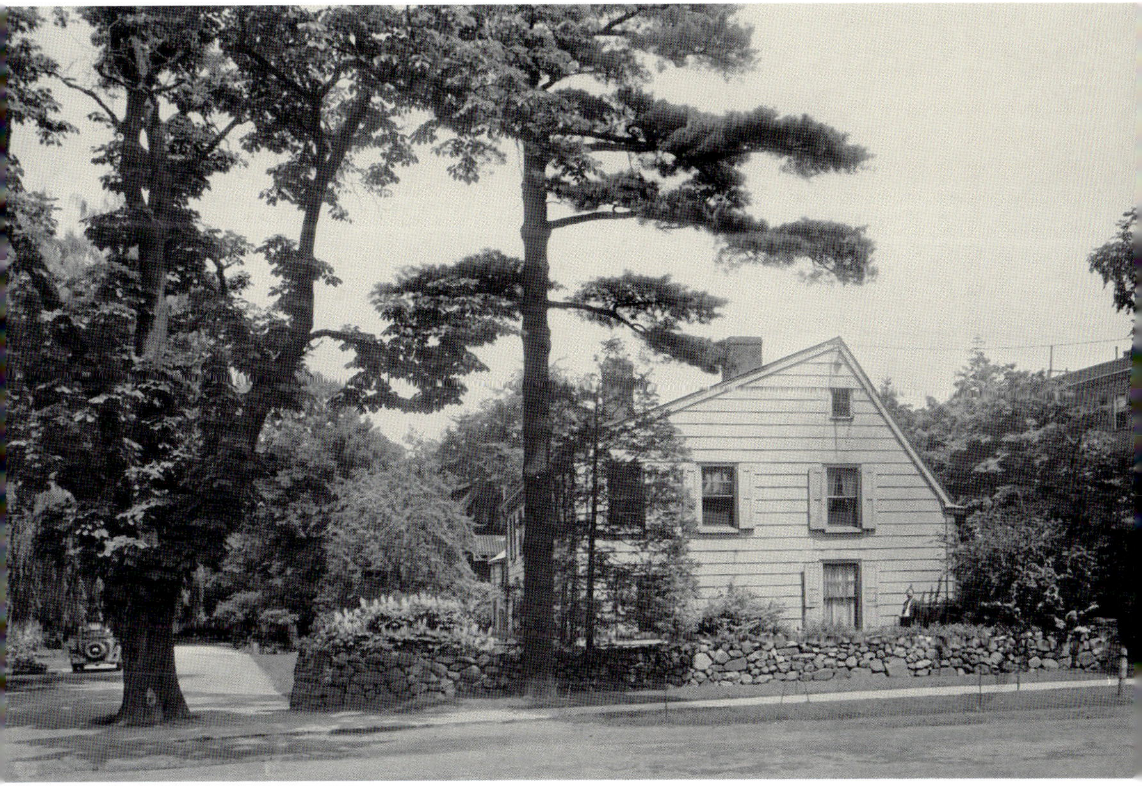

John Bowne constructed his home in 1661 on property that was purchased in 1651 from the Matinecock Native Americans. The Bowne House is the oldest standing structure in Flushing. His wife, Hannah Feake, was a devout Quaker and, through her influence, Bowne embraced the new religion himself. Practicing the Quaker belief was deemed illegal by Gov. Peter Stuyvesant causing the townspeople in 1657 to create the *Flushing Remonstrance*. It was here that Bowne courageously invited the Friends of Flushing to hold their religious meetings. (Courtesy of the Library of Congress.)

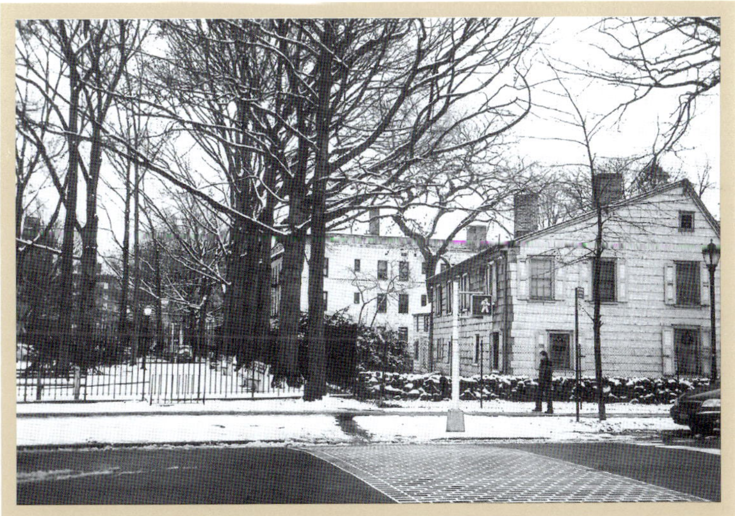

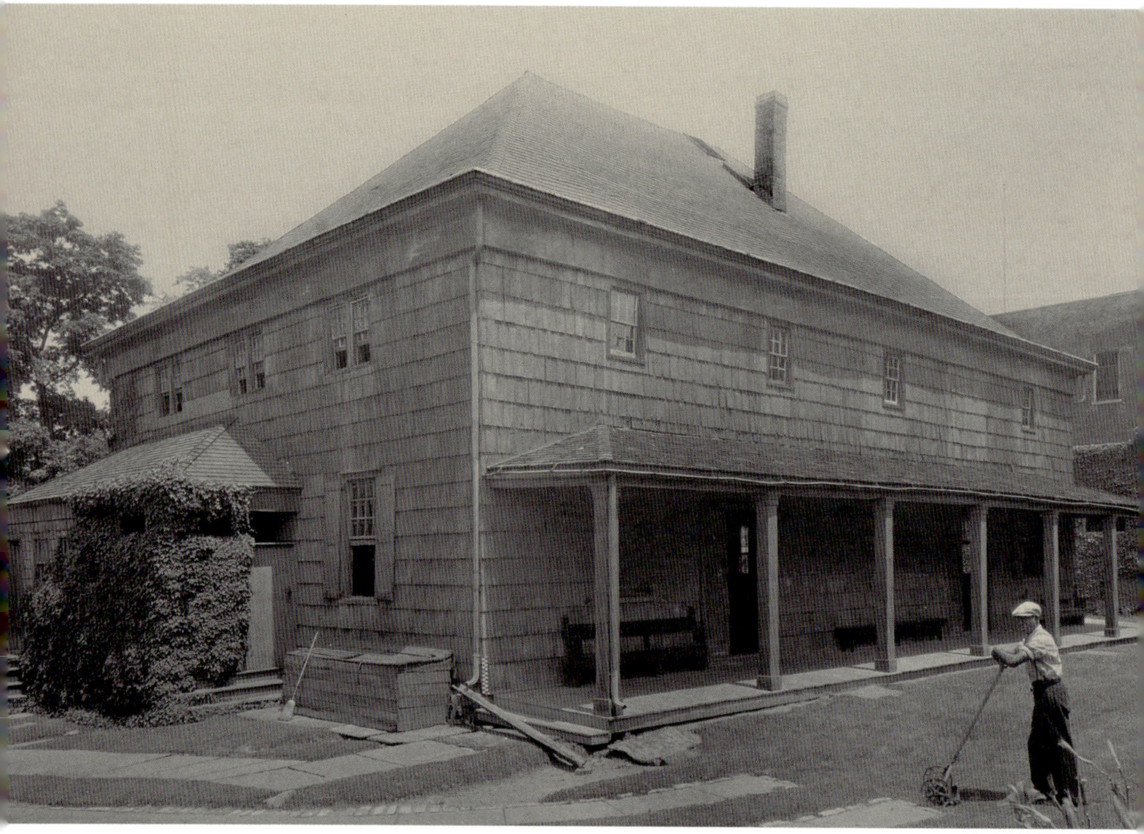

In 1663, restrictions on the Quaker religion were removed by the Dutch West India Company. Still in use today, the Quaker Meeting House, located at 137-16 Northern Boulevard, was erected by the Religious Society of Friends or Hicksites in 1694. It was the very first house of worship in the village. Three acres were purchased from John Ware for the site. The first document announcing the new house of worship was written in 1693 as follows: "It was agreed by John Bowne to employ workmen to get timber they shall see fitting ye house for raising next month." The first meeting was held on November 24, 1694. (Courtesy of the Library of Congress.)

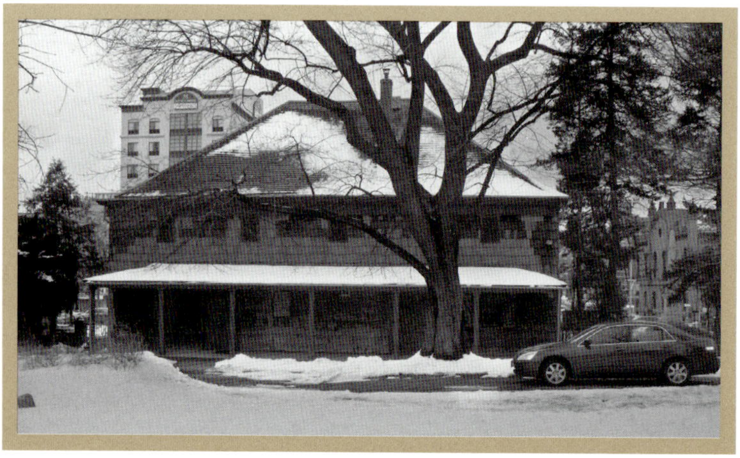

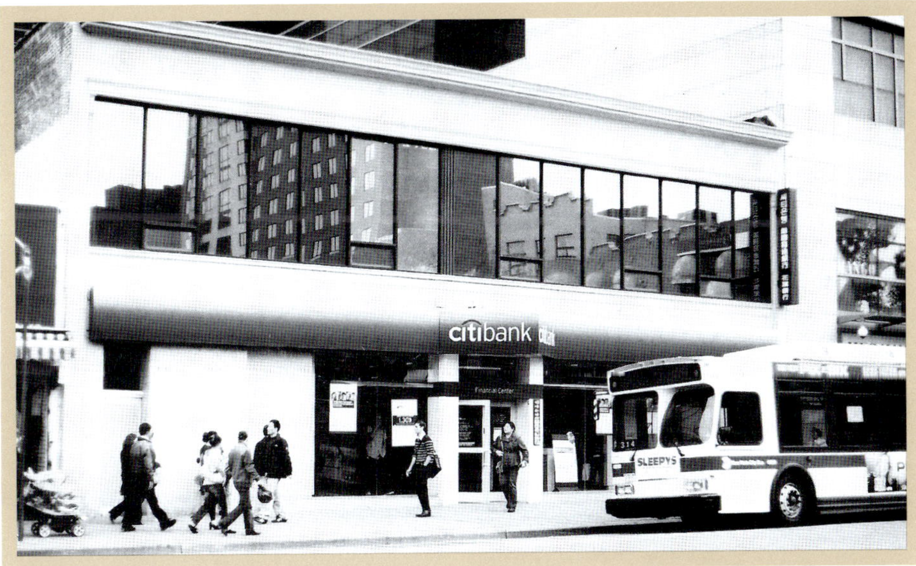

Garretson Homestead was located on Main Street directly opposite St. George's Episcopal Church. Owned by Garret R. Garretson and his wife, Eliza Bloodgood, the home was erected in 1659 and stood on the east side of Main Street between Lincoln Street (Thirty-eighth Avenue) and Locust Street (Thirty-ninth Avenue) with a large lawn. The interior featured two kitchens, six bedrooms, a living room, and dinning room. Garretson was a specialist employed by the Prince Nurseries. A branch of Citibank now occupies the site of the homestead, which was leveled in 1911.

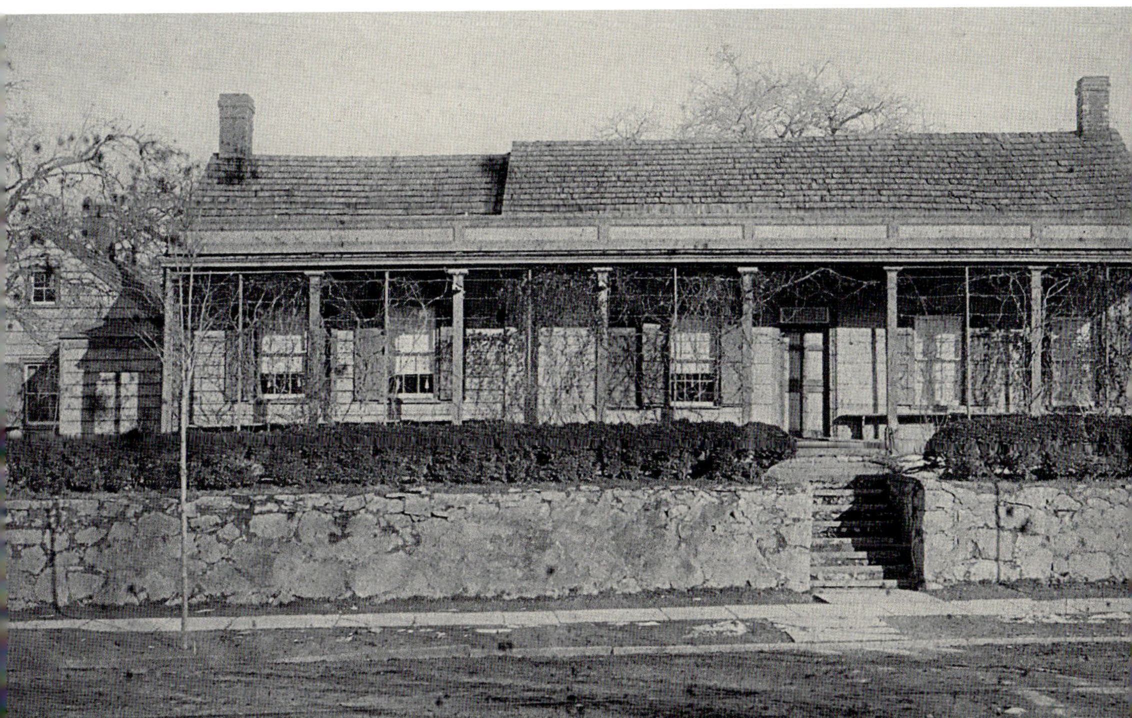

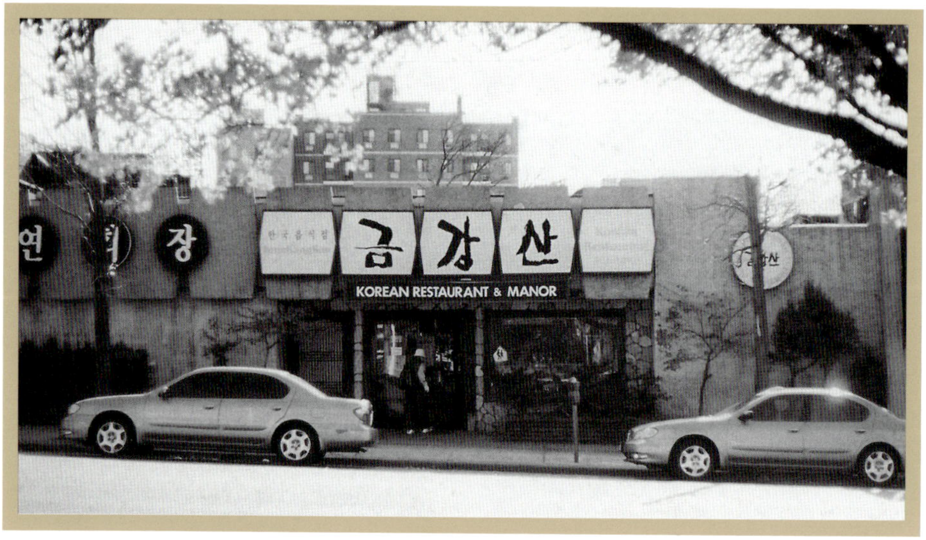

The Aspinwall House, which stood at 138-28 Northern Boulevard, was built by sea captain John Aspinwall, a founder of St. George's Episcopal Church, in 1762. Aspinwall's home was used as a headquarters for British officers during the American Revolution. During the Civil War, it was used as a station on the Underground Railroad for runaway slaves seeking passage to Canada. A secret tunnel connected the property with the Bowne House just a few blocks away. In 1846, it became the residence of Dr. Bloodgood. The house was demolished in the early 1950s and is now a Korean restaurant. (Courtesy of the Queens Borough Public Library, Long Island Division, Eugene L. Armbruster Photographs.)

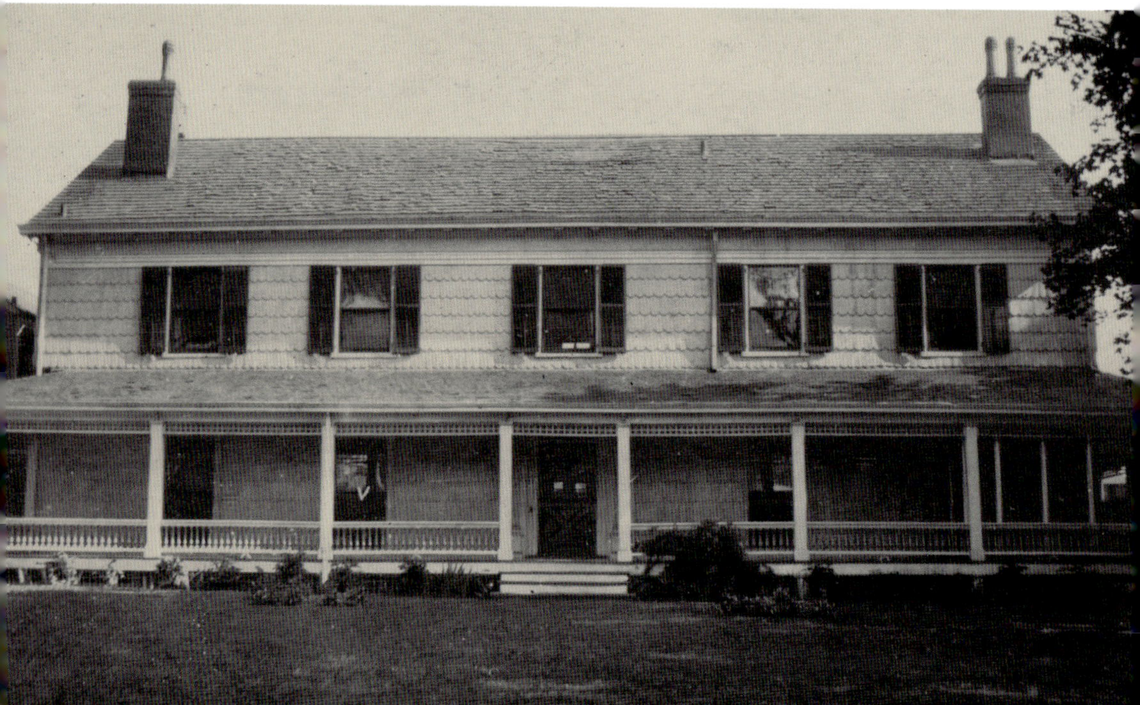

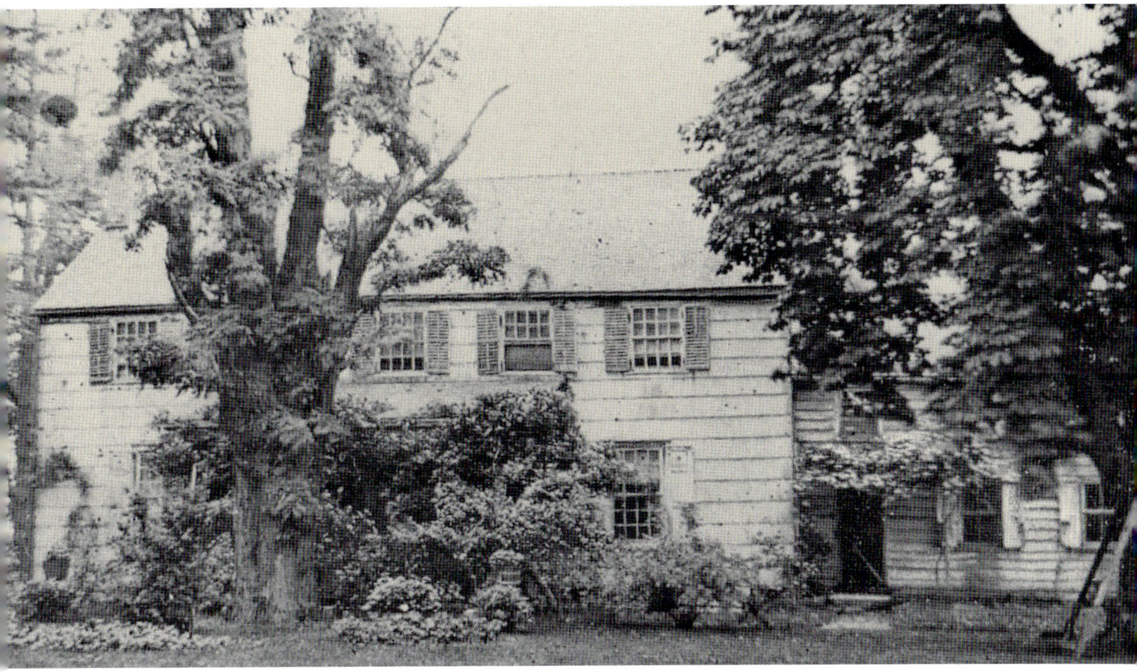

The Frame family, another notable name of early Flushing, erected this house in 1790 on what is today Francis Lewis Boulevard, just north of Crocheron Avenue. In 1902, the house and its 90-acre spread were purchased by the Van Dyke family who occupied it until 1905. The property was demolished and today is a heavily populated business and residential area known as Bayside West. A car wash now occupies the site.

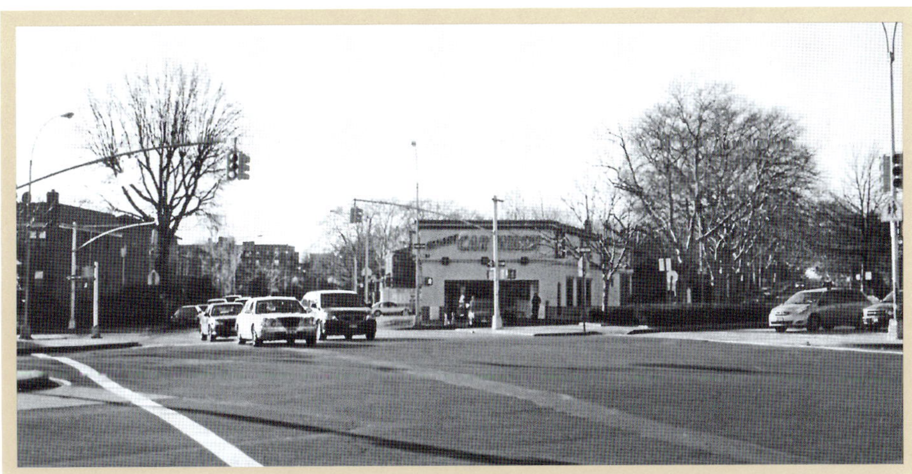

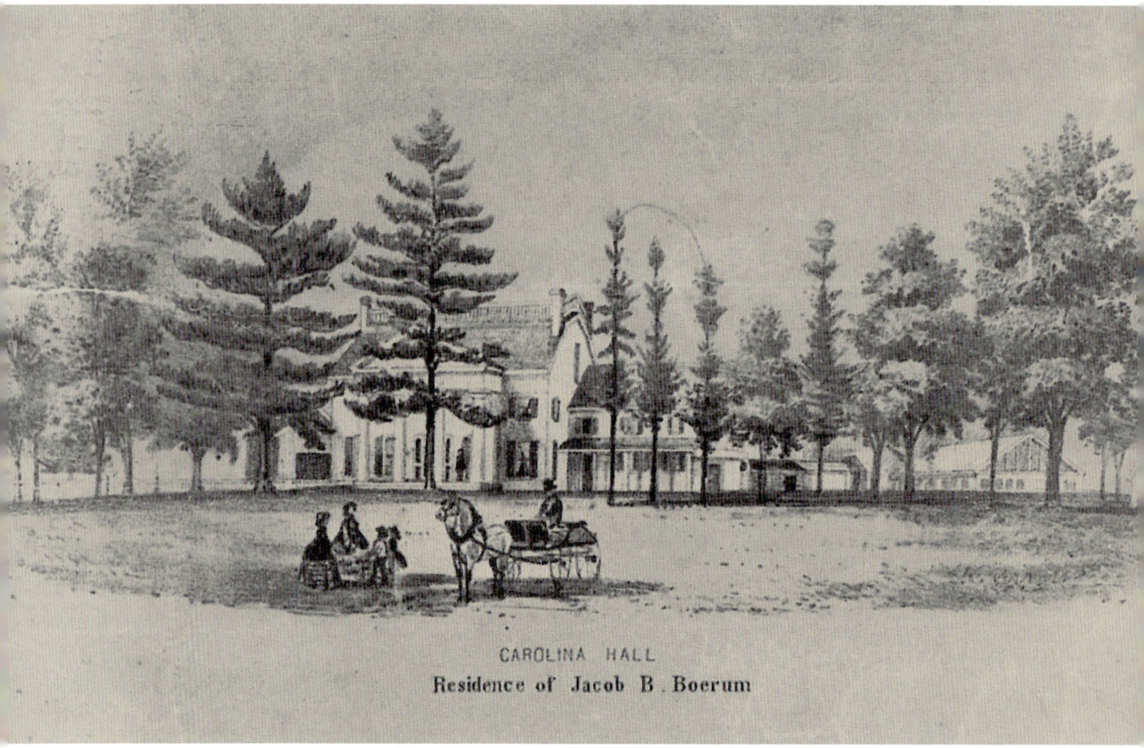

Carolina Hall, constructed in the 1840s by merchant Jacob R. Valk, was located at 149th Place and Thirty-fifth Avenue. The centerpiece of what was a 60-acre estate was also the residency of Jacob B. Boerum and featured a Southern-style design inspired from Valk's hometown of Charleston, South Carolina. Boerum was superintendent of the town of Flushing in the 1850s.

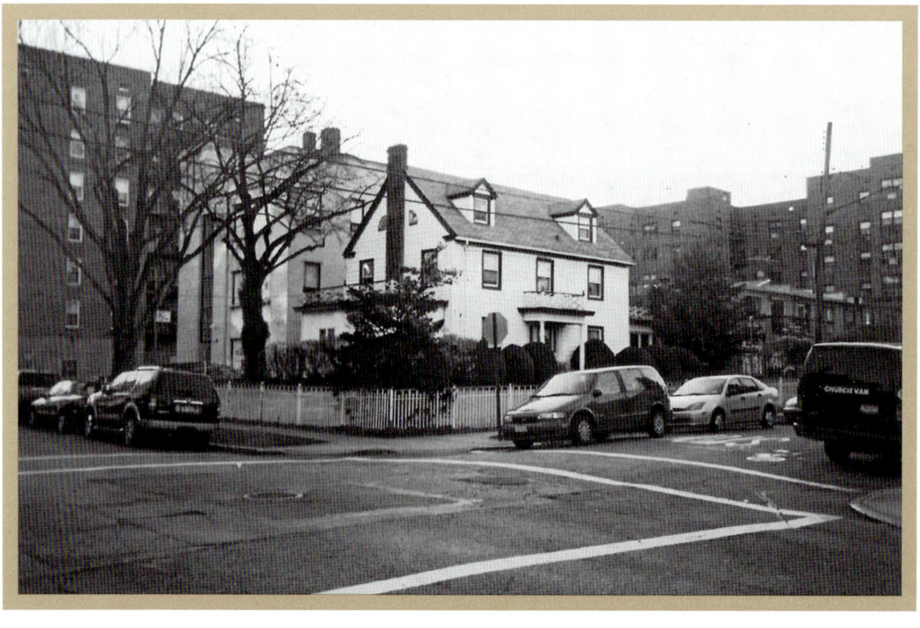

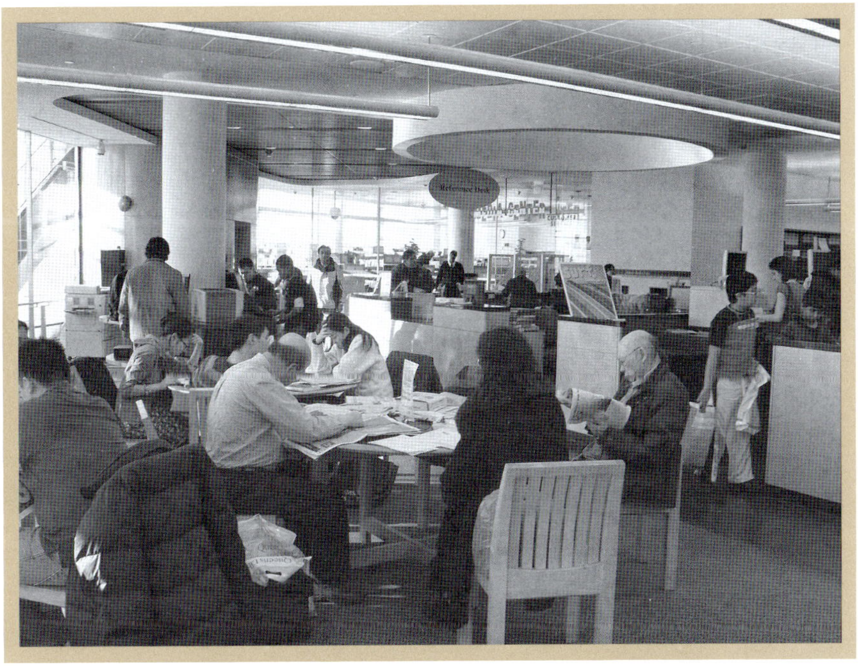

Founded in 1858 as a subscription service, the Flushing Library was incorporated on April 17, 1869. Mary Ann Shaw, the principal of the Flushing Female Association, helped to establish it as a free circulation library in 1884. In December 1901, the library joined the Queens Borough Public Library. In 1904, a new building funded by Andrew Carnegie was constructed at Kissena Boulevard and Main Street. The building seen here opened in 1906 and stood until 1955. Two subsequent buildings have stood on this site.

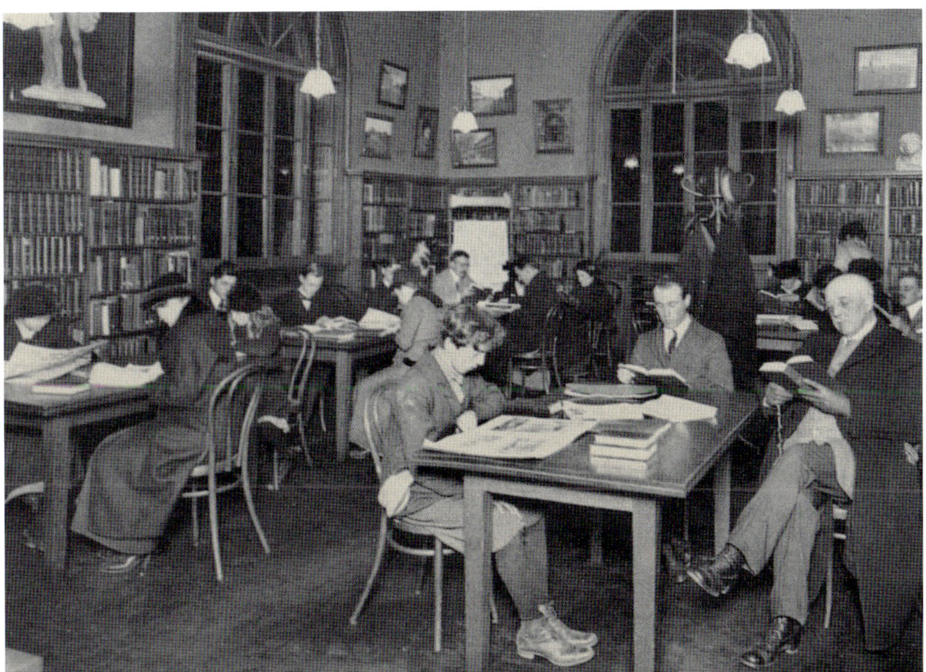

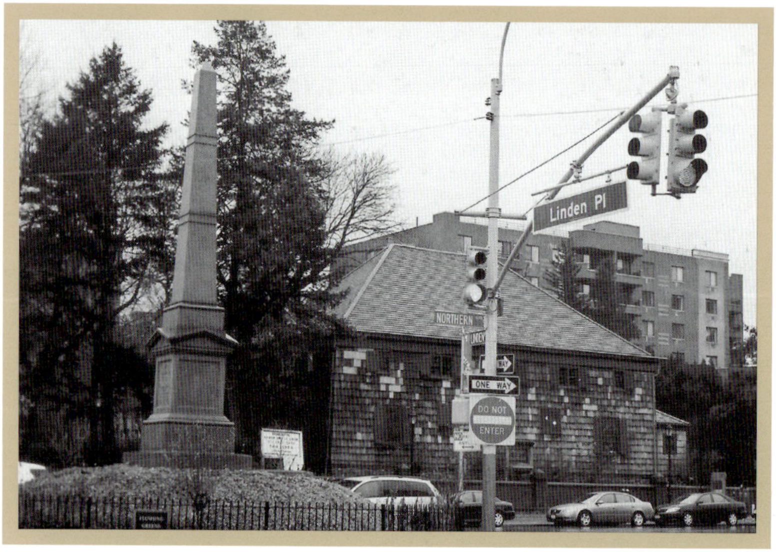

Even a town like Flushing was not immune to the effects of the Civil War. Constructed by R. E. Launitz and Company, the Civil War monument was erected on July 4, 1866, in the mall along Northern Boulevard by the Soldiers Monument Association. In this photograph taken by Sylvester Roe, orphans and widows still deep in mourning are shown attending the dedication, hosted by the Hamilton Rifles Light Artillery. The obelisk reads, "Erected in Memory of the Patriotic Volunteers from Flushing Who Sacrificed Their Lives in the War for the Preservation of Our Union 1861–1865."

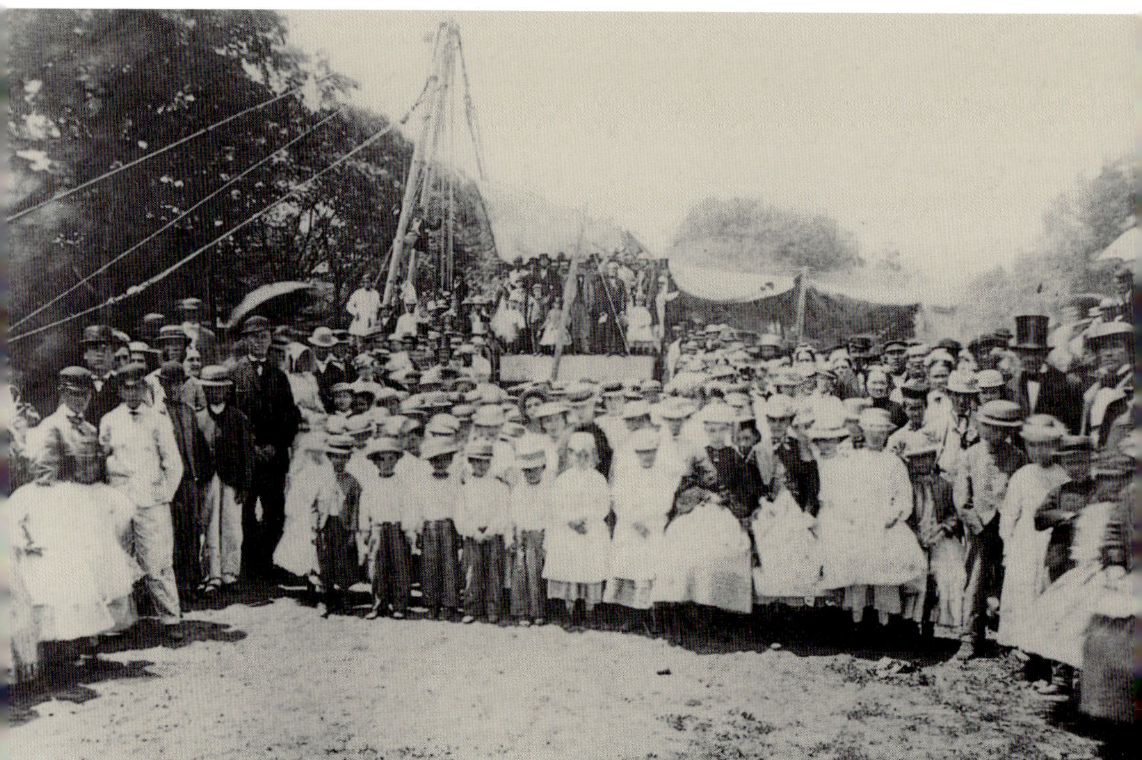

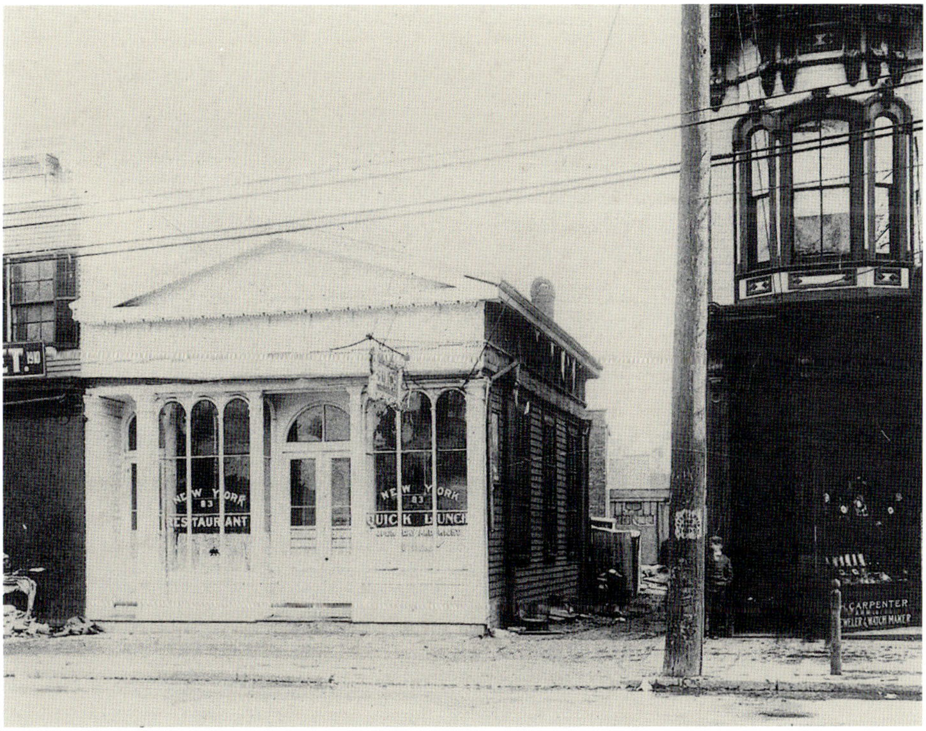

Trustees Hall (center) served as the seat of government in Flushing from 1844 until 1864. It was located in the center mall at the intersection of Northern Boulevard and Main Street, facing east. That same year, after the new town hall was constructed, the building was sold at public auction for $430 to Dr. J. H. Vedder and relocated to Main Street. The location was rented to various businesses such as the New York Restaurant and Quick Lunch stop, as seen in this photograph from 1910. One of Flushing's numerous municipal parking lots now occupies the spot. The modern view is looking west. (Courtesy of the Queens Historical Society.)

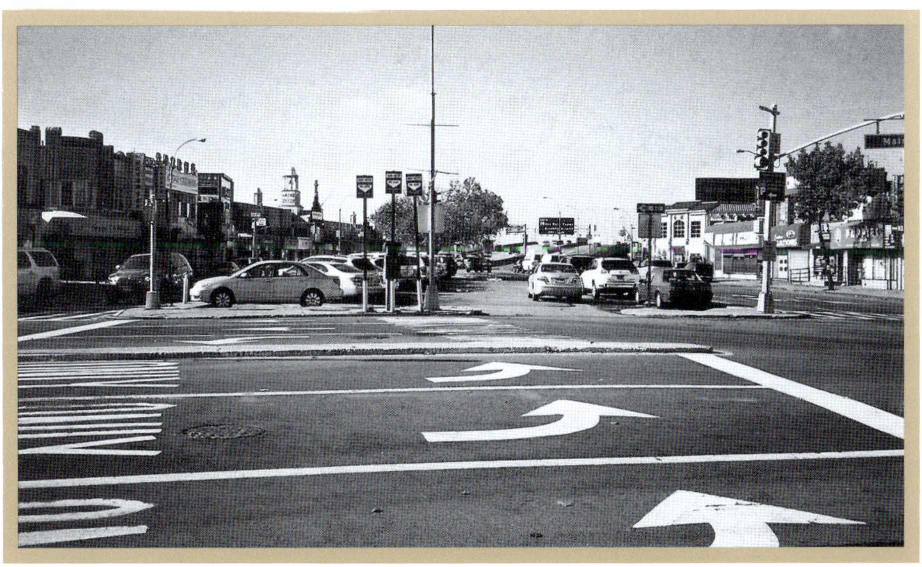

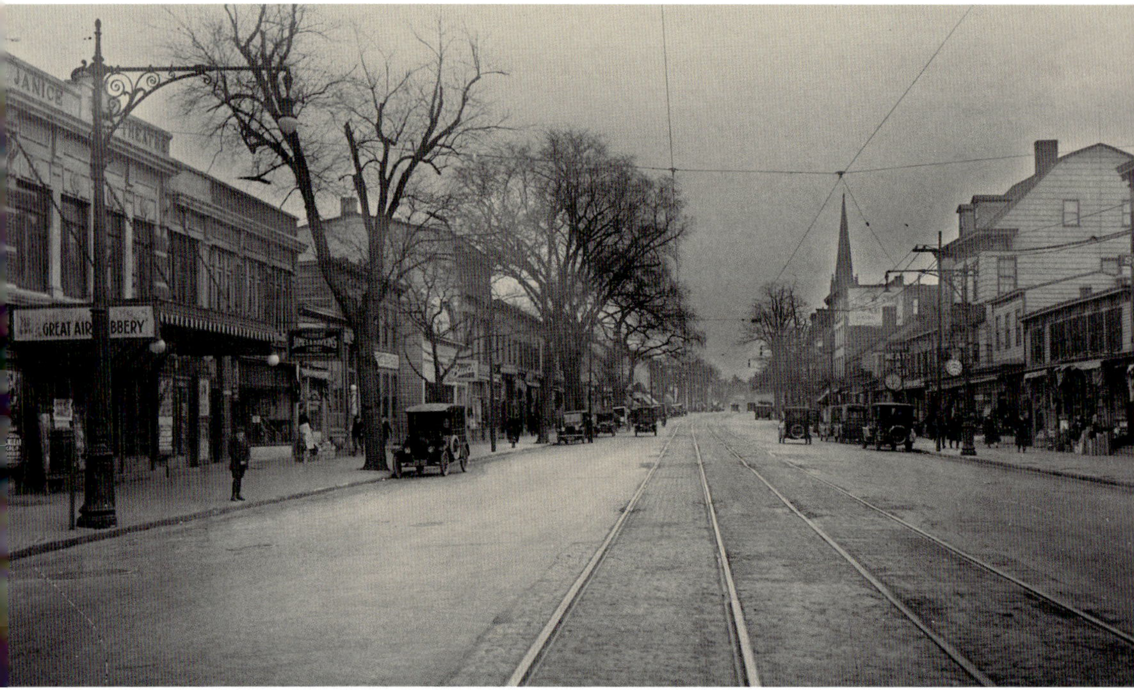

Main Street became a bustling row of stores, banks, and theaters in the late 1890s. Among these establishments that provided goods and services to the people of Flushing were George A. Smith's Stationery, Priggs Ice Cream and Confectionery, Whiting's Cigar Store, William Allen's Haberdashery, Fire Chief McCormack's Saloon, and James and Hawkins' Hardware Store just to name a few. On the left side is the old Janice Theater as seen in this photograph from April 1920. (Courtesy of the Queens Borough Public Library, Long Island Division, Frederick J. Weber Photographs.)

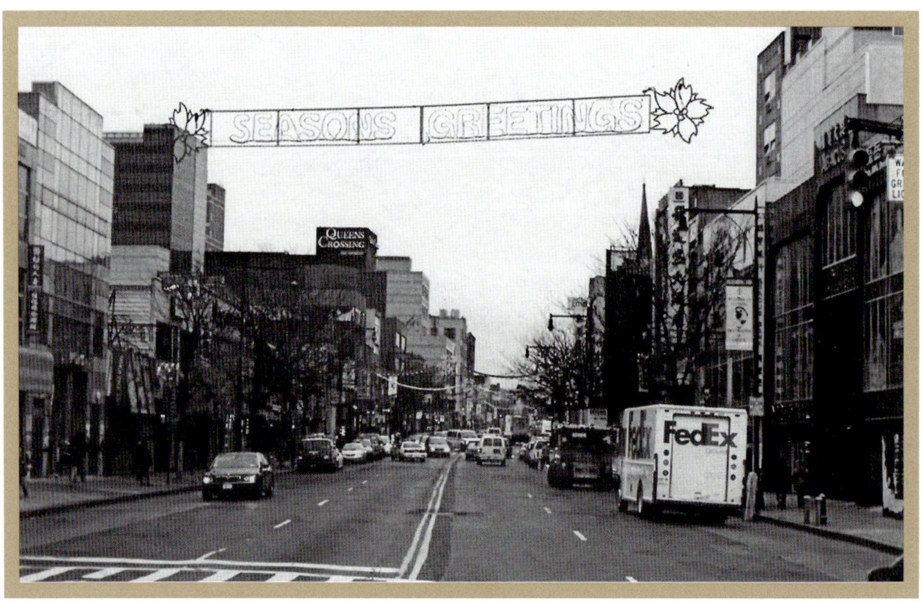

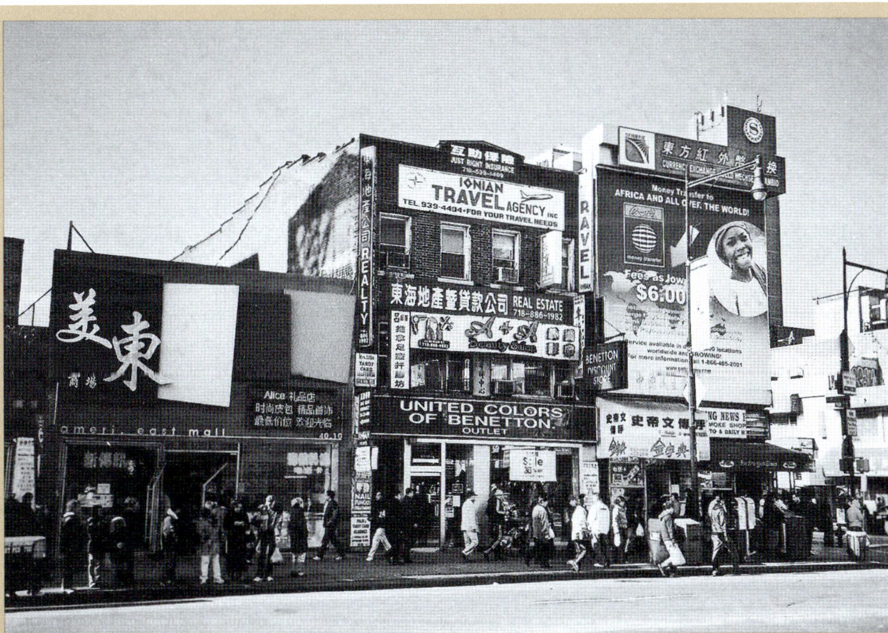

One of the earliest and most famous pharmacies to serve Flushing was Hepburn's Pharmacy, located on the west side of Main Street just south of Roosevelt Avenue. Dr. Alex Hepburn succeeded his father, John, who founded the drugstore in 1870. To the left is Geddes Painters Supplies Store, and a combination billiard hall and bowling alley is located on the right. The present-day variety of businesses is indicative of Flushing's cultural landscape. (Courtesy of the Queens Borough Public Library, Long Island Division, Eugene L. Armbruster Photographs.)

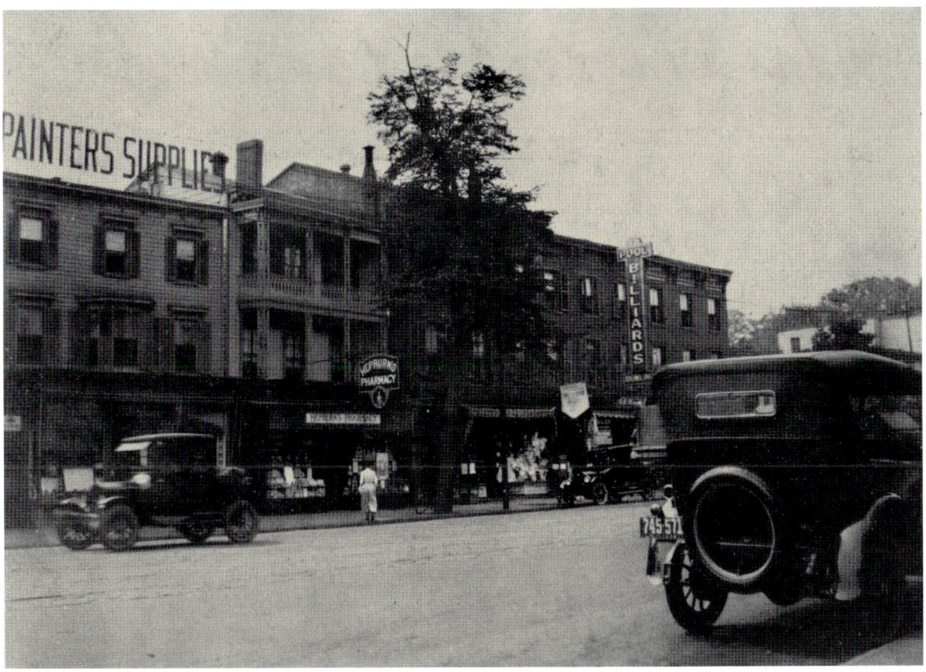

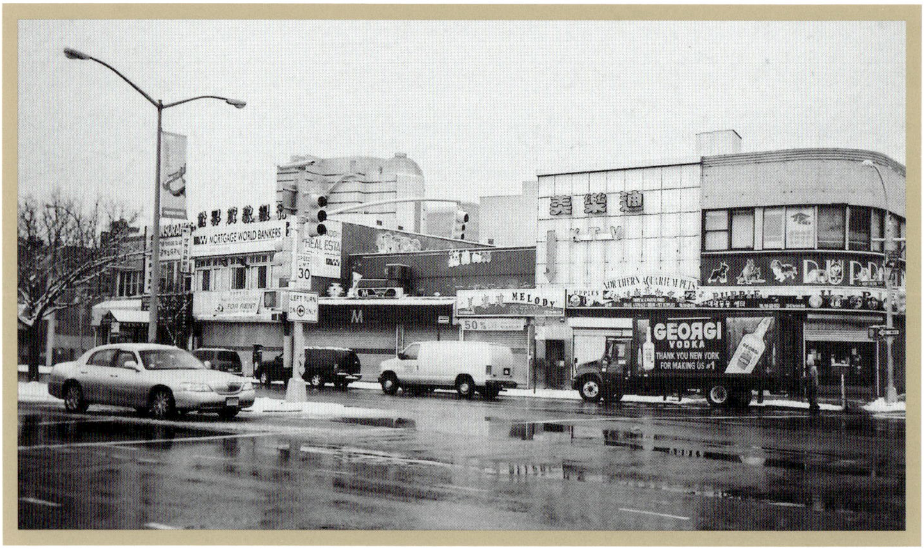

Henry Clement and Frank Bloodgood opened their store in March 1847 on the southeast corner of Northern Boulevard and Prince Street. It was a country store where anything was available. The original two-story building, owned by William B. Frey, was the location of Bloodgood's Pharmacy, the first one ever established in Flushing. This larger store, constructed in the early 1870s, sold ready-made clothing, boots, stationary, pharmaceuticals, flour, and feed. The building was yet another demolished for the widening of the boulevard. Occupying the same building on the left was Odd Fellows Hall.

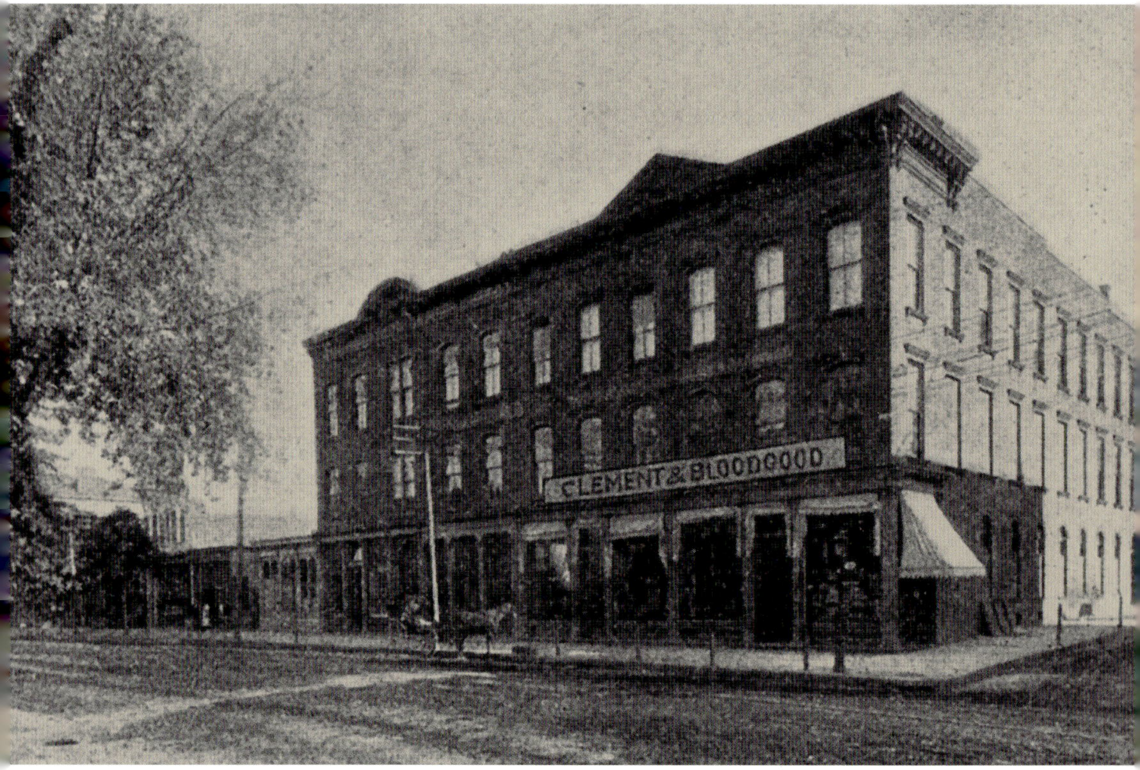

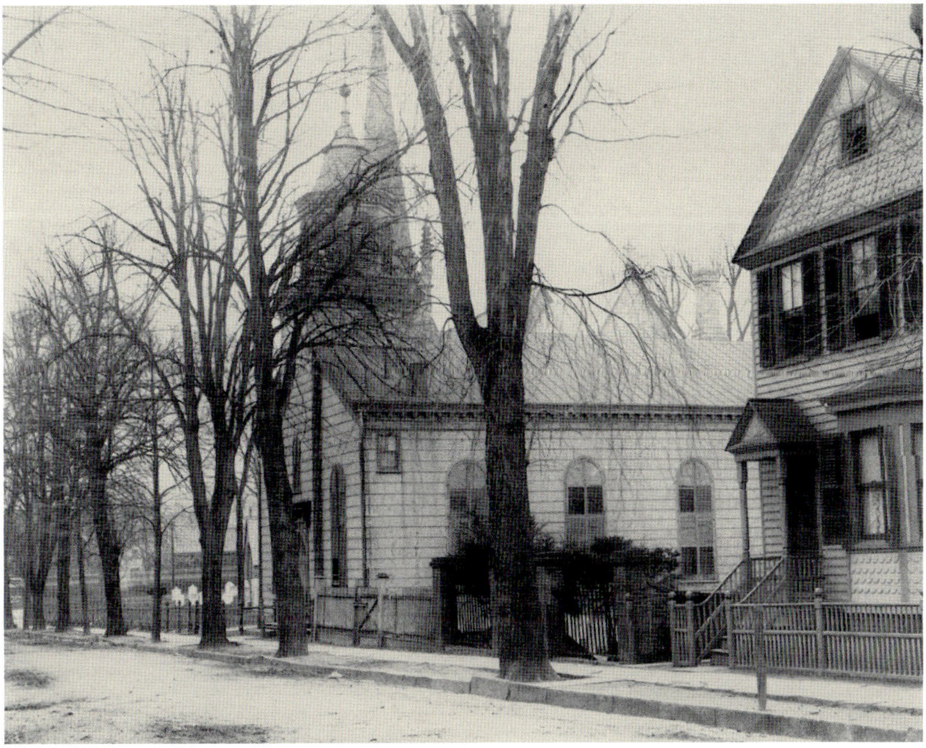

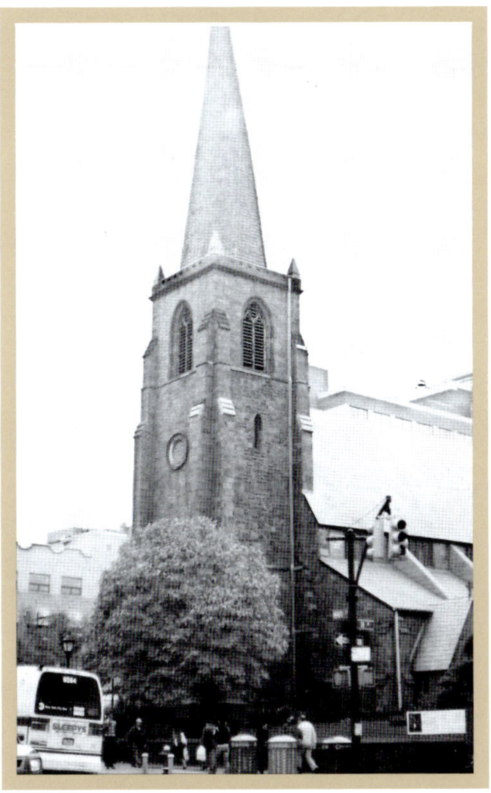

St. George's parish was founded in 1704 as part of the Church of England. The first version of the Episcopal Anglican church was built in 1821 and enlarged in 1838. As the Flushing community grew so did the church, and a new one was erected and consecrated on June 1, 1854, just around the corner on Main Street and Thirty-eighth Avenue. Still standing today, the church is made of Connecticut Bluestone and was designed in the Gothic style. The original wooden church was converted into a schoolhouse and then removed for an expansion of the present structure.

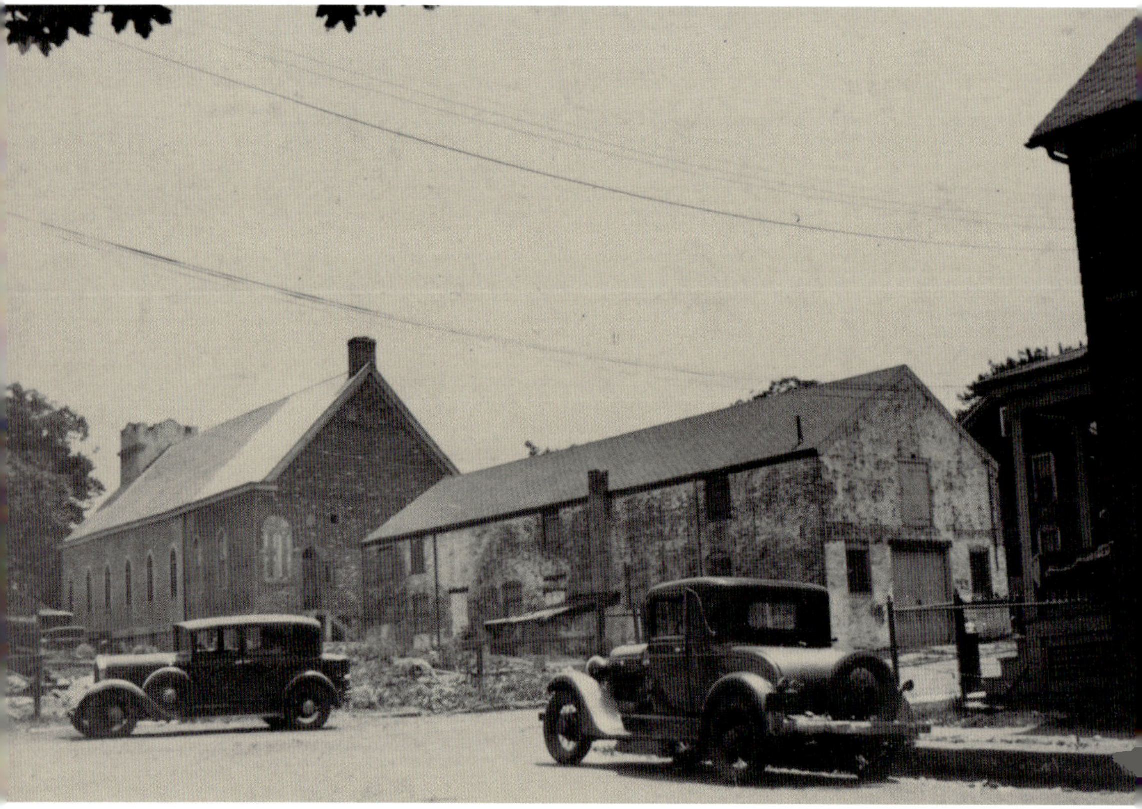

Flushing's rich religious history continued when the first Baptist church was built in 1870 on Thirty-sixth Avenue and Prince Street. Started by Mrs. Ellen Green, the Ebenezer Baptist Church grew in number in just a very short time. Rev. W. J. Bowman was the first pastor. In 1914, the church was completely destroyed in a fire and rebuilt for $16,000 and modified in 1920. The brick building to the rear, now a stonecutter, was used as a slaughterhouse. (Courtesy of the Queens Borough Public Library, Long Island Division, Eugene L. Armbruster Photographs.)

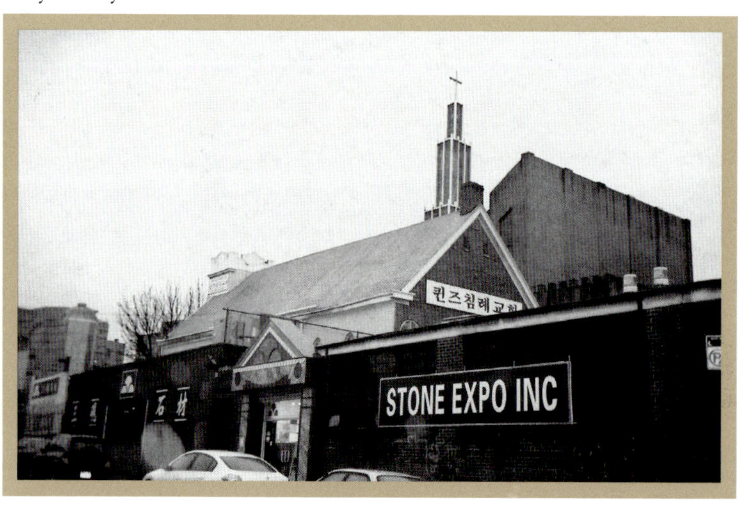

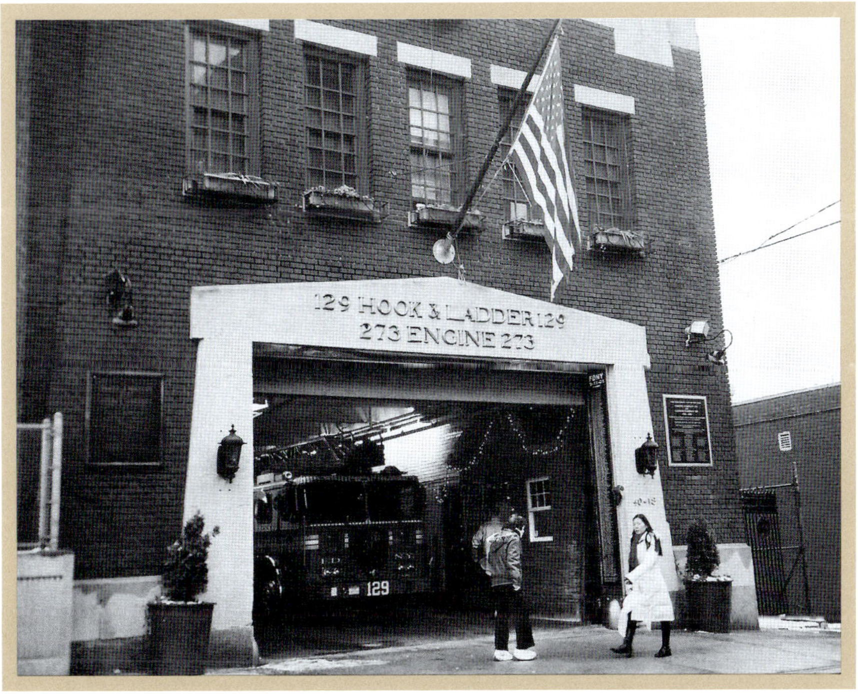

On March 24, 1809, the Flushing Board of Trustees passed "An Act of Extinguishing Fires in the Village of Flushing" into law. Firefighters were untrained volunteers, and Flushing Creek was the only water source. In November 1854, the village organized the first fire companies including Young America (shown below), Mutual No. 1, Murray Hill Hose Company No. 4, Rescue Hook and Ladder, and Empire House Company. The local companies were phased out in 1908 and replaced by the FDNY.

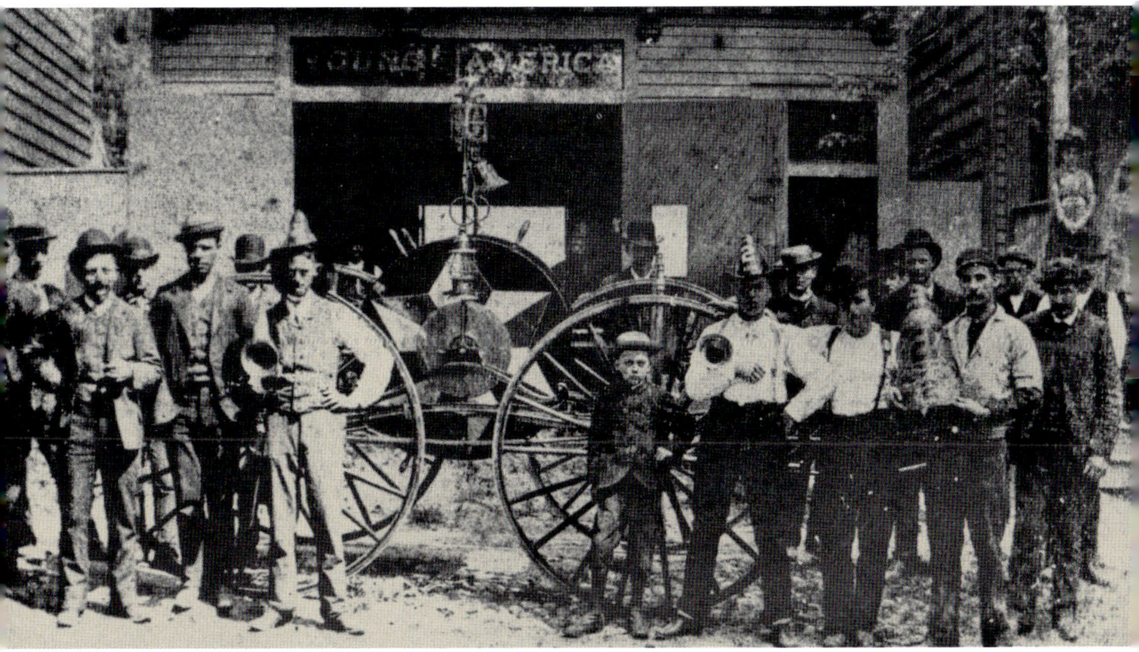

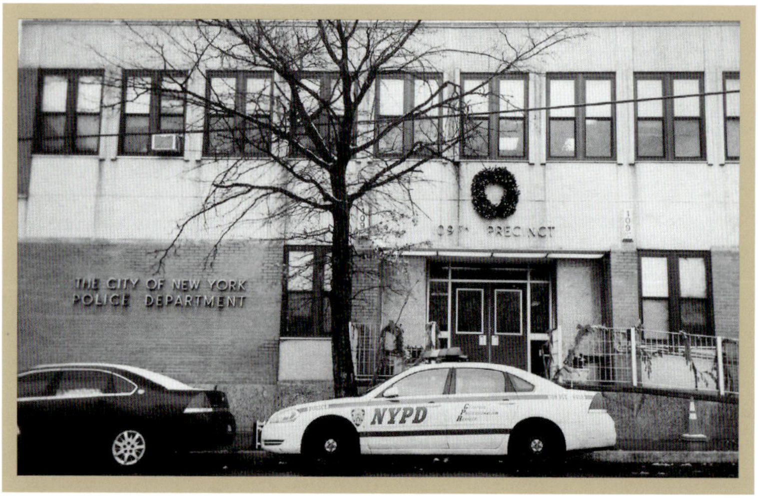

One of the first village police forces appeared in the 1880s. Original patrolmen Henry Thompkins, Joe Kinney, and Joseph Stillwagon were led by Capt. Charles Hance. They wore blue uniforms with big shiny buttons, a badge, and a high crown hat. This image from 1924 shows the 65th Precinct of the NYPD. Originally located on Prince Street and Thirty-fifth Avenue at the former Winter Estate, it became the 109th precinct in 1929 before relocating to Union Street in the late 1960s—early 1970s. (Courtesy of the Queens Borough Public Library, Long Island Division, Frederick J. Weber Photographs.)

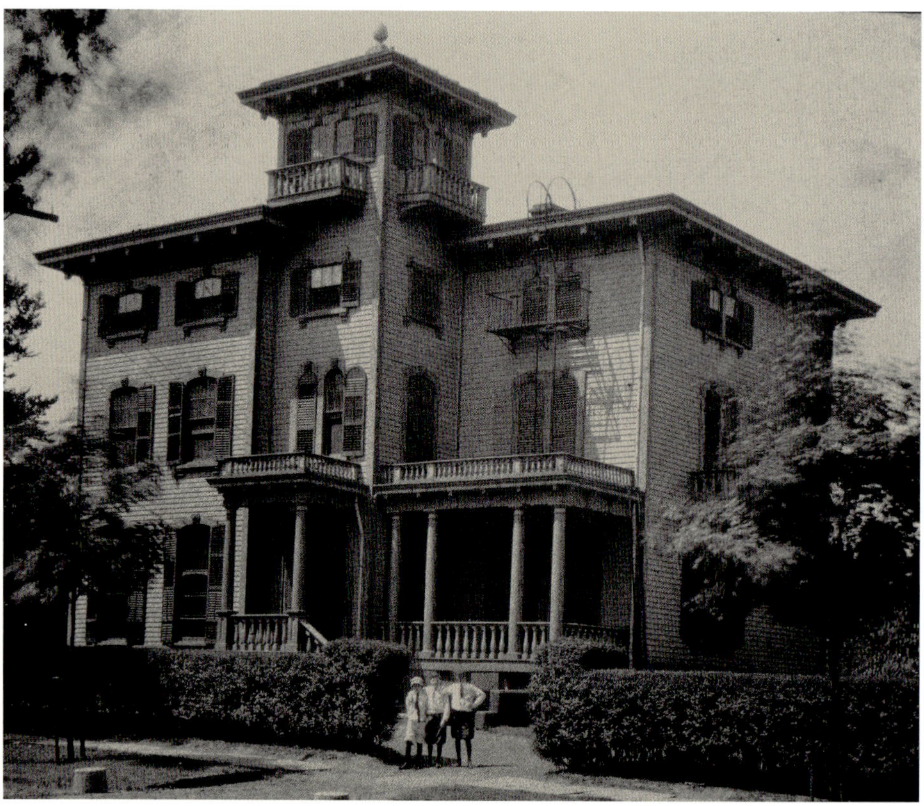

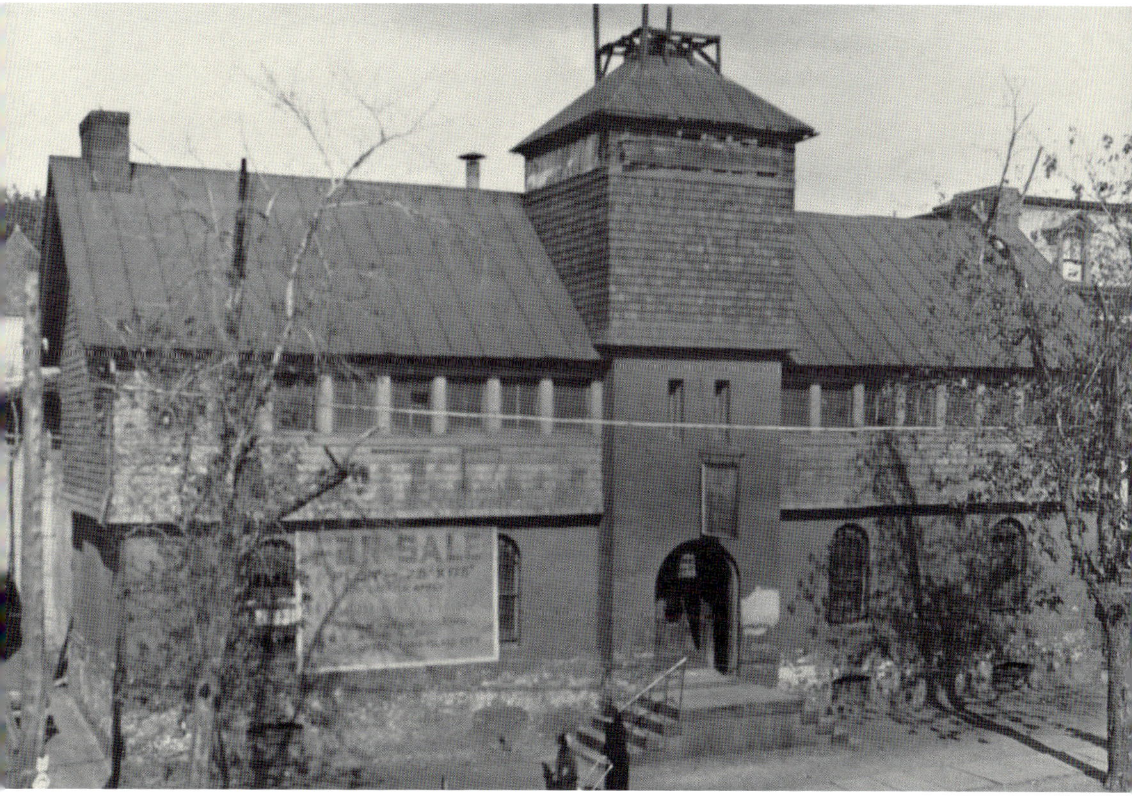

The 17th Separate Company of the State National Guard Armory was headquartered on the north side of Roosevelt Avenue, between Main Street and Union Street. The cornerstone was laid by the Order of the Masons on Memorial Day, 1884. Constructed for $12,000, the armory was named Fort Christensen after Brig. Gen. C. T. Christensen who, at that time, commanded the Second Brigade that was attached to the 17th Separate Company. The former location is now the Lippmann Arcade. (Courtesy of the Millstein Division of U.S. History, Local History and Genealogy, the New York Public Library, Astor, Lenox, and Tilden Foundations.)

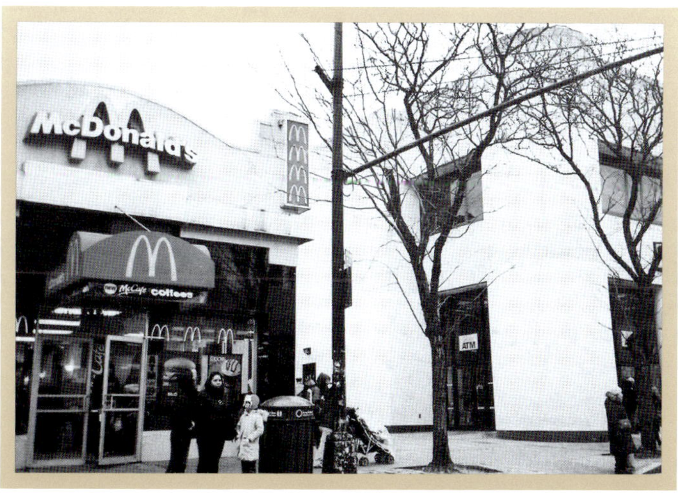

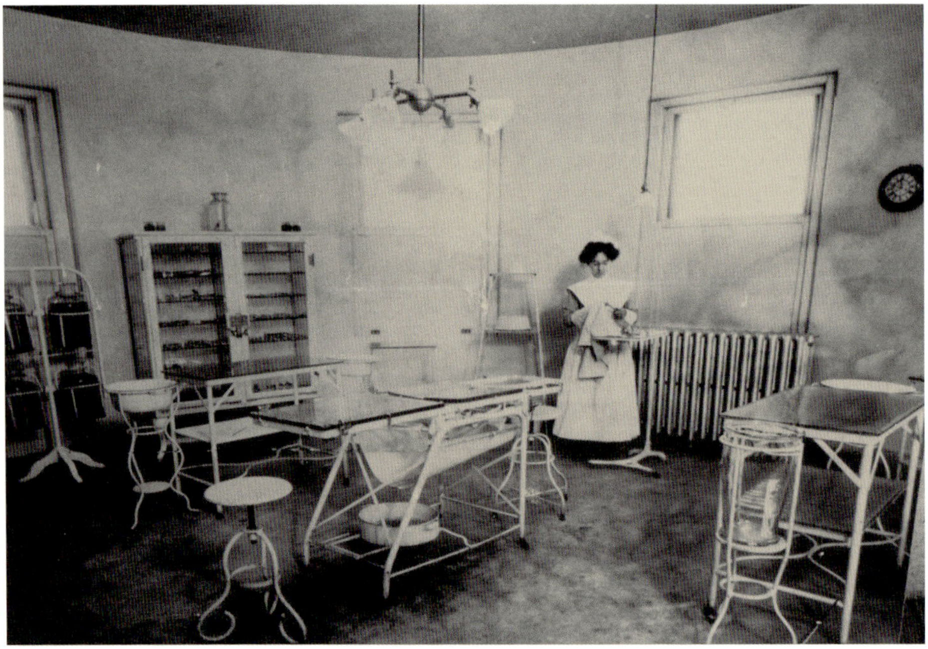

Over 130 years ago, the only place a resident of Flushing could receive medical attention was in Kings County. When the maid of Mr. John Gihon died in the winter of 1882 en route to Brooklyn he started a movement for establishing a village hospital. Flushing Hospital opened on May 30, 1887. The building consisted of two wings, one for men and the other for women. Shown here is the operating theater in 1912—an amazing comparison with the medical advancements of today. (Courtesy of the Queens Historical Society.)

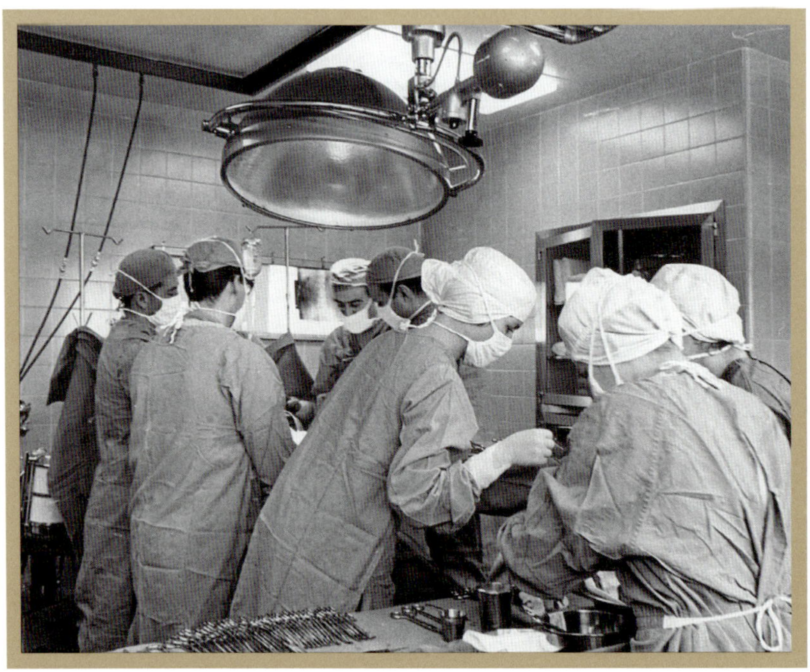

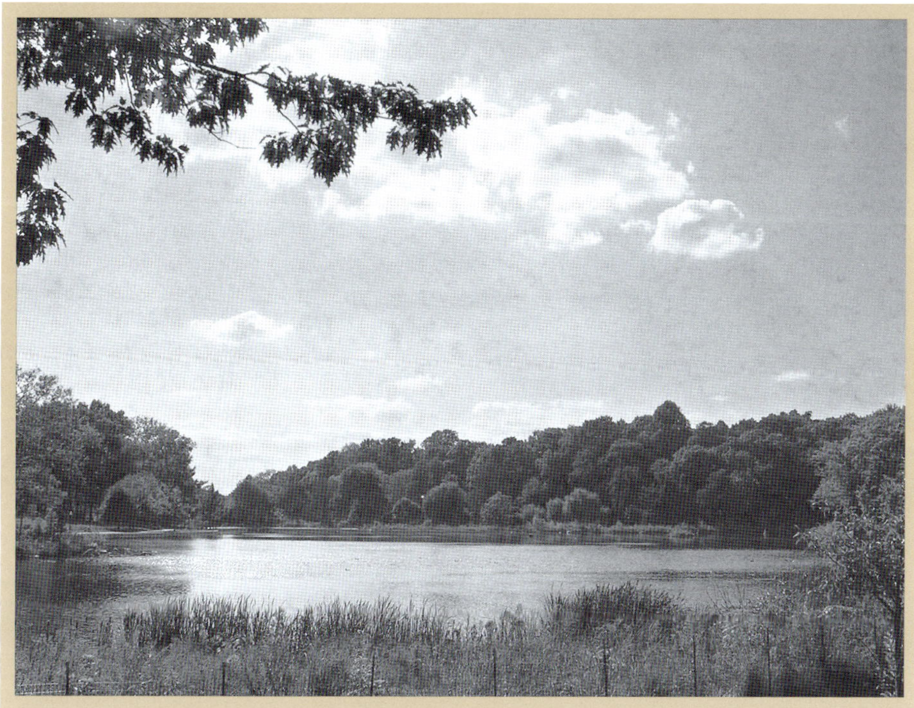

The Flushing Carnival was a favorite annual tradition. The festivities, sponsored by the Flushing Hospital Benefit Association, were held in Kissena Park, as shown above, and also in the village proper at Parsons Avenue (Boulevard) and Elm Street. More than 3,000 people turned out for opening night of the first carnival on June 6, 1906. The program proclaimed, "Wrestled from the jungles of Sweden, Elmhurst, Africa, College Point, Asia and the corner of Main Street and Broadway comes hordes of ferocious lions, tigers, elephants, bears and mosquitoes!"

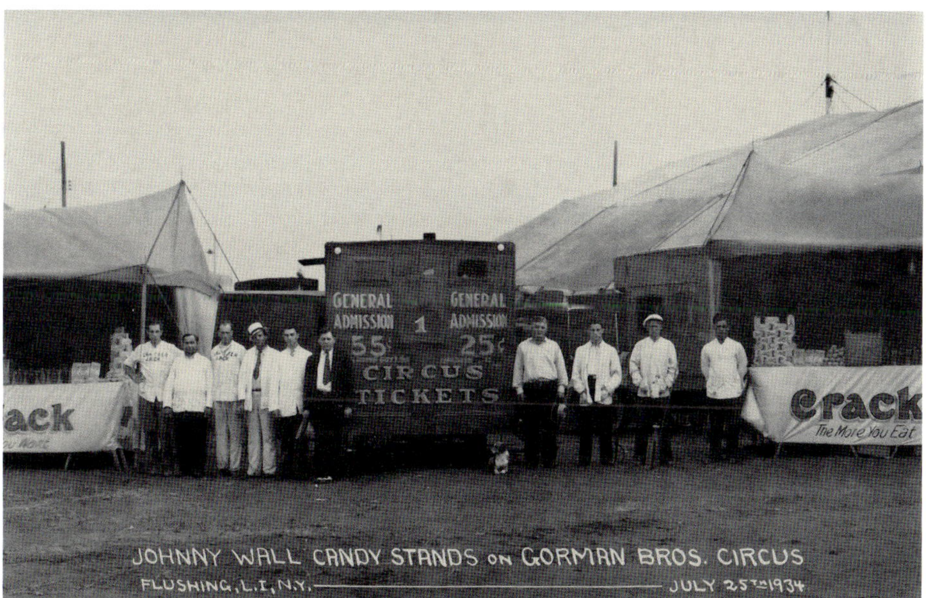

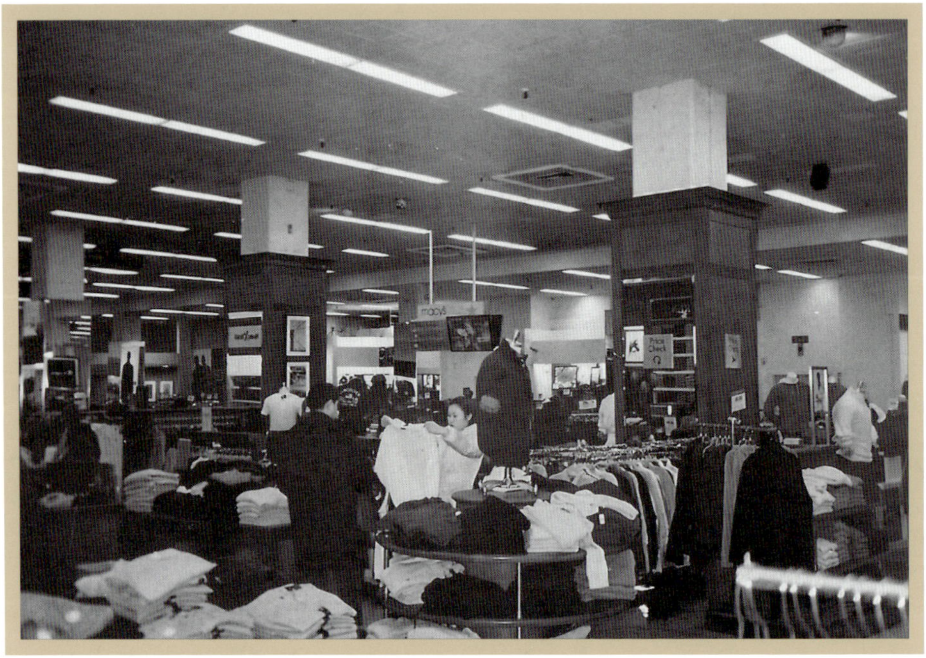

In 1828, Rev. Dr. William Augustus Muhlenberg started a private academy known as the Christian Institute of Flushing. Fearing that the title prejudiced against other faiths, the name was changed to the Flushing Institute. The cornerstone was laid on August 11, 1827. In 1842, it became St. Ann's Hall and reverted to its original name in 1846. Under the leadership of Ezra and Elias Fairchild, the institute became the most successful preparatory school in the country. Shown here on November 24, 1860, the institute stood 100 feet back from the east side of Main Street just south of Roosevelt Avenue until 1925. Macy's department store now stands in its footprints.

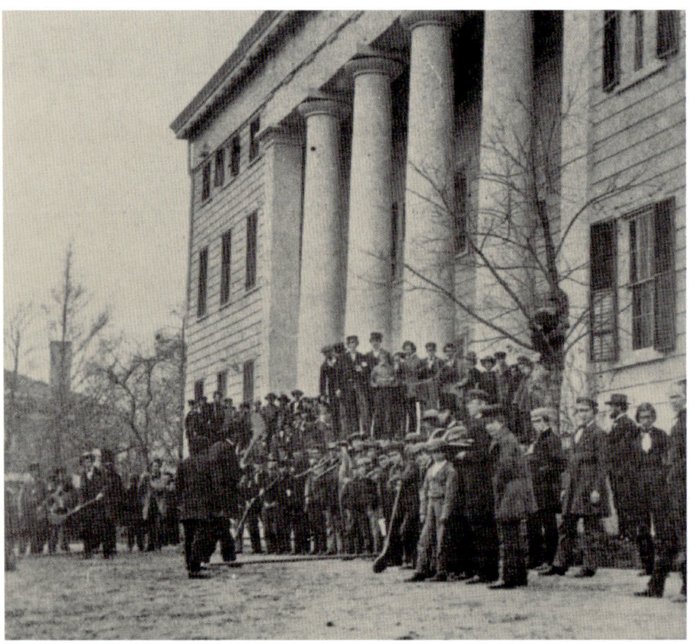

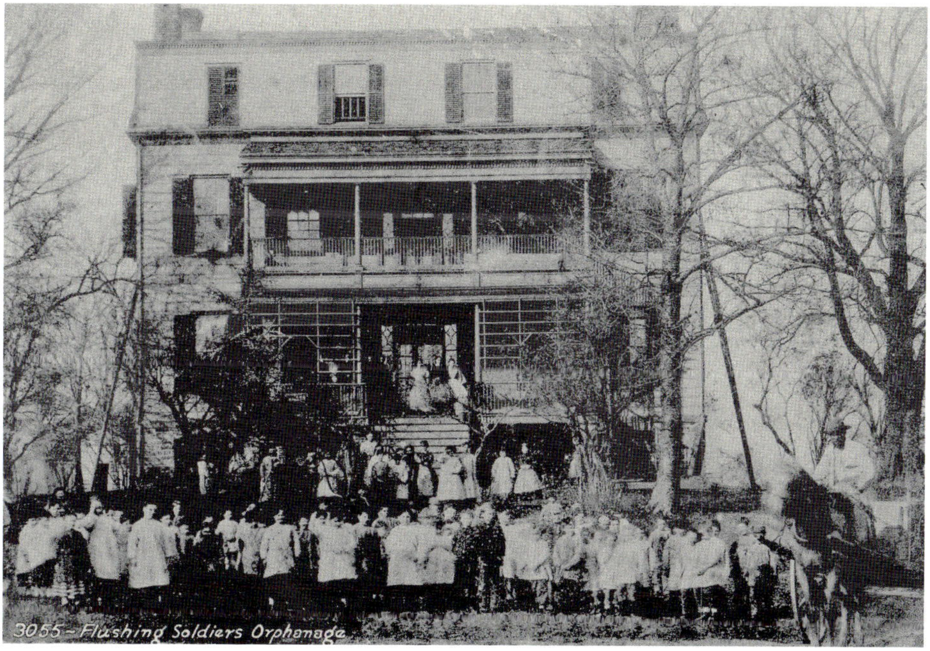

In April 1864, the C. Miller house, located at what is today the northeast corner of Thirty-third Avenue and Downing Street, was purchased for $20,000 and turned into the Patriot Orphan Home. Over 200 orphaned children, whose parents were killed in the Civil War, lived here at one time. Joseph Bodine was the superintendent, and the staff included two teachers, two English seamstresses, four young Irish domestics, and one nurse. The area is now completely dominated by industrial facilities.

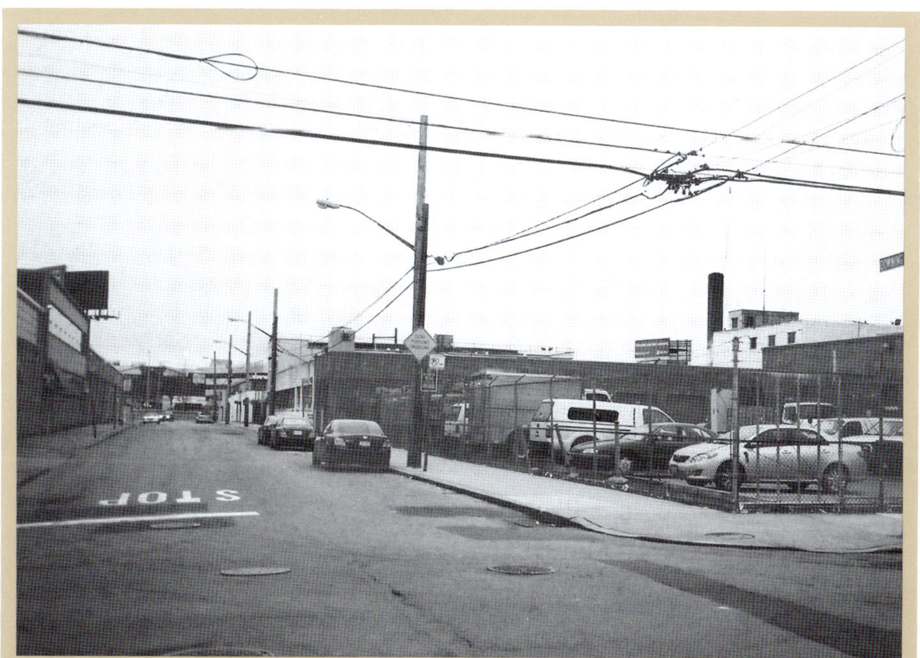

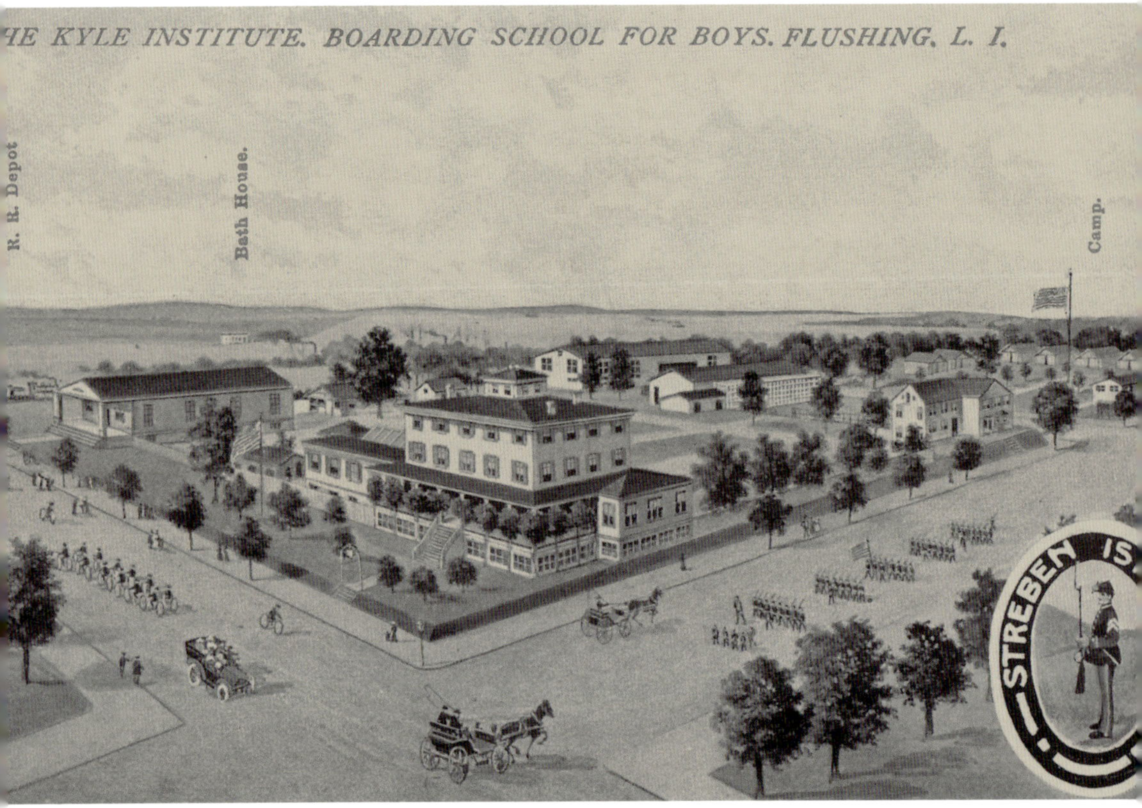

Architect Gilbert Hicks built this large handsome house on the northwest corner of State Street (Thirty-fifth Avenue) and Farrington Street in 1856 for the Linnaean Hill Seminary. In 1857, it became St. Mary's School before changing into the residency of Hicks from 1873 until 1891. It was handed over to Prof. Paul Kyle for his military school known as the Kyle Institute. Cadets came here from Queens and around the country. This postcard view shows the main building, gymnasium, and swimming hole. It was closed in June 1914 and demolished in the 1930s.

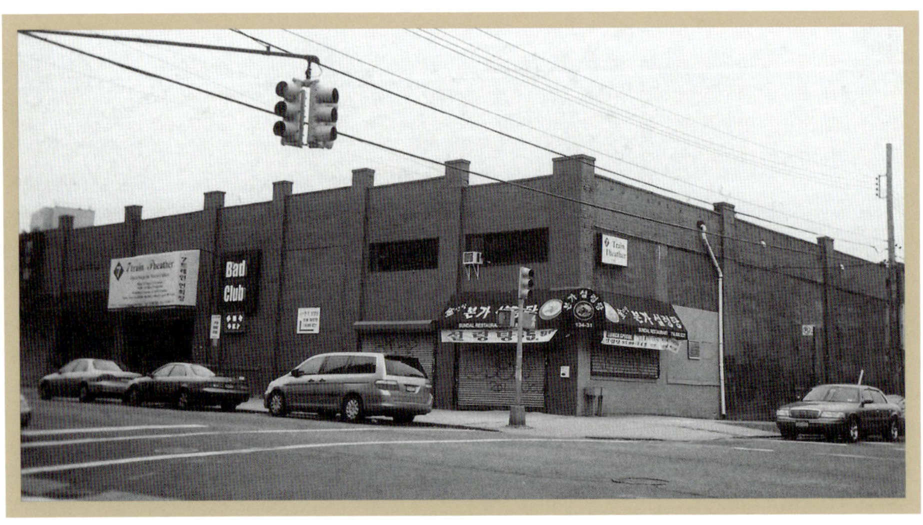

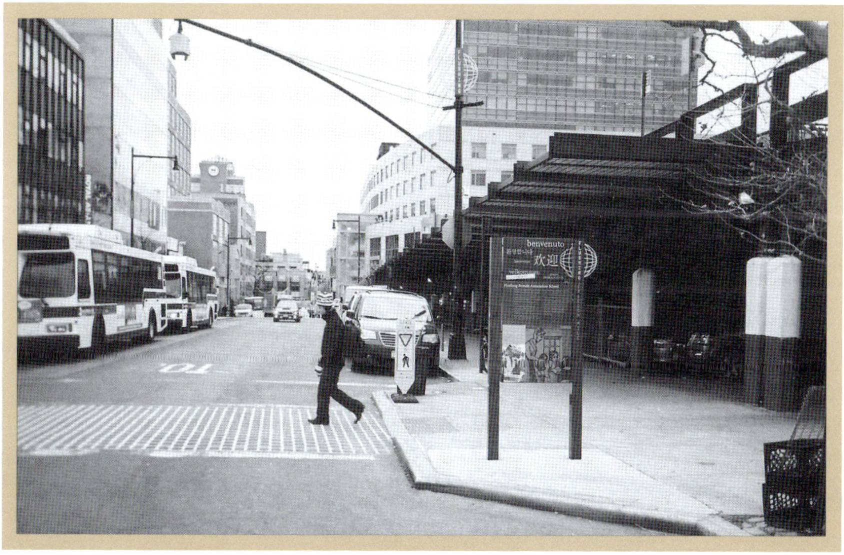

The Flushing Female Association schoolhouse opened on April 1, 1814, and provided free education to the African American community. It was located at 136-60 Thirty-eighth Avenue between Washington Street and Main and Union Streets. In its final years, it was regarded as one of the oldest nonreligious charity organizations in the country. The building was leveled in order to construct the parking lot for the Interborough Rapid Transit subway. A Flushing Freedom Mile marker was erected in its place. (Courtesy of the Queens Borough Public Library, Long Island Division, Eugene L. Armbruster Photographs.)

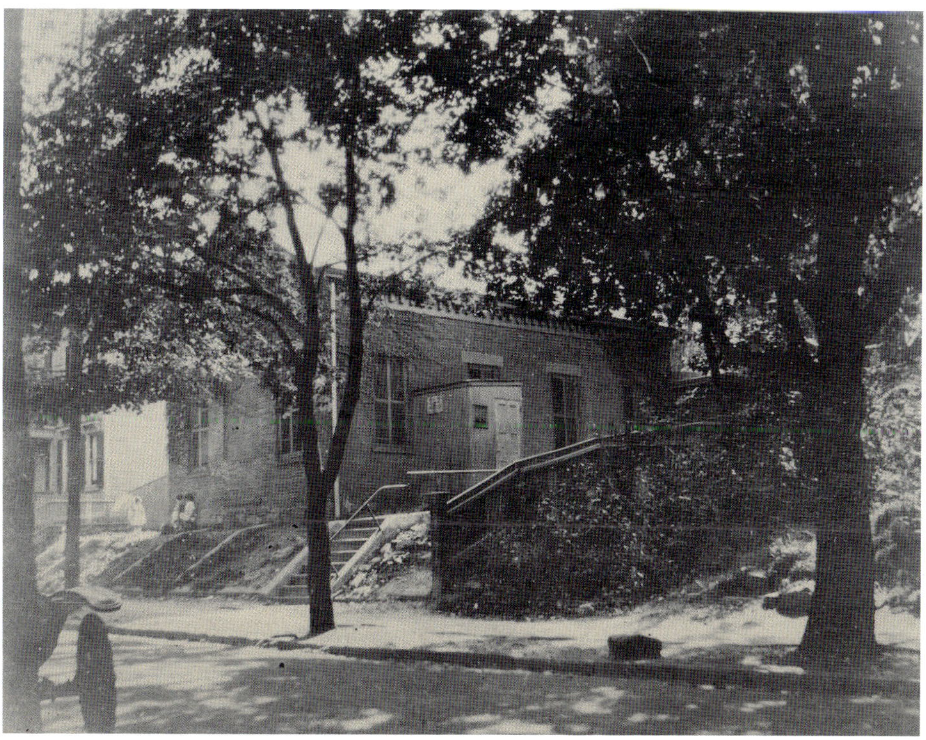

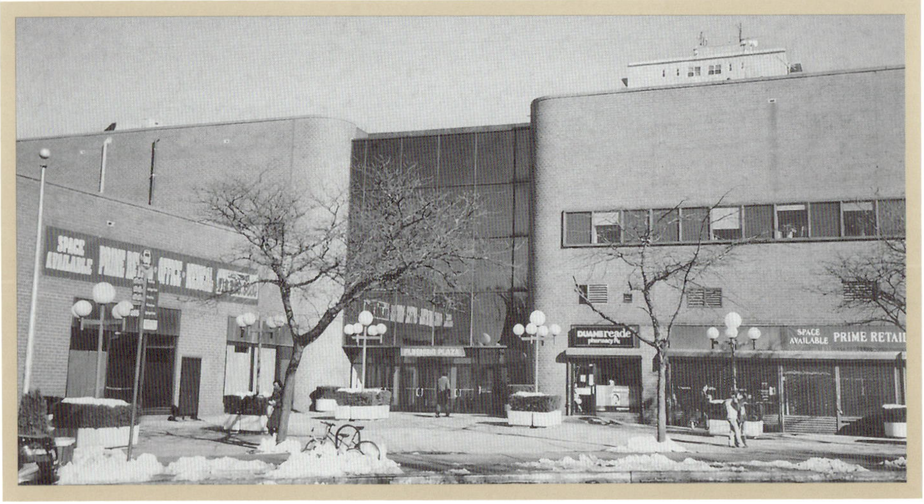

In 1860, the Sisters of St. Joseph's Convent moved from their location in Brooklyn to the serene setting of Flushing. They occupied a large framed building known as St. Thomas' Hall. During the Civil War race riots of 1861, the sisters allowed many African Americans from the area to remain on the convent grounds where they could be safe. In 1877, a new wing containing a dinning room, an exhibition hall, and dormitory rooms for pupils of the new boarding school was constructed. Located at 41-61 Kissena Boulevard and Sanford Avenue, St. Joseph's Home for Girls was demolished by fire in the 1960s and replaced by an E.J. Korvette department store, also gone.

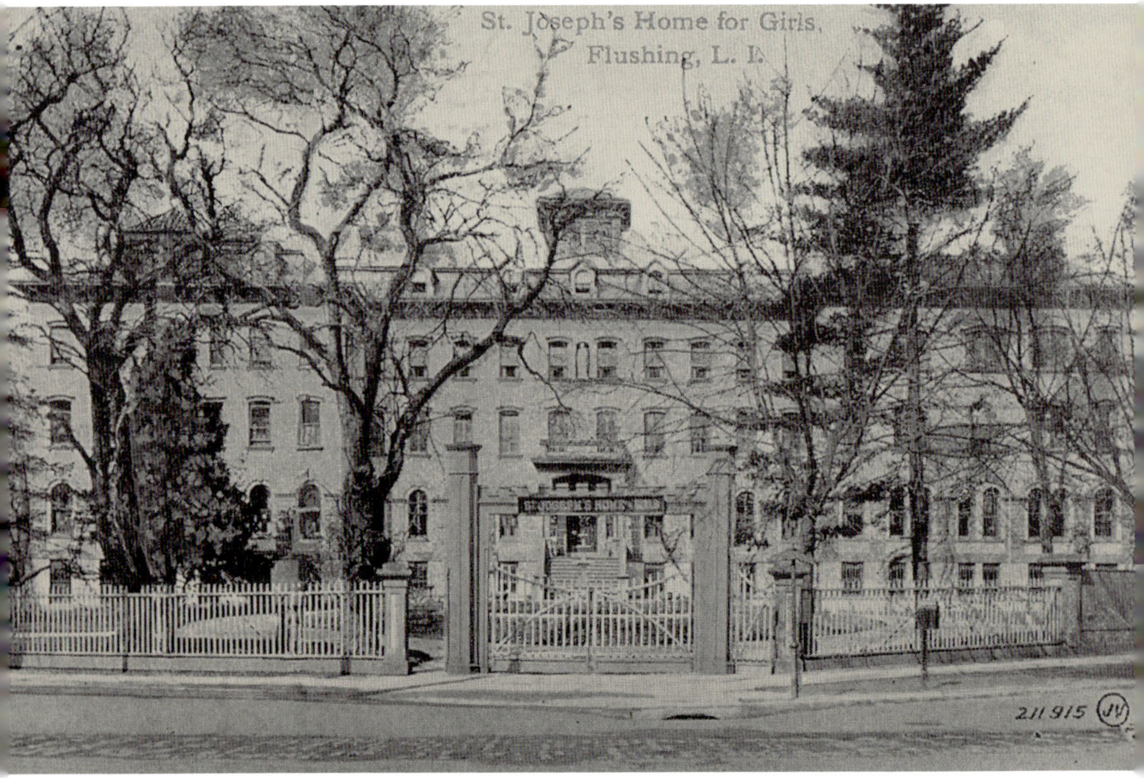

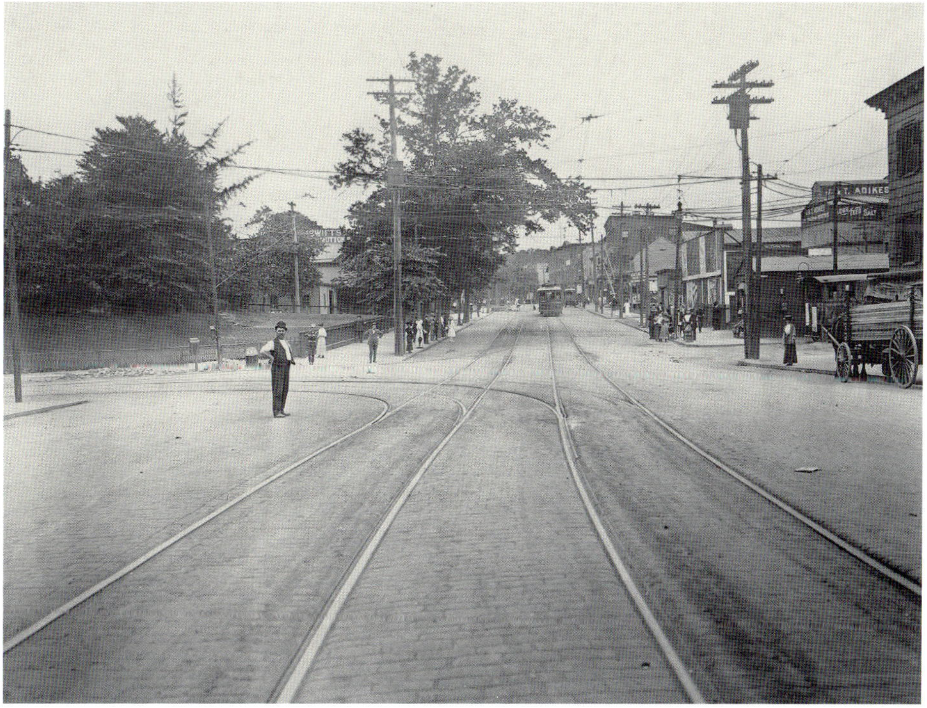

A typical day in Flushing is captured in this extraordinary photograph looking east down Bridge Street (Northern Boulevard) from Lawrence Street (College Point Boulevard) on June 25, 1912. To the left is the heavily wooded property of the Prince homestead and the Linnaean Nurseries. On the right is John and Thomas Adikes Grain, Flour, and Feed store. After that is the Flushing Luncheonette. Trolleys in the background approach the grade crossing of the Whitestone Branch of the Long Island Rail Road. Today there is not one surviving structure. (Courtesy of the New York Transit Museum.)

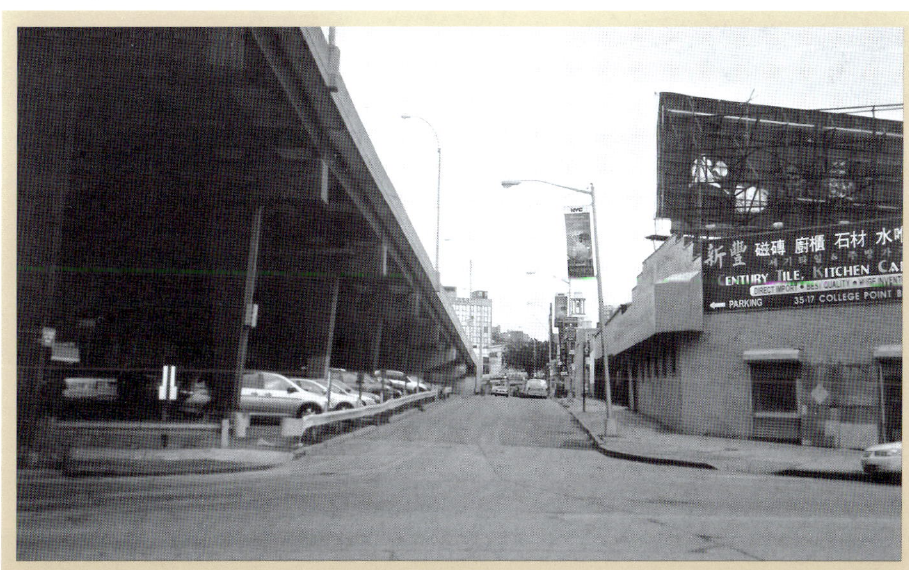

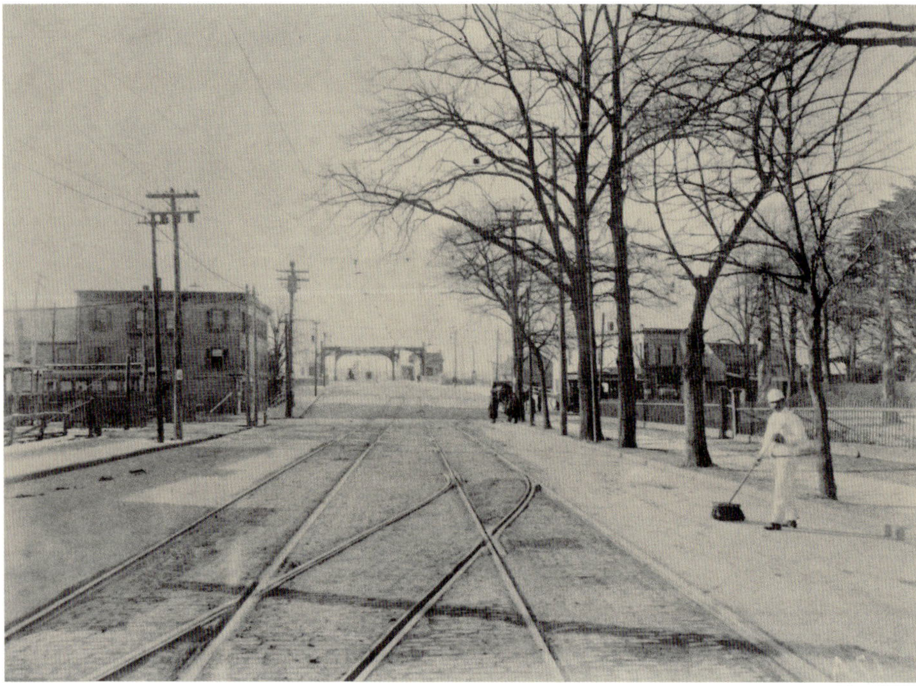

Northern Boulevard and College Point Boulevard are shown again looking west on the approach to Flushing Creek Bridge in 1912. A street sweeper can be seen on the right. The bridge was eliminated in 1937, when Northern Boulevard was widened up to 150 feet. The approach still has a familiar resemblance with the exception of the surrounding buildings. Factories now dominate the Linnaean Nurseries on the right, and Germain's Restaurant (constructed in 1873) on the left was completely eliminated for the right-of-way for the current bridge named after the Prince family who brought America's first commercial nursery to Flushing.

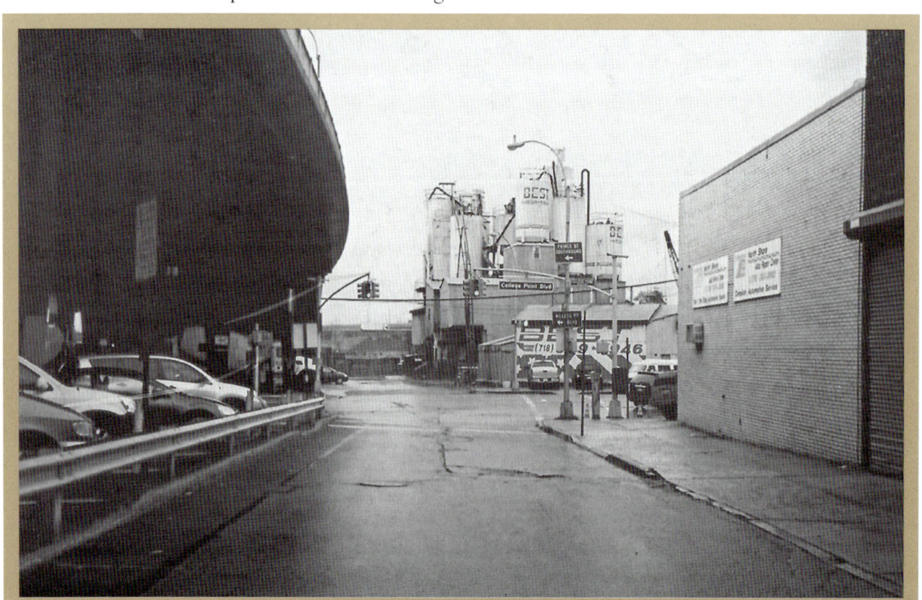

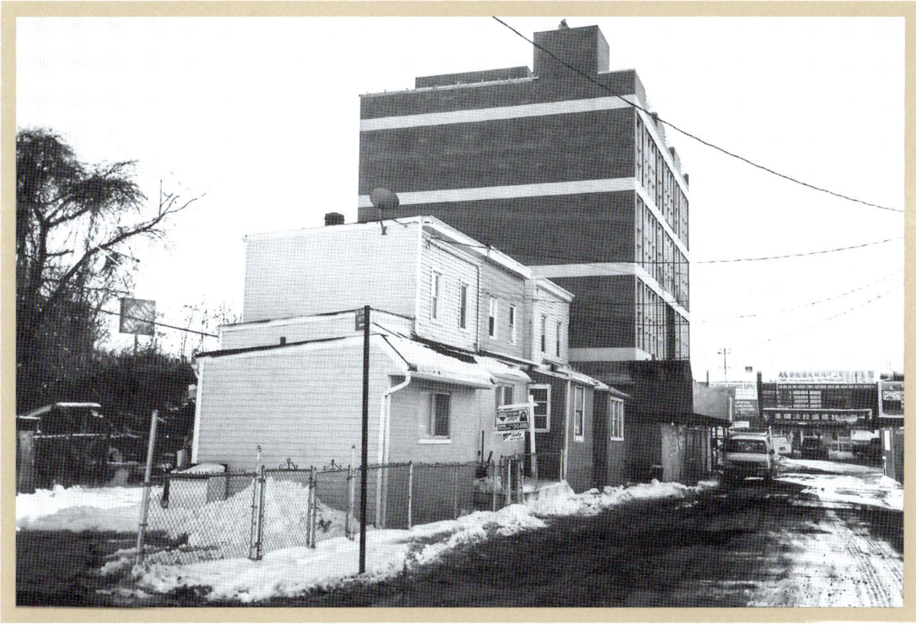

Flushing Creek was the location of the very first settlers 365 years ago. The creek was deeper, wider, and open for both private and commercial shipping traffic. West of the creek was heavily wooded on the high ground with impassible swampland down below. Shown here in a rare photograph from 1897 are early dwellings along the creek. Most of the river has been altered by landfill. Only a handful of homes from the late 19th and 20th centuries remain, as a new Target, Best Buy, and BJ's wholesaler now occupies the site. This current view looks southwest at the foot of Fortieth Road. (Courtesy of the Queens Borough Public Library, Long Island Division, Eugene L. Armbruster Photographs.)

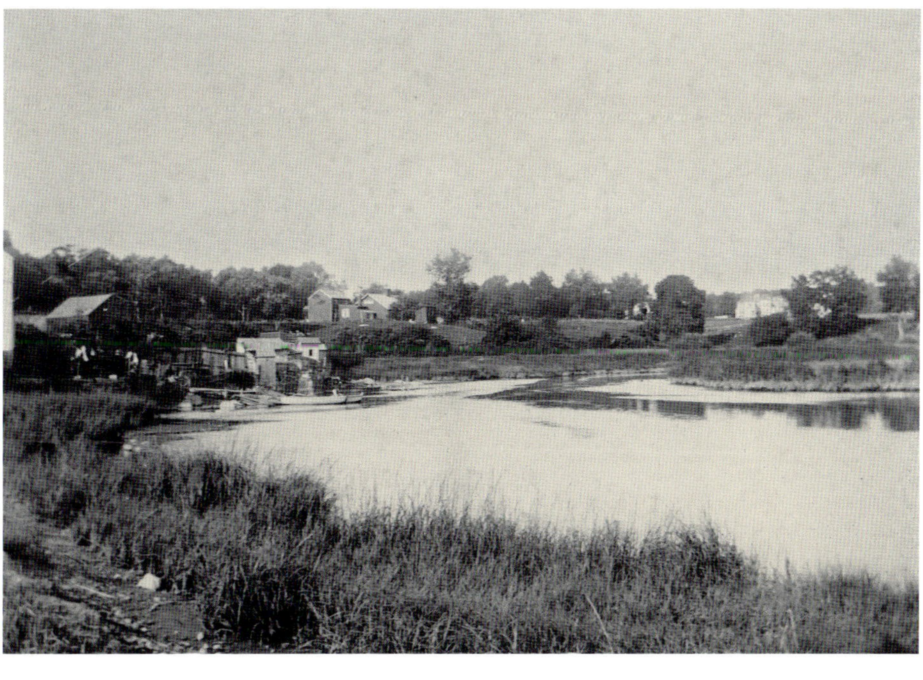

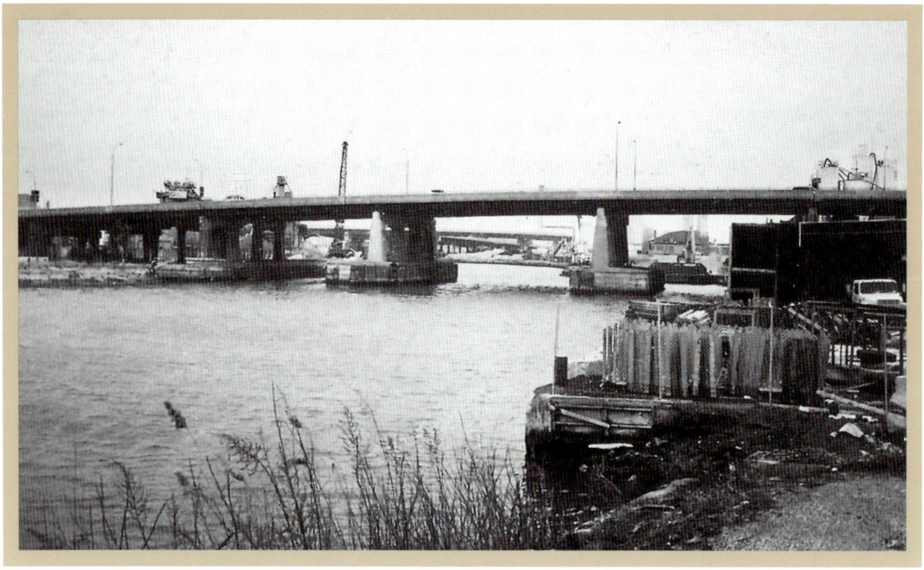

In the late 1790s, William Prince II organized a company to construct the first bridge over Flushing Creek in order to provide a shorter stage route to New York City. Originally the western area was so impenetrable that travelers had to go via Brooklyn. The Flushing and Newtown Road and Bridge Company was incorporated on March 21, 1801. The company maintained two tollhouses, one on Flushing Bridge and the other on Thirty-seventh Avenue between 112th and 114th Streets in Corona. Here is the third version of the bridge, which was built in July 1866 as a wooden swing bridge.

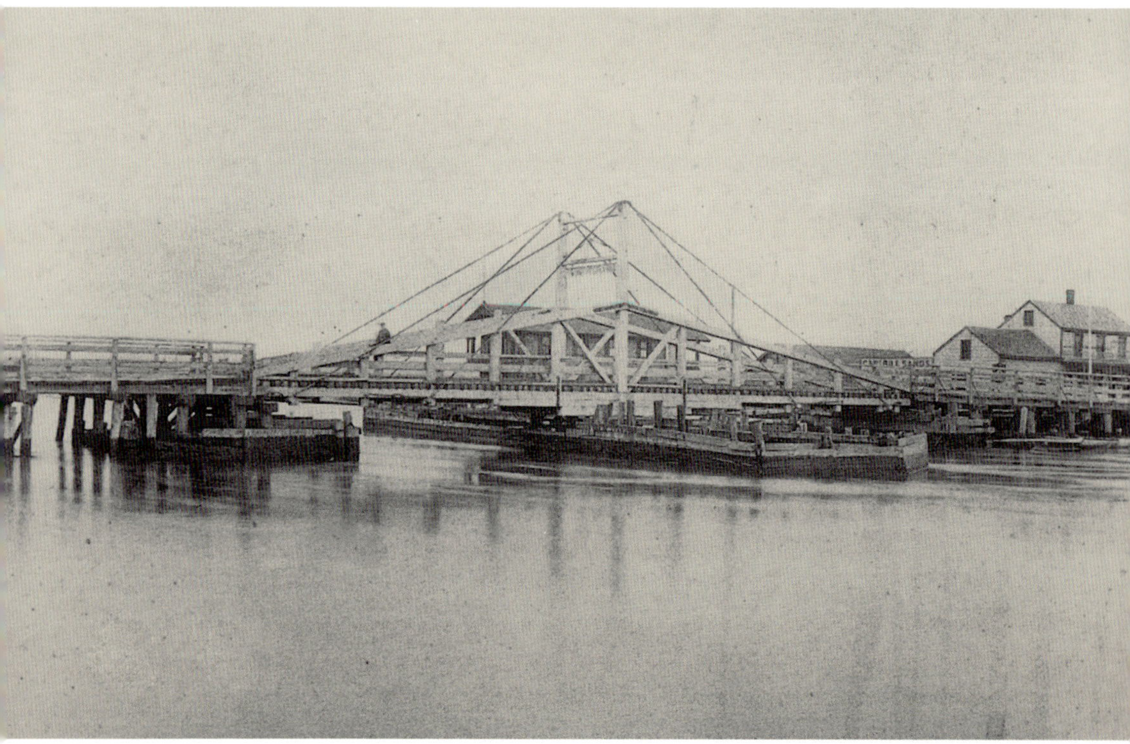

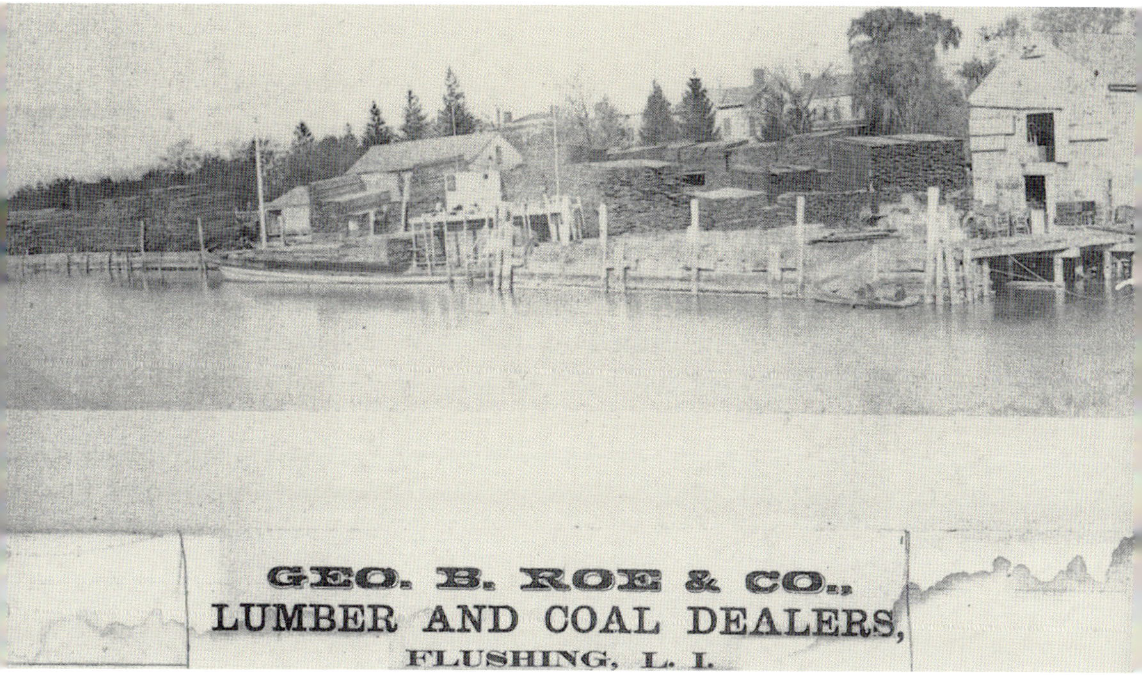

This is a rare view of the waterfront steamboat wharf and docks located on Flushing Creek. Isaac Peck and his family purchased the property around the time of the American Revolution. On February 4, 1865, this portion of land along present day College Point Boulevard at the foot of Northern Boulevard was sold at auction to Capt. George B. Roe and Company for $11,750. The company was the main supplier of lumber for most construction projects in Flushing. The shoreline is now dominated by asphalt mixing plants and even a small lumberyard.

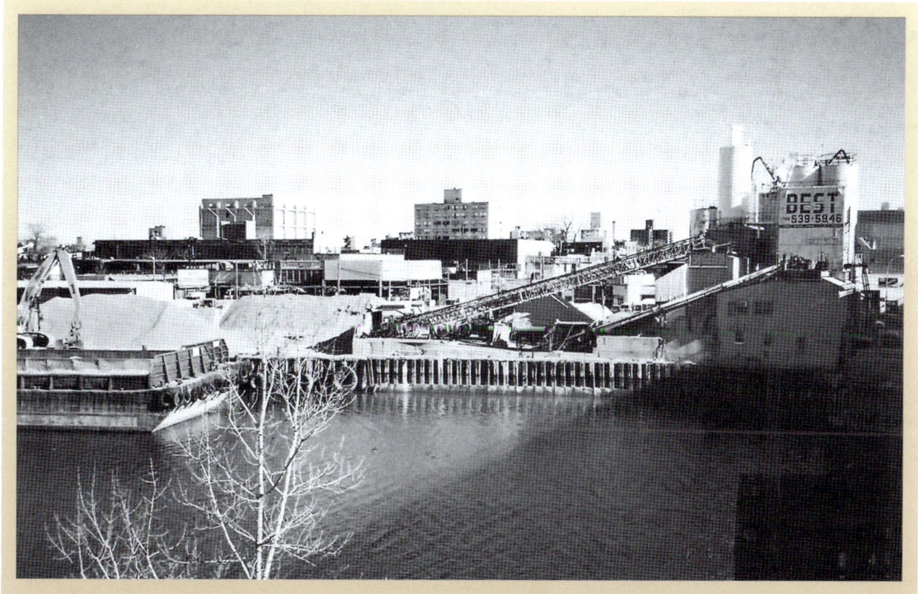

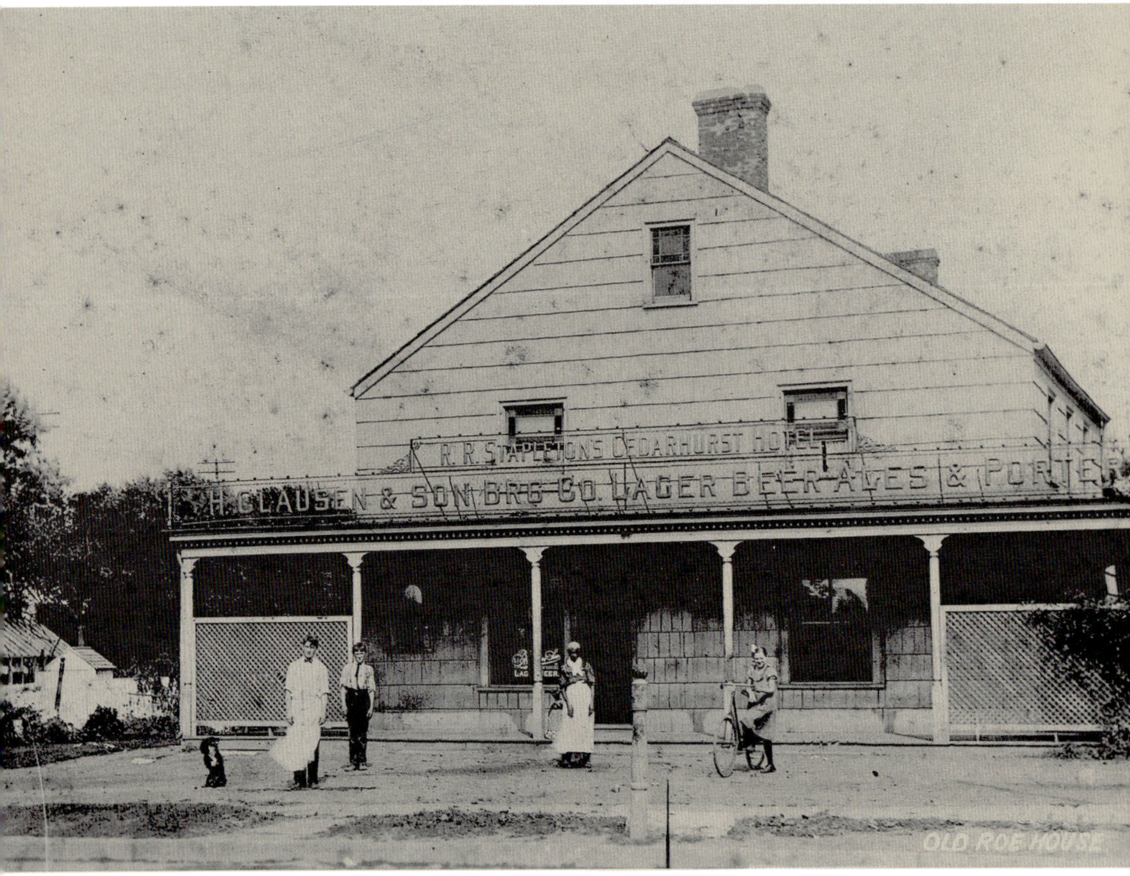

The old George B. Roe family home was located on the south side of Myrtle Avenue (Thirty-second Avenue) just east of the intersection of College Point Boulevard, which was then known originally as Clinton Avenue. In the late 1890s, it became R. R. Stapleton's Cedarhurst Hotel. Most of the area is now dominated by dozens of factories featuring glass cutters, food manufactories and distributors, cement and gravel refineries, and storage warehouses. The Whitestone Expressway approach is visible to the left.

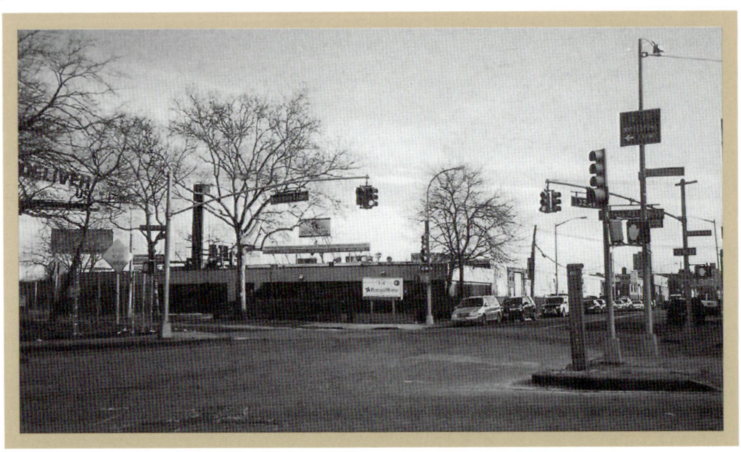

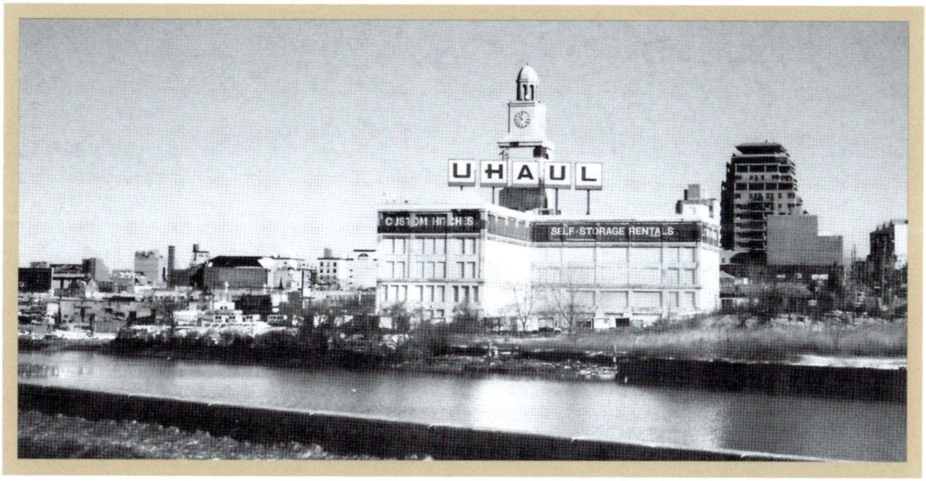

William Lawrence first came to Flushing in 1635 from Ipswich, Massachusetts, and became one of the original patentees of Flushing. His grandson John Lawrence built the family homestead known as Willow Bank in the early 1790s on Old Lawrence Street (King Road), a short diagonal path that connected Broadway with Lawrence Street. In 1830, it was destroyed by fire. The new Willow Bank was constructed in 1836 on the west side of College Point Boulevard and stood for almost 100 years until its destruction in 1926. (Courtesy of the Queens Borough Public Library, Long Island Division, Borough President of Queens Photographs.)

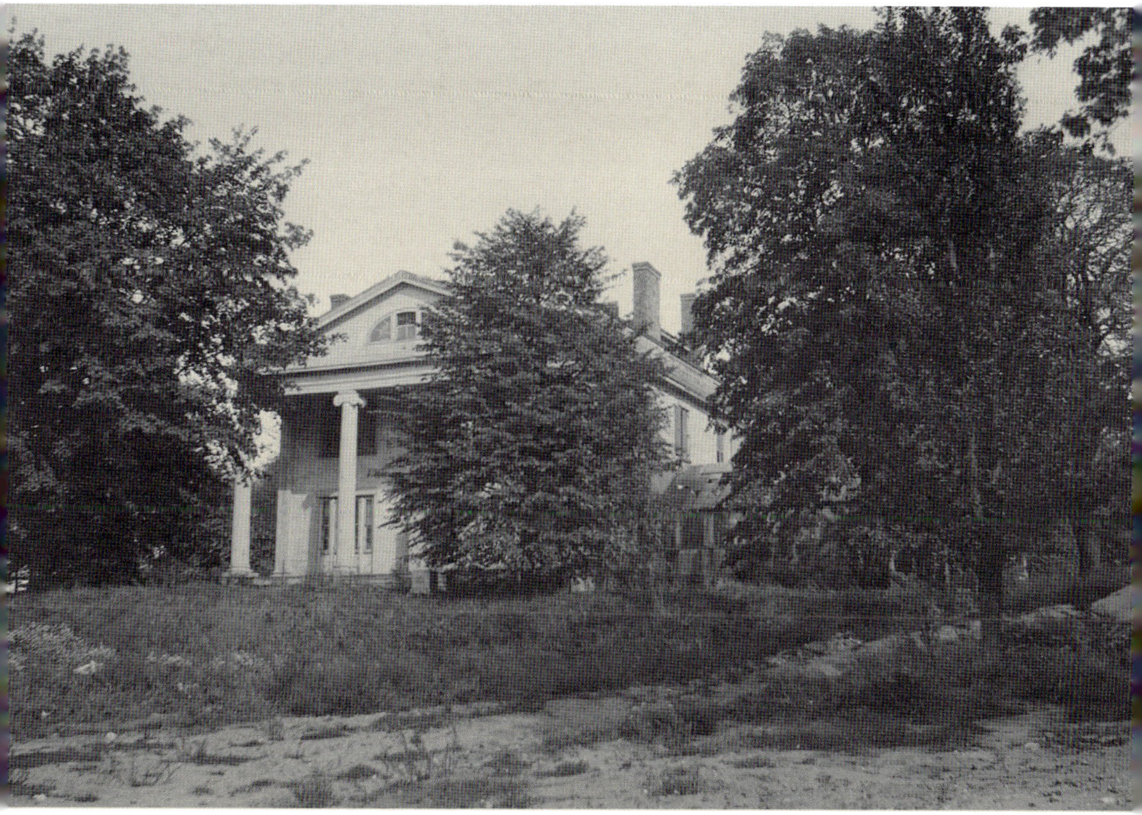

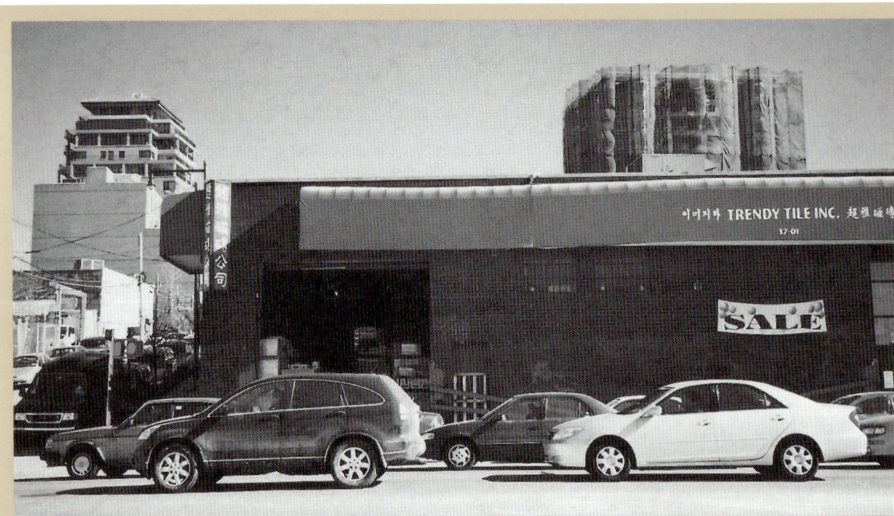

The estate of attorney Henry Augustine Bogert was located at 72 Lawrence Street and designed by prominent New York architect Richard M. Upjohn in 1878. It was named Robinshurst by the eldest daughter, Mary, because of the plentiful amount of robins that nested on the property. The property sat atop a hill near the southeast corner of Thirty-seventh Avenue and College Point Boulevard. The Bogert family was a very prominent family in Flushing, owning many properties throughout the town.

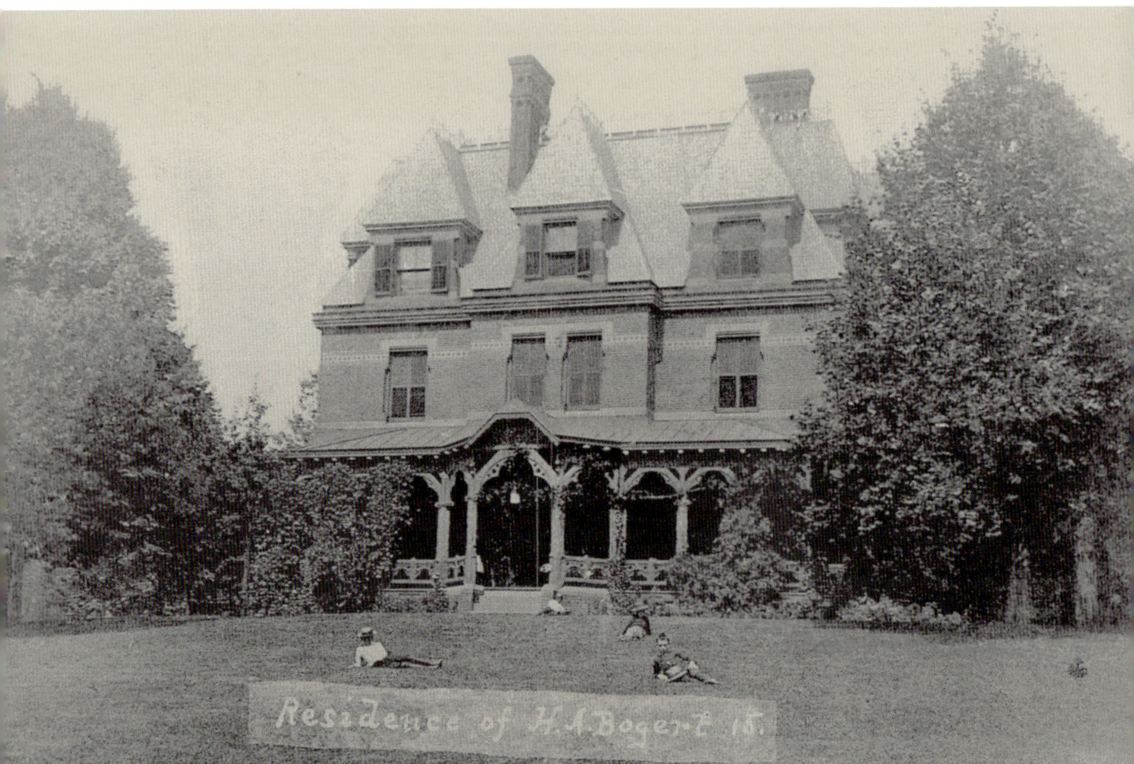

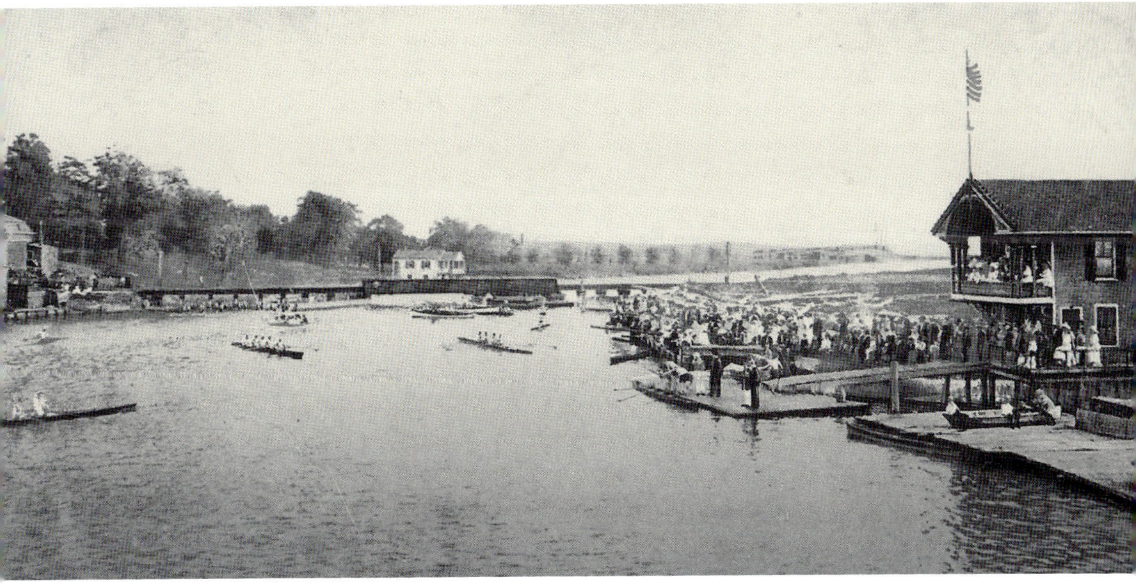

Wahnetah Boat Club was located just south of the bridge on the west side of Flushing Creek. It occupied the boathouse of the former Nereous Club and was organized in 1900. Hundreds of people turned out to watch the rowing talents of Joseph G. Dondero, Henry Hilbers, William R. Lawson, Thomas, Joseph, and Angelo Cleary, as well as William and Lawrence Halleran. On August 28, 1915, the Wahnetahs won four races including the trophy at the 29th Annual Regatta of the Long Island Rowing Association. In the background is the rail bridge for the Whitestone Branch of the Long Island Rail Road.

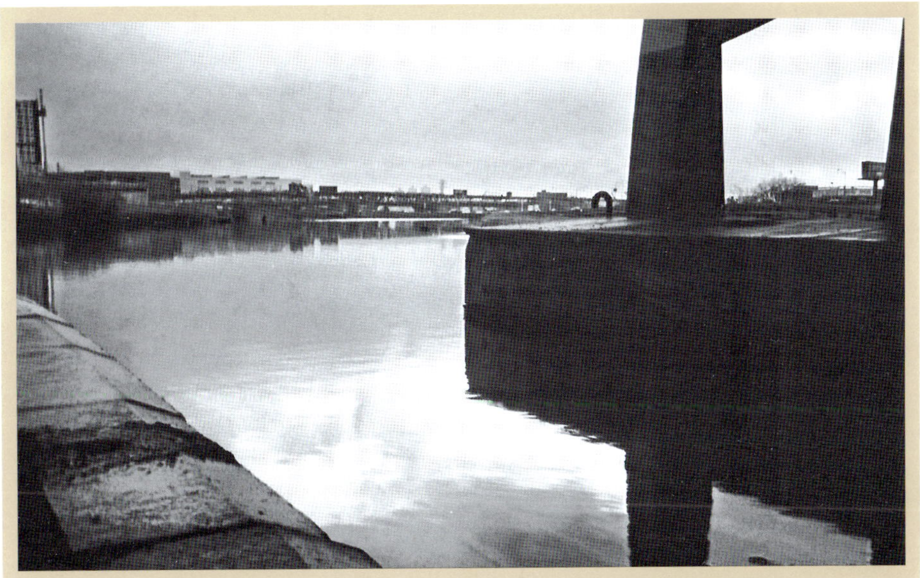

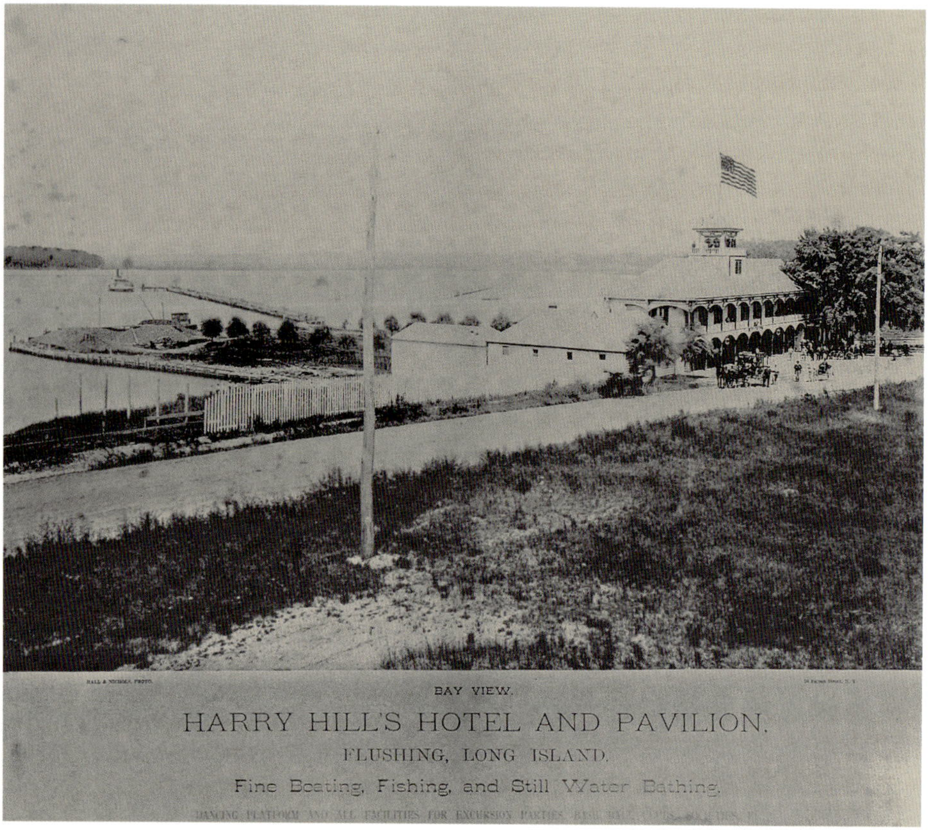

Harry Hill's Hotel and Pavilion opened on Tuesday, October 14, 1879, near Northern Boulevard at the mouth of Flushing Bay. Measuring 150 feet in length, it featured a dining hall, bowling alley, and shooting gallery. British forces occupying Flushing during the American Revolution used this location as the headquarters for the 37th British Regiment on what was originally the site of the Lent Farmhouse. The Pavilion burned to the ground on October 25, 1891, when a loose dog knocked over an oil lamp. The site is now occupied by the World's Fair Marina.

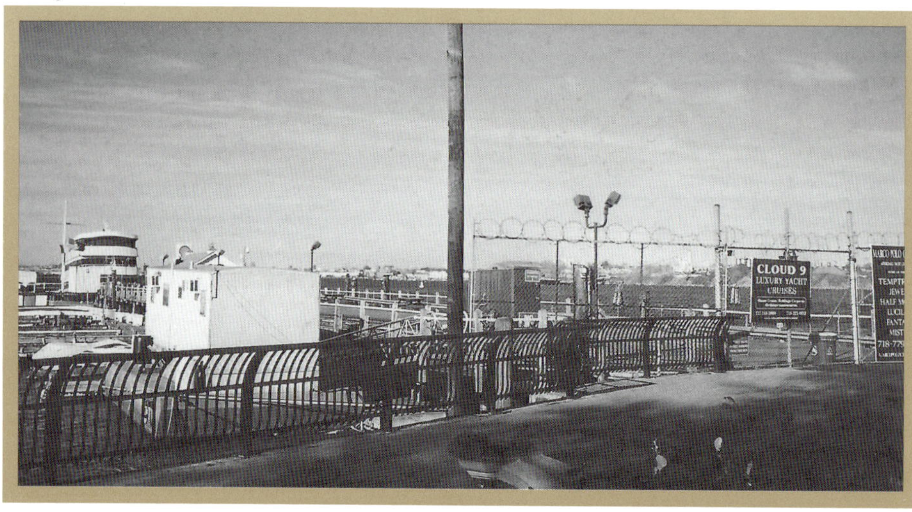

CHAPTER 2

Flushing and Its Environs

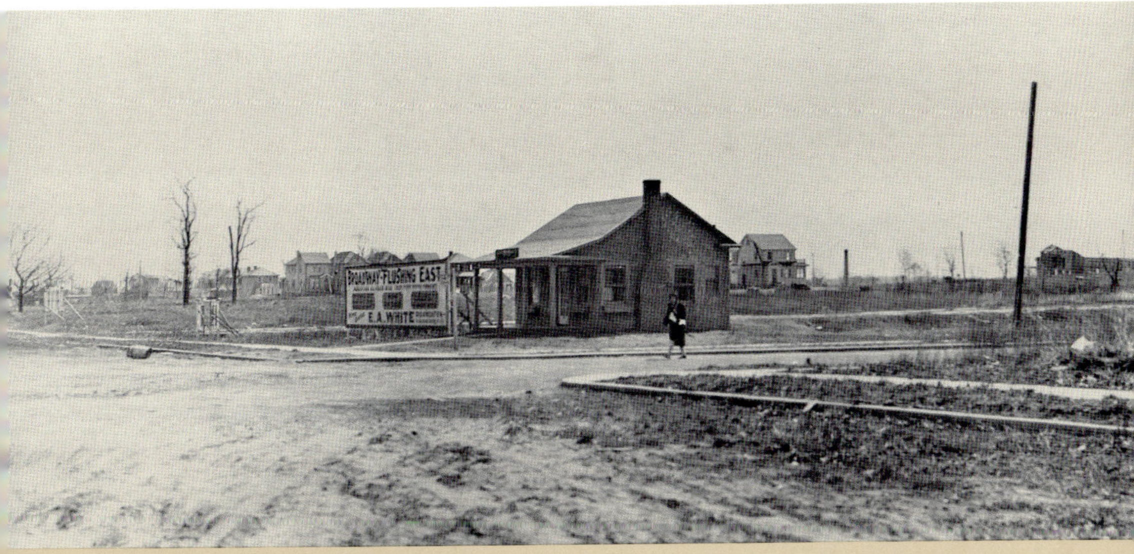

As the population of Flushing grew so did the town's geography. By the beginning of the 20th century, the following suburbs and villages would become part of Greater Flushing. These included Little Neck, Douglaston, Bayside, Auburndale, Murray Hill, Broadway, Waldheim, Kissena Park, College Point, Malba, Beechhurst, Whitestone, Flushing Heights, Fresh Meadows, Springfield, Oakland Gardens, Hillcrest, and an additional two-dozen subdivisions located within the township. Here, a real estate office, located on the former Bowden property on the southeast corner of 192nd Street and Northern Boulevard, sold property for the Broadway section. (Courtesy of the Queens Borough Public Library, Long Island Division, Borough President of Queens, Percy Loomis Sperr Photographs.)

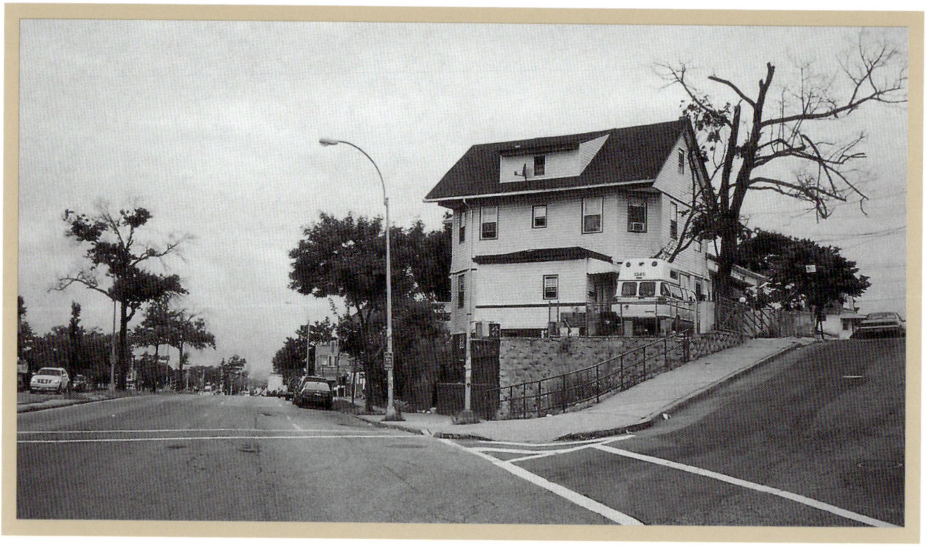

Corona, originally known as West Flushing, was first settled in 1655 by Robert Coe. One of the most notable sites in early Corona was the National Race Course, which opened June 26, 1854. The area finally received its official name in 1870 from Thomas Waite Howard, a real estate developer who suggested that Corona was "the crown of Queens County." This scene is looking west on Astoria Boulevard between 105th and 104th Streets in 1905. To the right is a path leading to Wenzel's Bathing Pavilion.

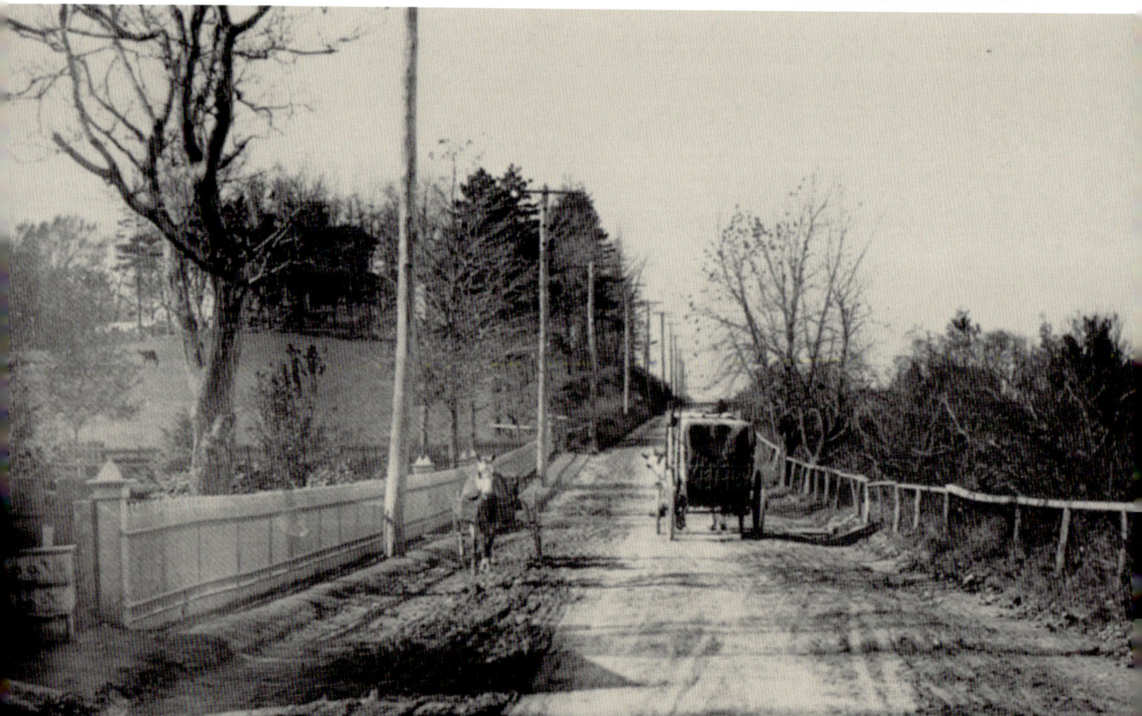

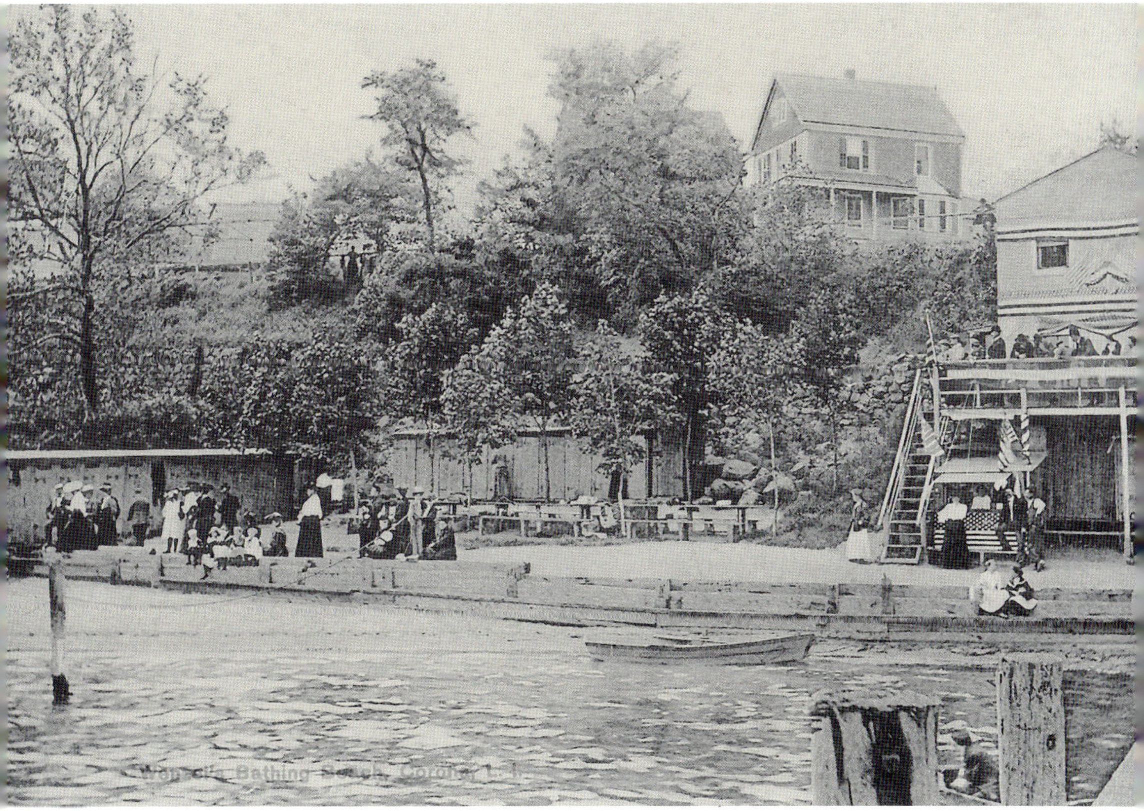

Wenzel's Bathing Pavilion, operated by the actor Frederick Wenzel, was a popular spot for summer recreation on Flushing Bay. A resident of Corona, Wenzel was a stage actor for 45 years. In 1911, the Board of Health demanded that all bathhouses install sterilization plants for suits and towels. These demands were beyond the means of the owners. Together with the increasing pollution of Flushing Bay, Wenzel's was forced to shut down. The waterfront property is today, incredibly, the Grand Central Parkway.

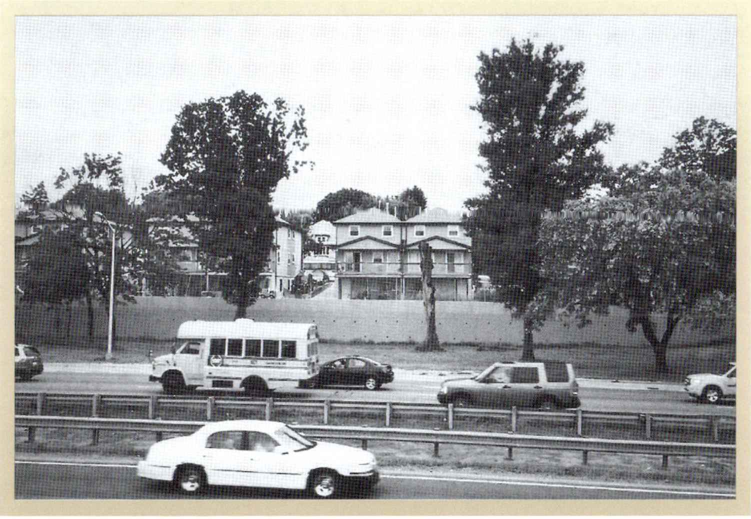

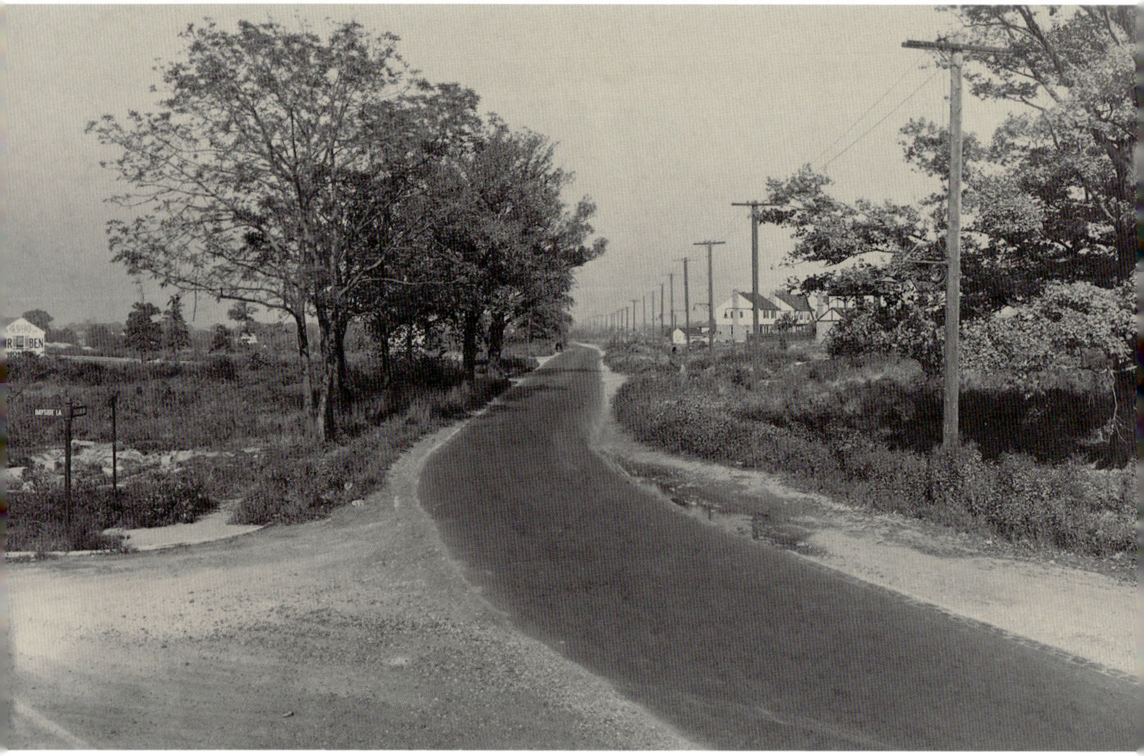

Cross Island Boulevard (Francis Lewis Boulevard) was originally a narrow thoroughfare that wound its way south toward the Rockaways. Widened in the late 1930s, the boulevard is shown here looking north entering Auburndale, which was developed in 1901 on farmland owned by Thomas Willett, who was the first mayor of New York City. The neighborhood expanded shortly after the Long Island Rail Road opened a station at 192nd Street and Thirty-ninth Avenue. To the east is Bayside, which was developed by the Lawrence and Bell families. (Courtesy of the Queens Borough Public Library, Long Island Division, Chamber of Commerce of the Borough of Queens Records.)

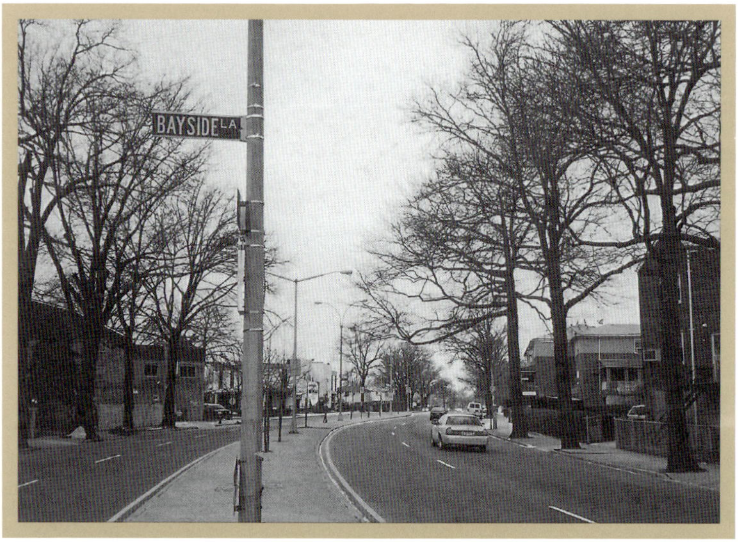

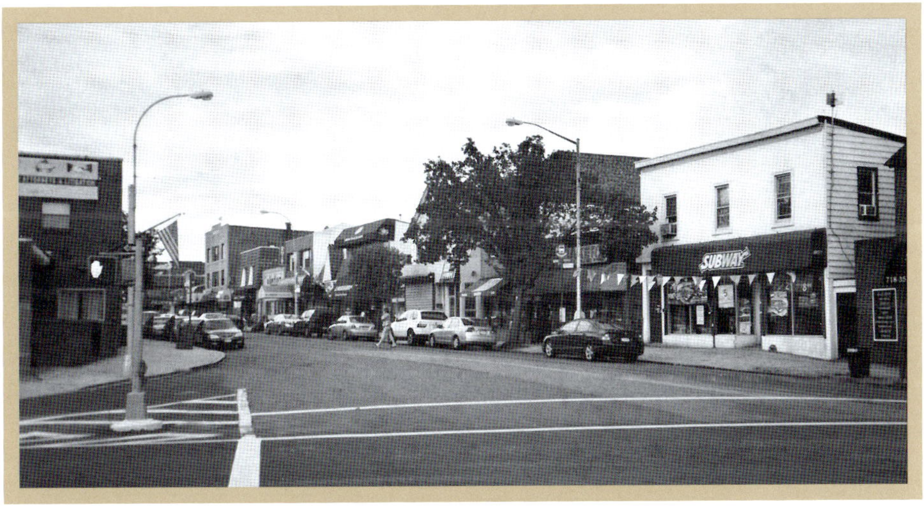

Whitestone was settled around 1645 by Dutch farmers who purchased it from the Matinecock for the price of one ax for every 50 acres. Named after a large white boulder found at the seashore, it also once was known as Cookie Hill. One day a woman from Manhattan who baked delicious cakes and cookies, as the legend goes, was accidentally put ashore by the steamer *Lynneus*. Unable to get home, she earned money by selling out her stock of sweets and crullers to a crowd of local men and boys. The village was incorporated in 1869. This view looks north up 150th Street.

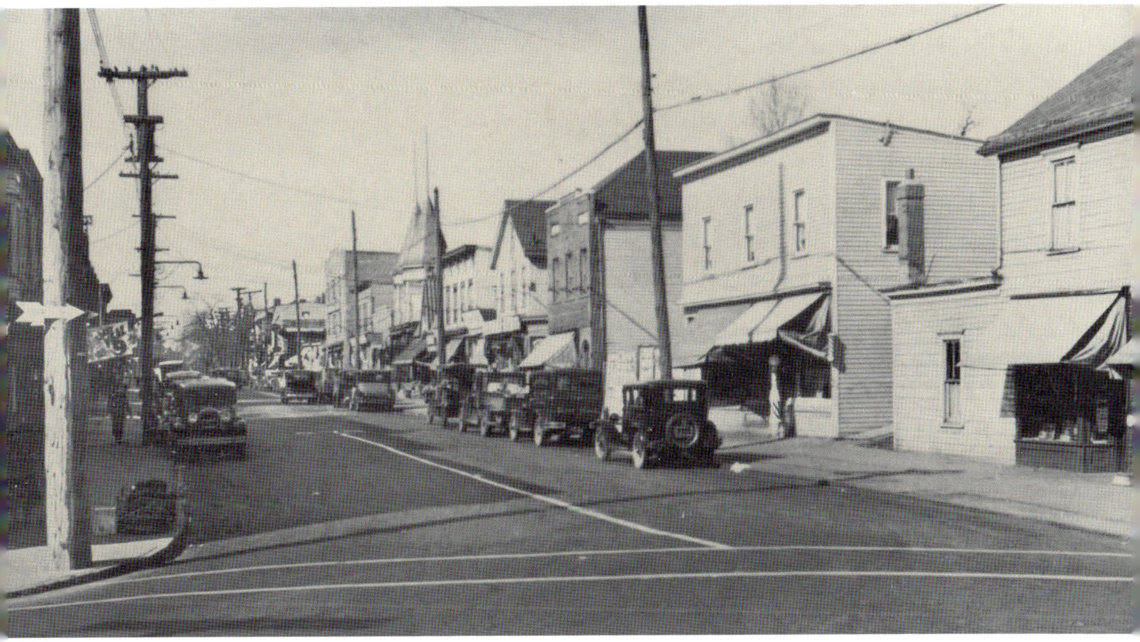

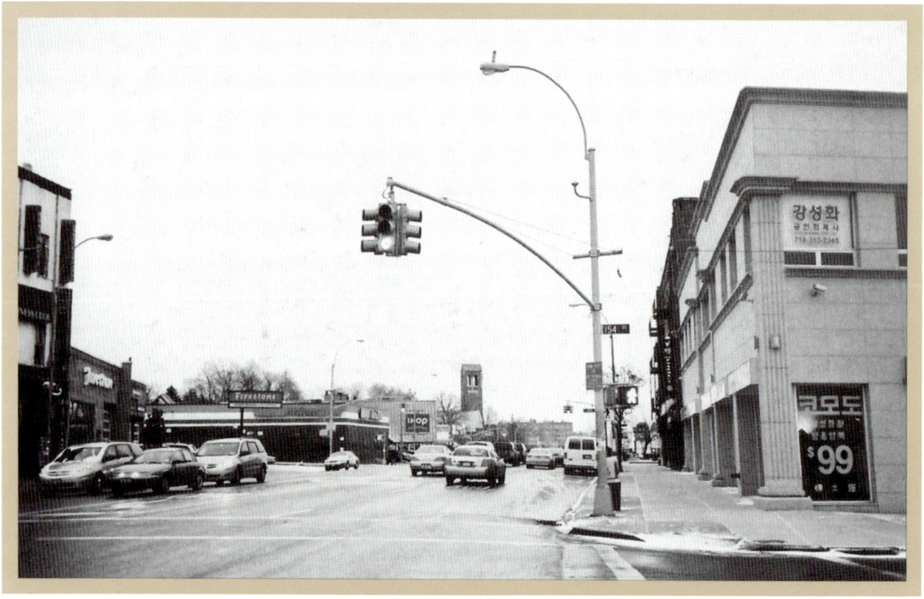

The Ritz Theatre was built in Murray Hill in 1917 on the southeast corner of Northern Boulevard and 154th Street. It was a small theatre with only 150 seats. The small cinema fell victim to the post–World War I recession and became an auto repair garage until 1923. The owner of the Janice Theatre converted it back into a cinema before it closed in 1927. Advertisements for the new Roosevelt Movie Theatre can be seen on the side of the closed cinema.

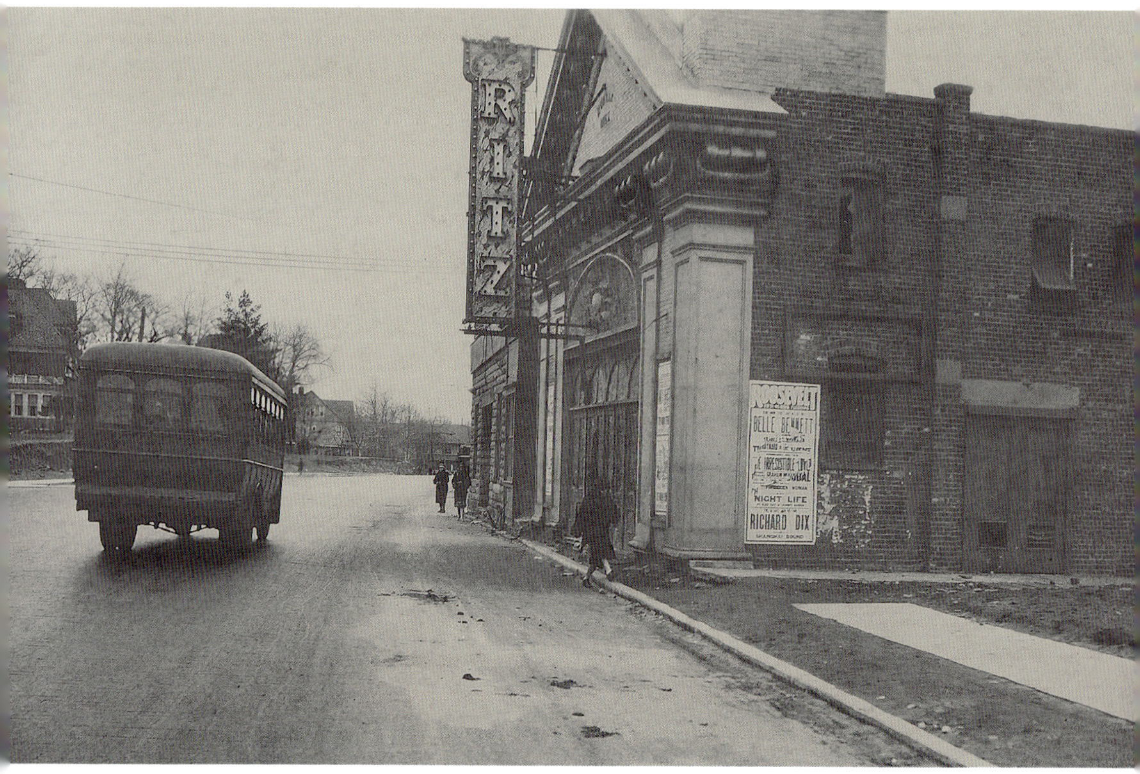

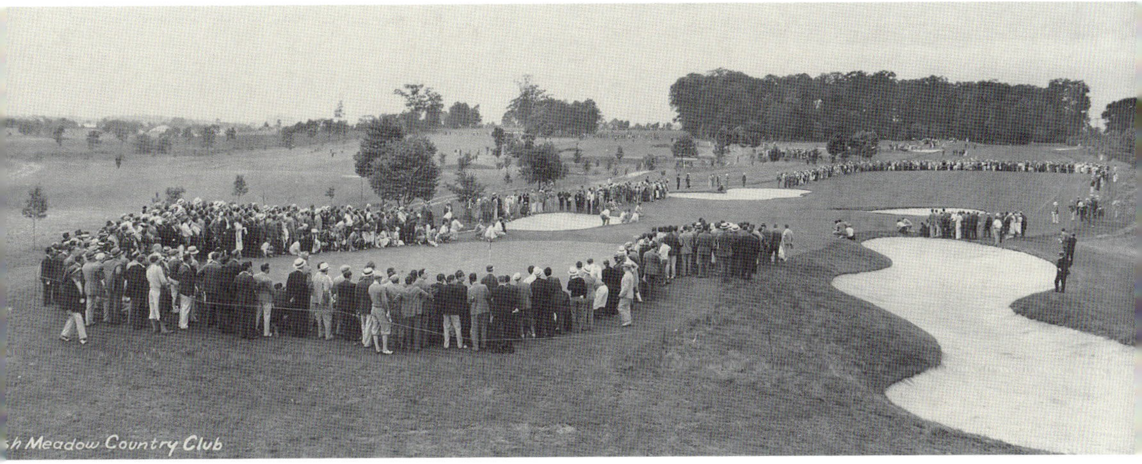

Fresh Meadows was known in colonial days as Black Stump, because local farmers marked their land boundaries with rows of blackened tree stumps. Benedict Arnold hid in the area during the American Revolution. In 1923, Benjamin C. Ribman purchased Klein's farm and opened the Fresh Meadows Country Club. The golf course became the setting for the National and Professional Golf Association Opens. In 1946, the 141-acre club was sold to the New York Life Insurance Company for a residential development that opened in 1949. (Courtesy of the Queens Borough Public Library, Long Island Division, Borough President of Queens Photographs.)

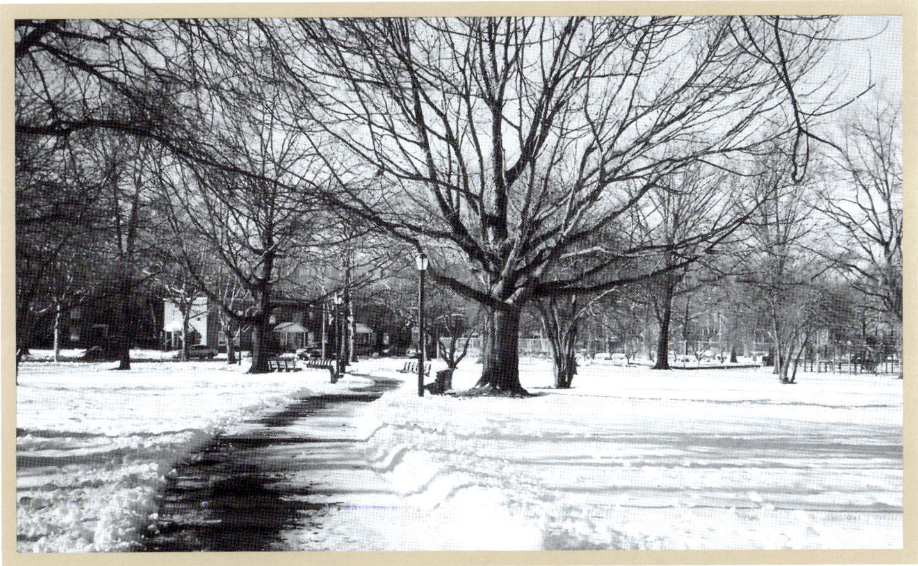

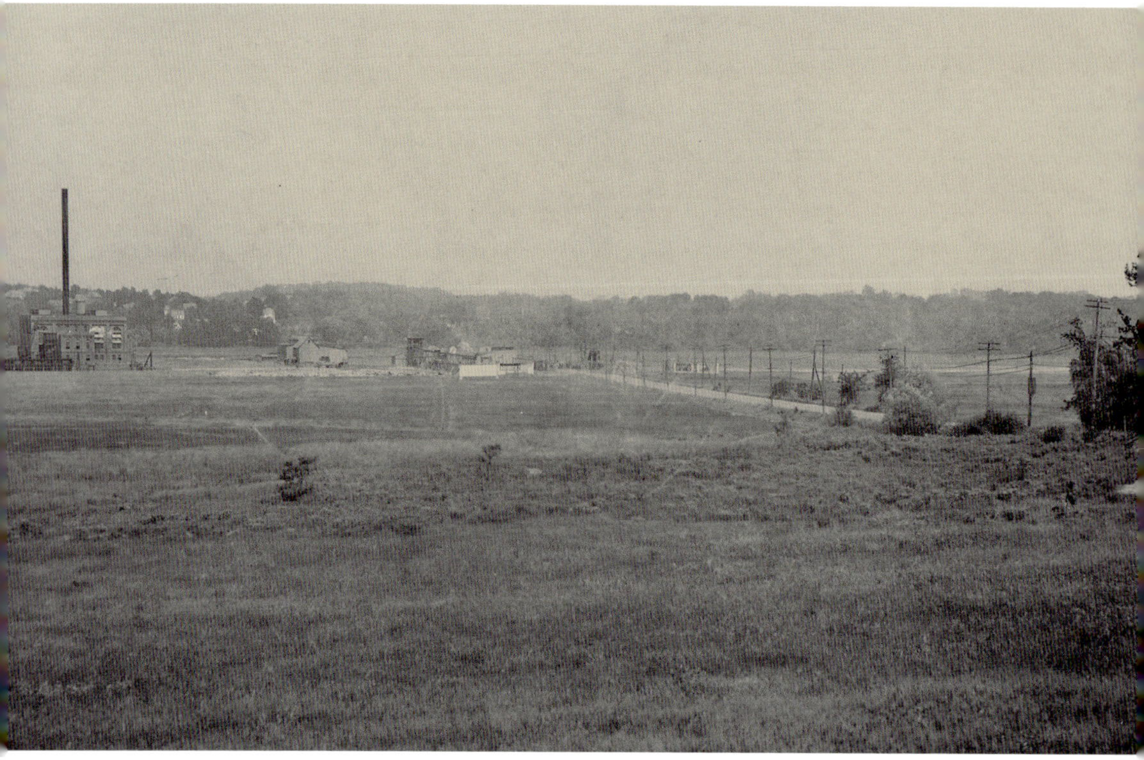

Douglaston and Little Neck make up the eastern frontier of Flushing Township. Located on the borderline of Nassau County, Little Neck received its name from the peninsulas that formed when the Wisconsinan Glacier broke and descended from Connecticut millions of years ago. Douglaston received its name from William P. Douglas who settled in the area in 1835, which he purchased from Wyant Van Zandt. It was developed by the Rickert-Finlay Company in 1906. This view looks east toward Alley Pond and Douglaston. (Courtesy of the Douglaston and Little Neck Historical Society, Nathaniel J. Palzer Collection.)

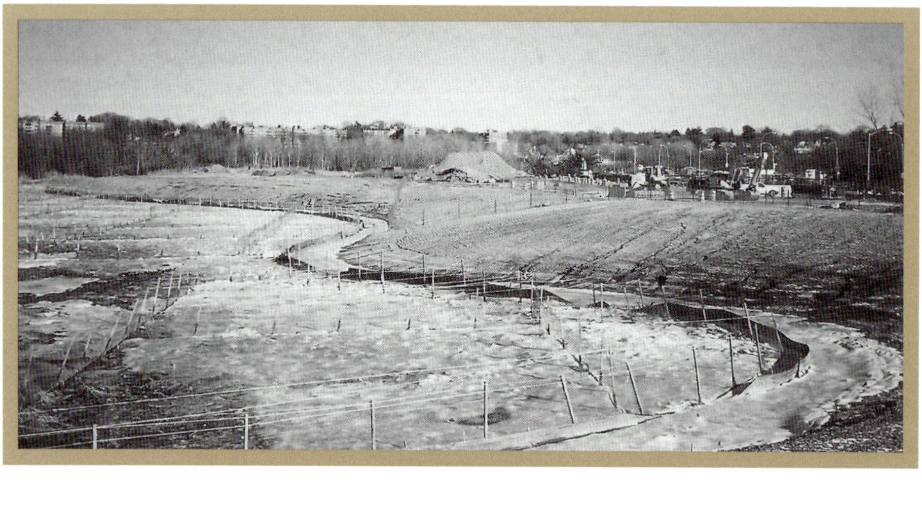

CHAPTER 3

THE RAILROAD COMES TO TOWN

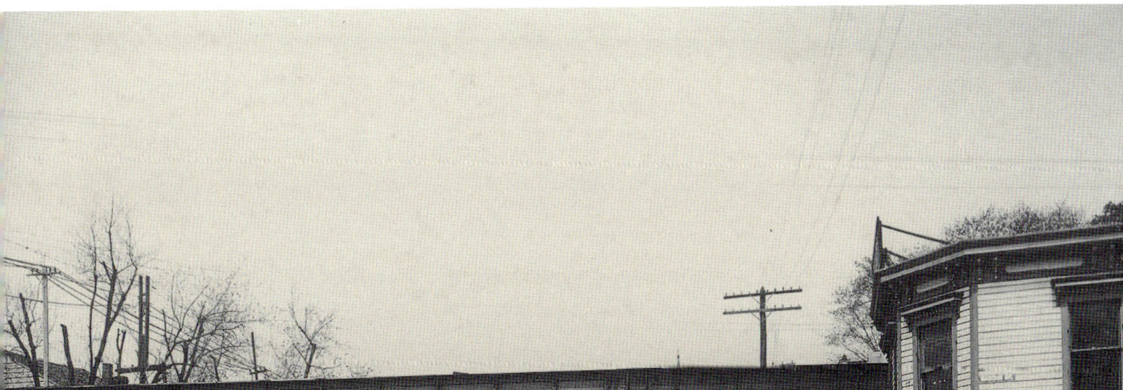

On June 26, 1854, the railroad came to Flushing. The stagecoach gave way to the New York and Flushing Railroad. Everyone in town gathered and cheered with jubilee as the first locomotive, bearing the name *Flushing*, pulled into the Main Street station. Shown here in this photograph from April 25, 1913, is the newly built overpass of the Port Washington Branch of the Long Island Rail Road (LIRR). The tracks were raised after the line was electrified in 1912.

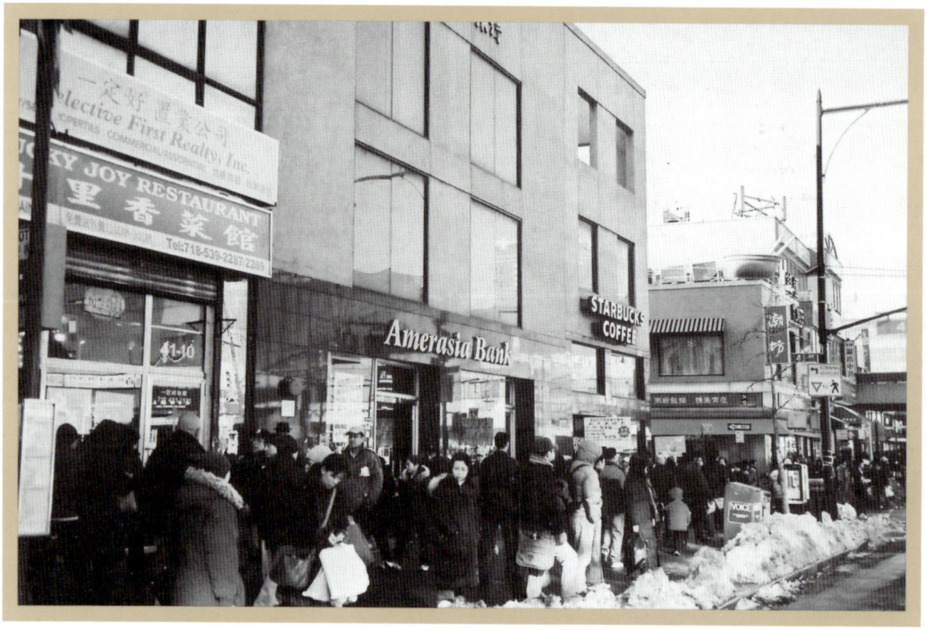

On November 10, 1873, the Newtown and Flushing Rail Road opened for business. The cars were painted white, and from this circumstance it received the popular name of "The White Line." The first station was in Newtown Village. The track then traveled east along the old Horse Brook before arriving at the Corona Park station at Corona Avenue and 111th Street. The train then turned northeastward across Flushing Creek before terminating at this small station on the west side of Main Street between Sanford Avenue and Forty-first Avenue. (Courtesy of the Queens Borough Public Library, Long Island Division, Eugene L. Armbruster Photographs.)

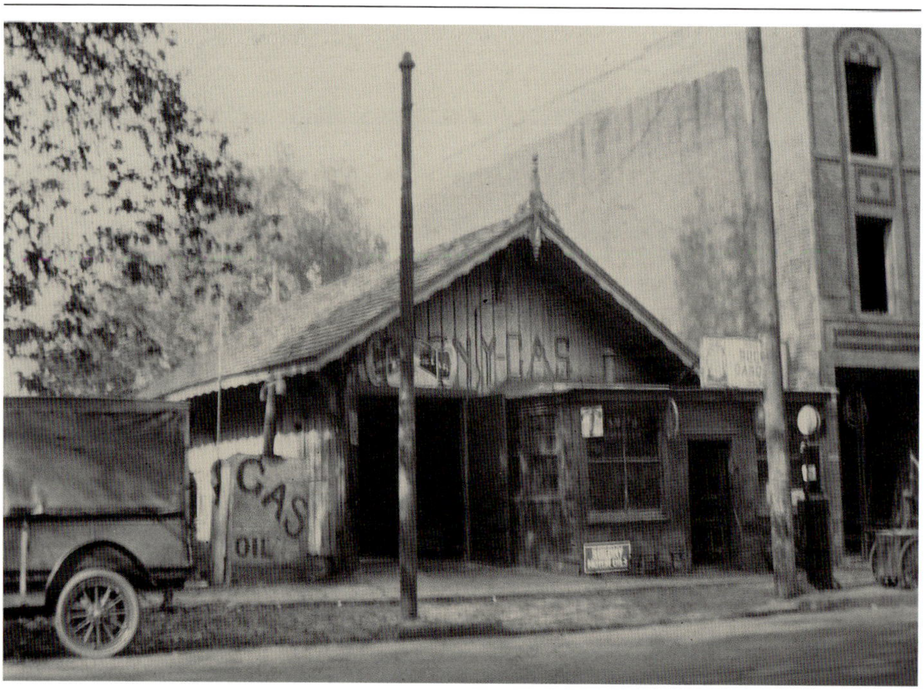

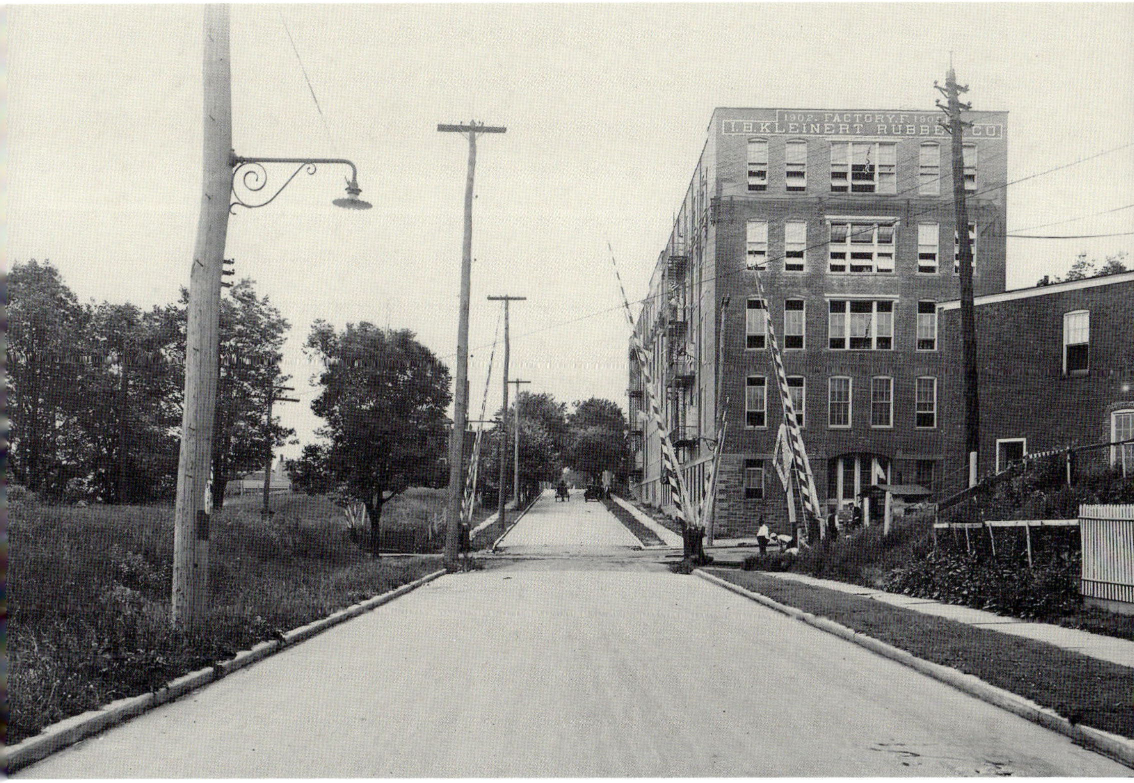

The Whitestone Branch, originally called the Flushing and North Side Railroad before it became part of Long Island Rail Road, was founded in 1869. It would originate at Whitestone Landing before moving onto Whitestone Village, Malba, and then College Point, as seen here on June 28, 1917. The grade crossing at Twentieth Avenue passes in front of the I. B. Kleinert Rubber Company on the approach to the College Point station, which was located on 127th Street and Eighteenth Avenue. The station, a two-story brick building, opened for use on August 14, 1869, and was demolished in 1934.

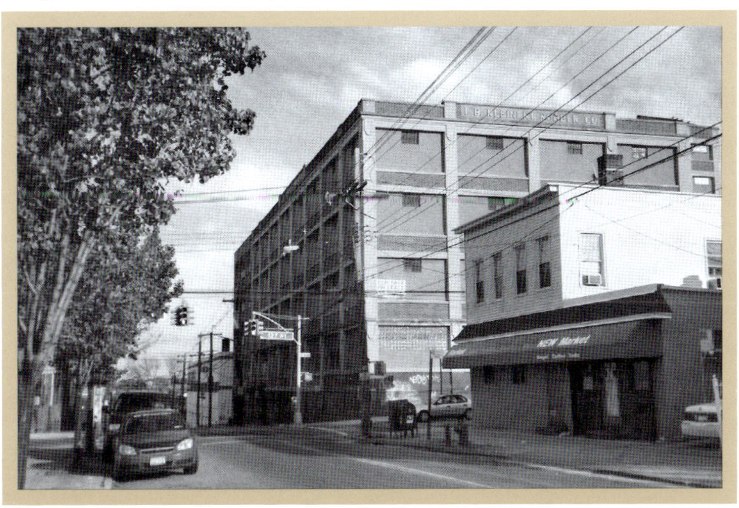

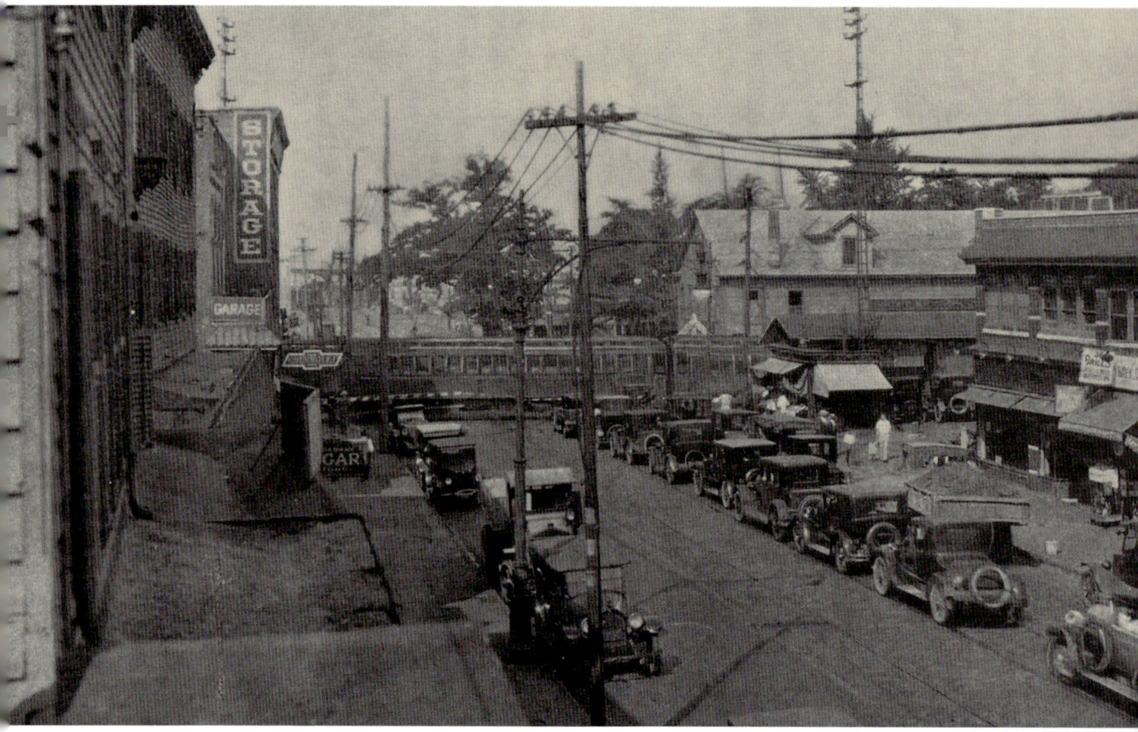

After leaving College Point, the train headed south across a wide-open frontier, which is today the Whitestone Expressway. It would cut through Farrington's Meadows, the current site of the Pathmark Shopping Center, before arriving at the Bridge Street station just north of Northern Boulevard. Opened on August 14, 1869, the station lasted until service was terminated on February 15, 1932, along with every station on the line. This view was taken from atop John J. Halleran's Real Estate Agency, which as mentioned before, was demolished along with other structures to widen the boulevard.

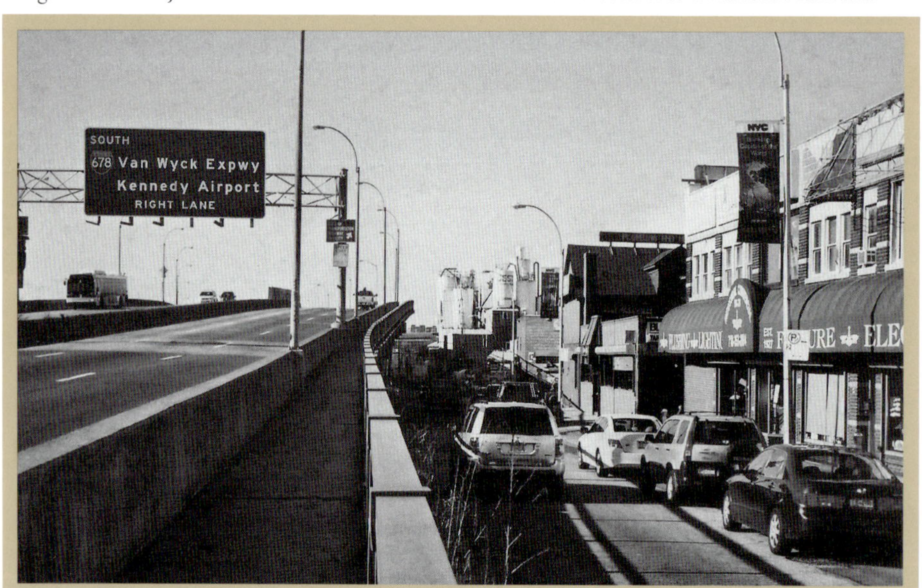

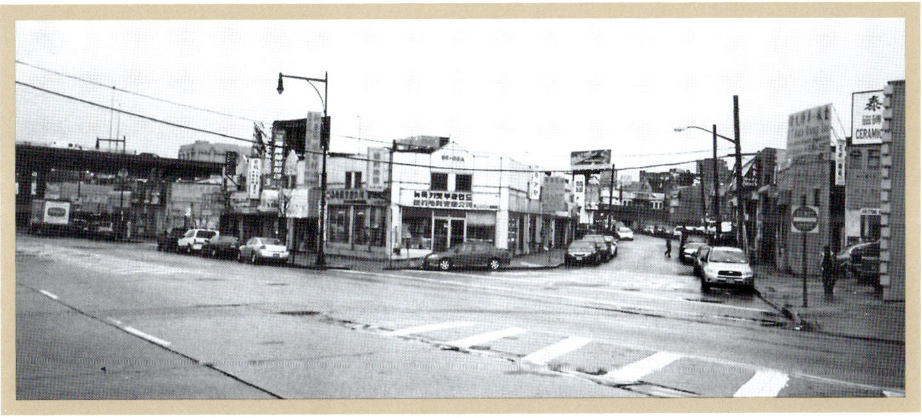

The train would continue west over Old Lawrence Street (King Road) and then cross Lawrence Street heading west toward Manhattan. This amazing photograph, taken on September 5, 1910, shows a serene country setting before the area became heavily industrialized in the 1940s. To the right is a building of special interest. The Flushing Pavilion was Flushing's premier hotel from the 1840s until the 1860s. It was three stories and featured 30 guest rooms. It would become the headquarters for John and Thomas Adikes' grain and feed business.

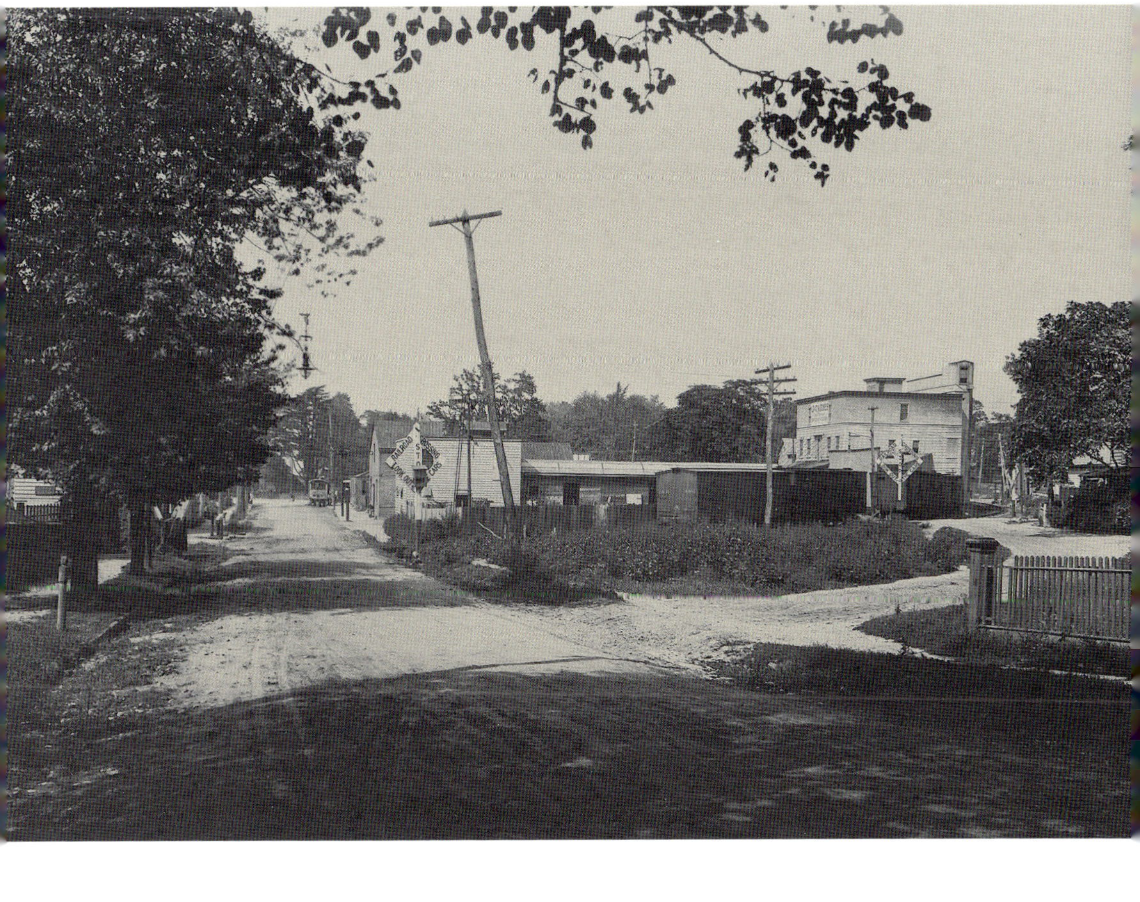

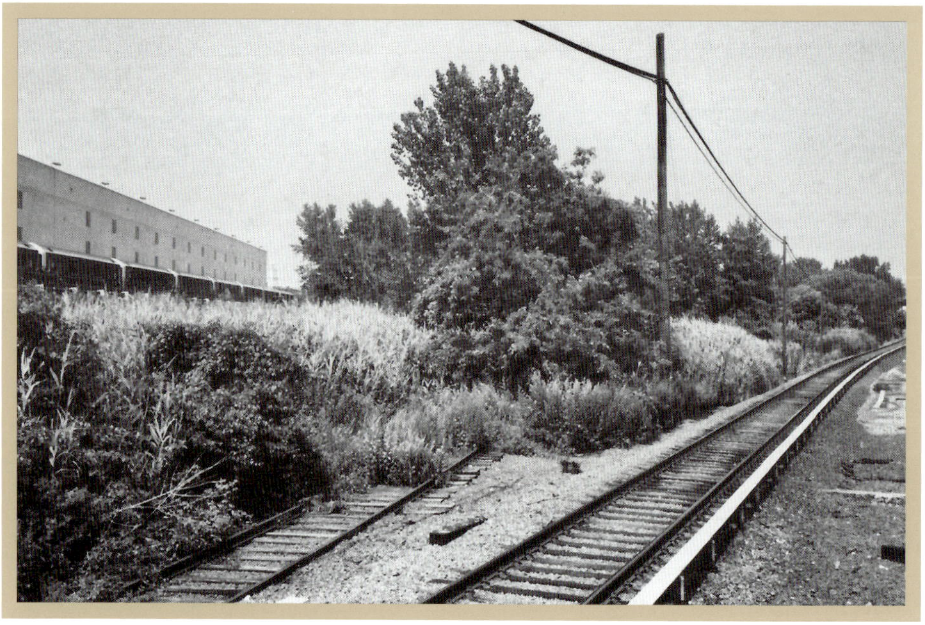

Taken on October 9, 1911, this photograph shows workmen tending to the tracks of the Port Washington Branch of Long Island Rail Road on the approach to Flushing Village. Formed out of the Flushing and North Shore Railroad in 1876, the line finally made its way to Port Washington by 1898. This view looks east near what would become the future Willets Point station in 1928. Today, remains of the old Whitestone Branch can still be seen from the platform. (Courtesy of Brian Merlis/Brooklynpix.com.)

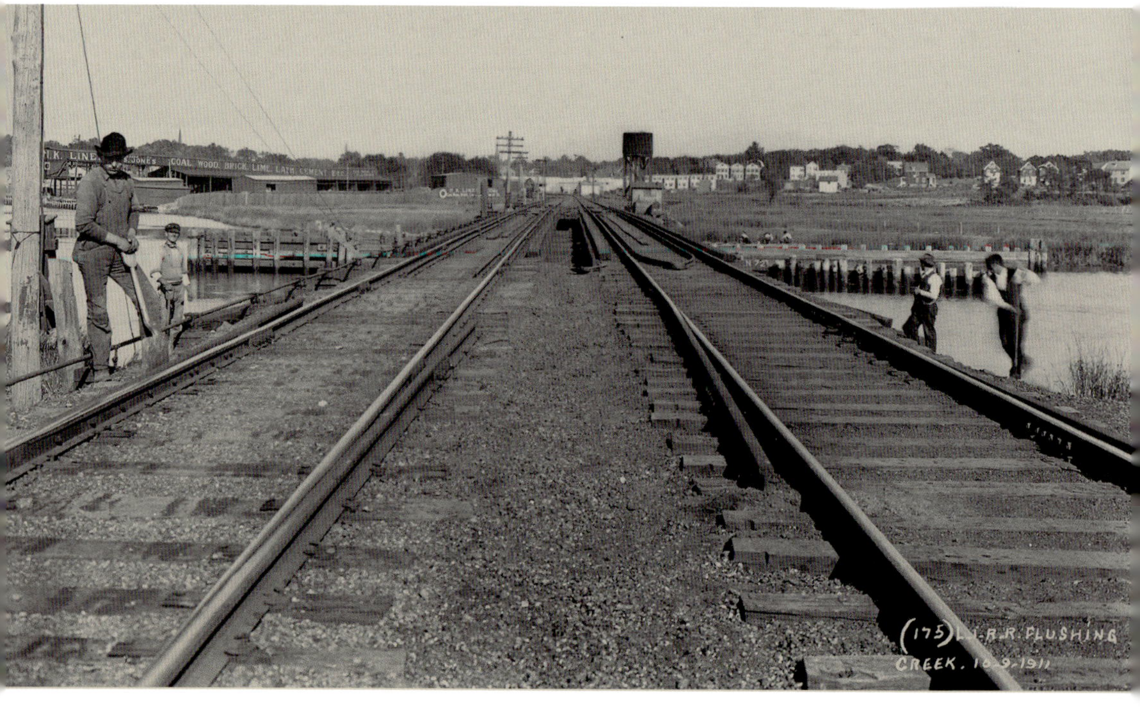

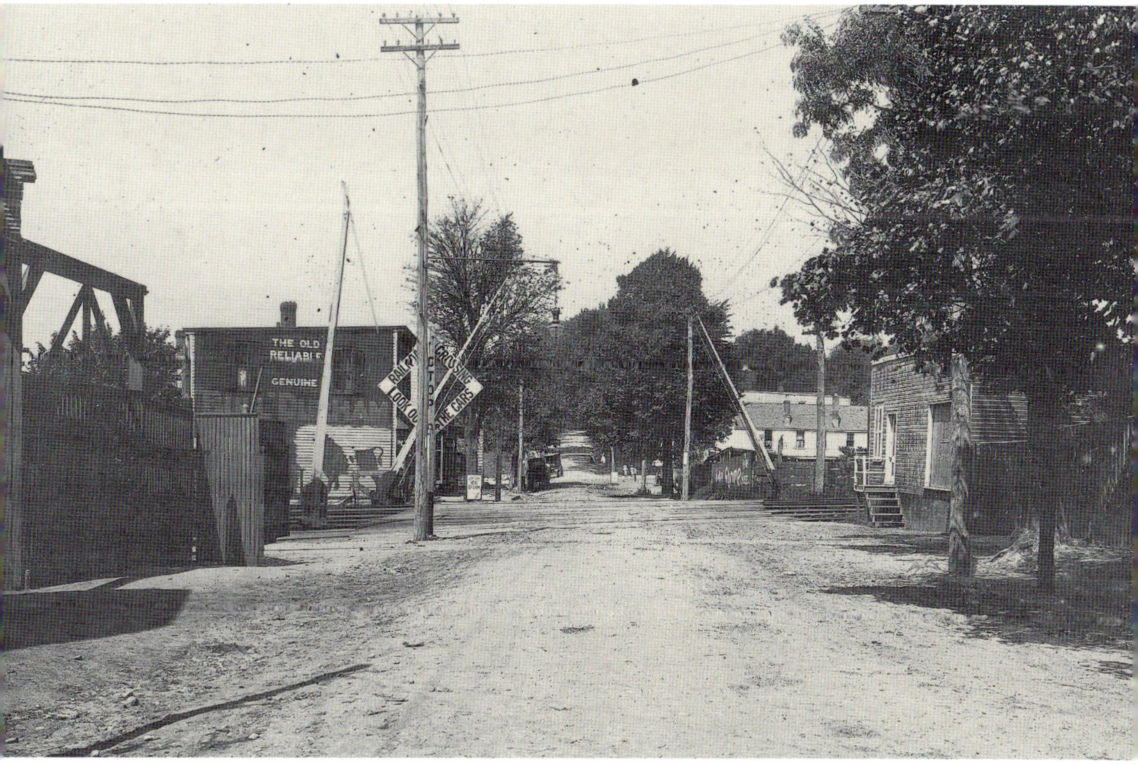

This photograph is looking north on College Point Boulevard near Forty-first Avenue on November 5, 1910, at the Long Island Rail Road grade crossing of the Port Washington Branch. The tracks were elevated at this point three years later because of collisions with horse-drawn wagons and pedestrians. To the left is a painted advertisement for "The Old Reliable" Bull Durham cigarettes. The company was founded in the 1860s by James R. Green of Durham, North Carolina. It quickly became a popular product of the period.

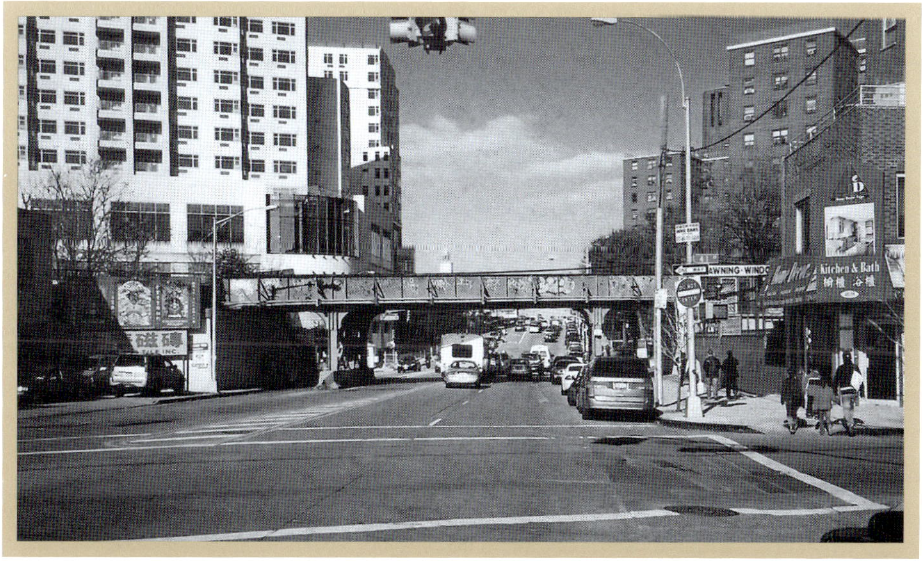

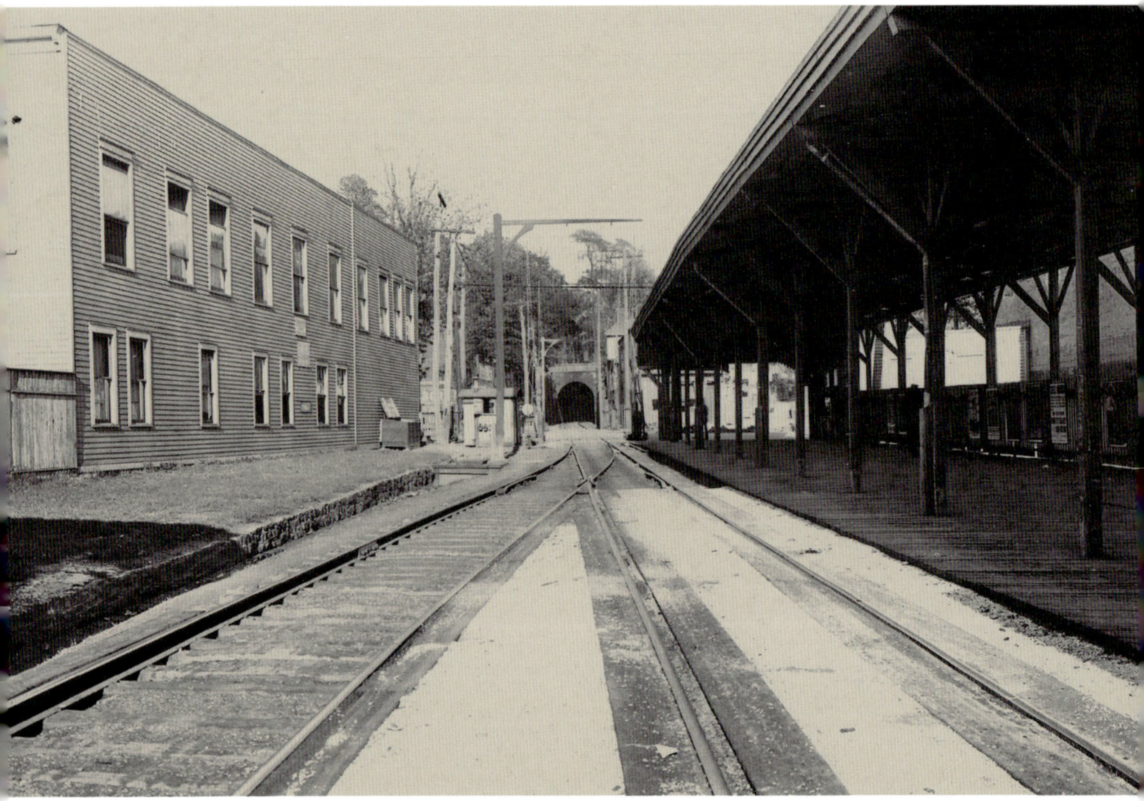

The Main Street depot of the Flushing Railroad was located on the west side of Main Street between Fortieth Road and Forty-first Avenue on a site donated by William Redwood who owned a mansion just north of the tracks. The first depot was built by Sylvester Roe in December 1853. The station burned down on October 30, 1864. A second depot was constructed in 1865, and a third in 1870. It was removed in December 1912 after electrification of the North Side line. Today the space once occupied by the station platform and its approach is now the James Allan Bland Playground. (Courtesy of Brian Merlis/Brooklyn.com.)

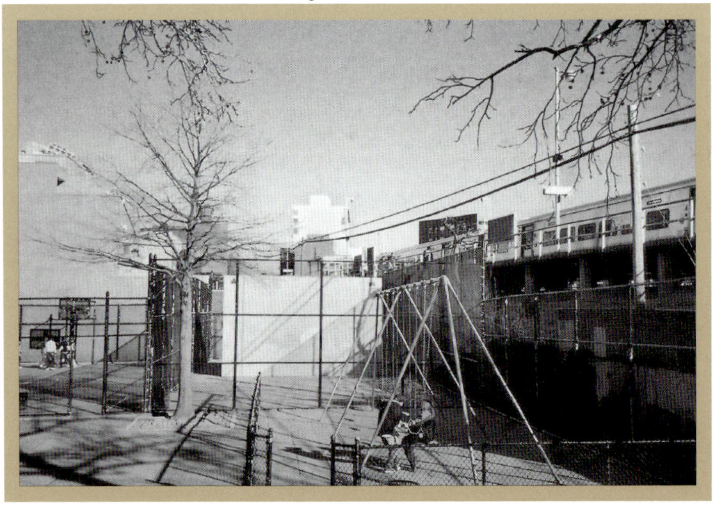

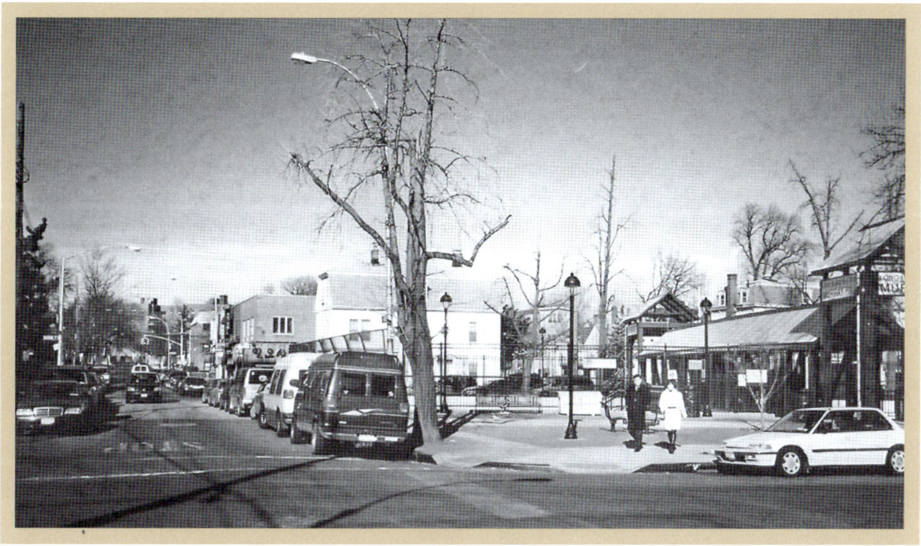

Wilson Avenue (149th Place) is seen looking north on September 14, 1910, on the approach to the Long Island Rail Road station at Murray Hill. The area, which consisted mostly of nurseries owned by the Parsons, King, and Murray families, was developed in 1889 by Frederick Dunton. In April of that year, Dunton, who was on the LIRR's board of directors, had the station built. To the left is a drinking fountain for horses, which was a common sight in Flushing when horses were used in everyday forms of transportation.

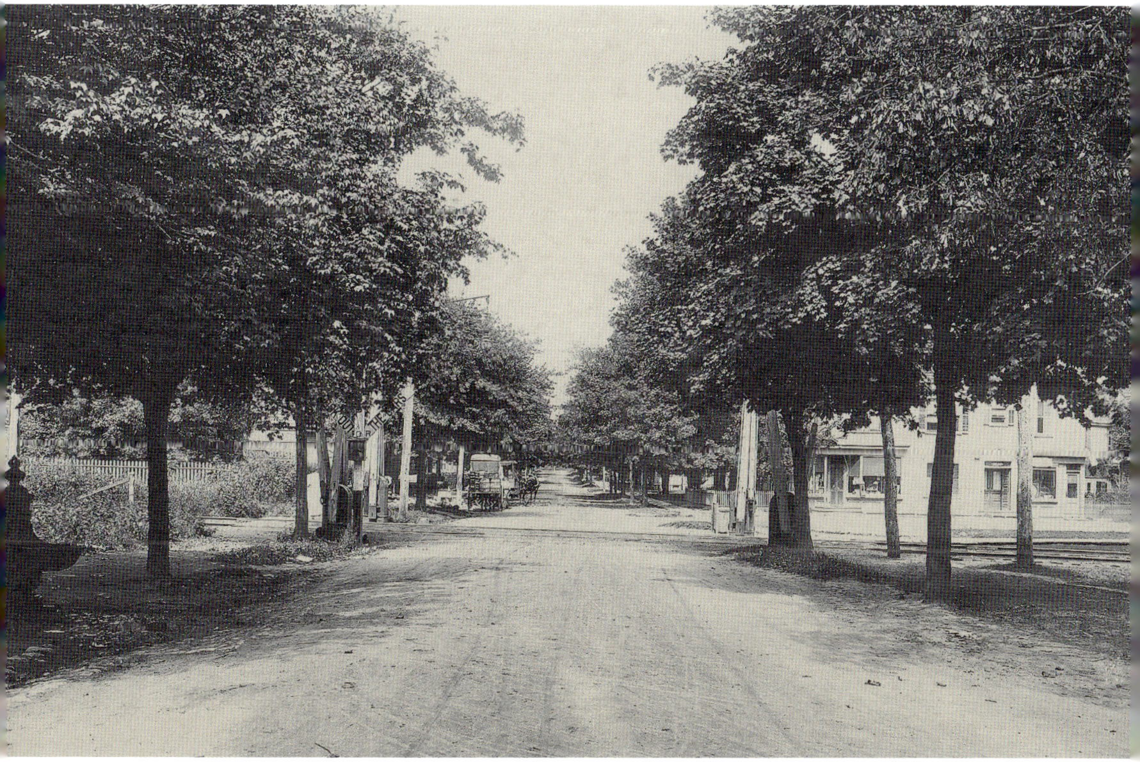

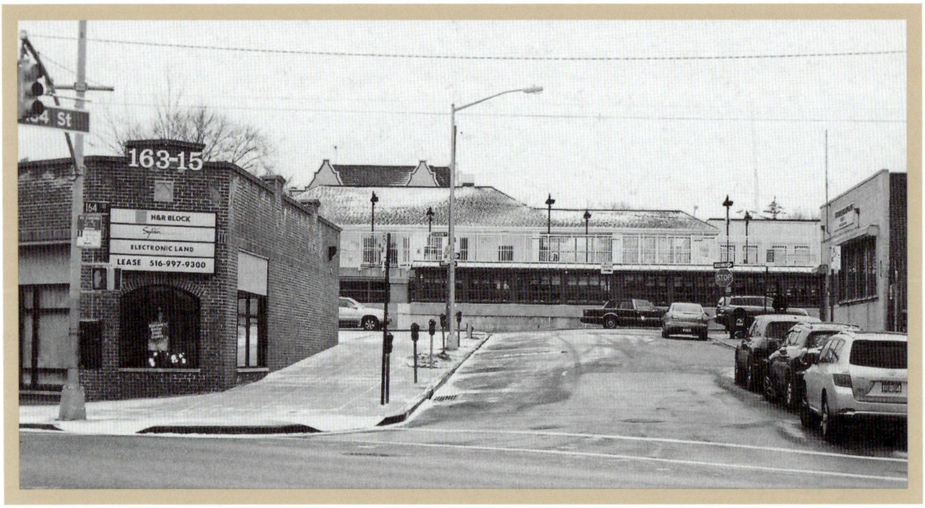

The next stop, Broadway station, is shown here in this photograph taken on December 18, 1911, looking north up Twenty-fourth Avenue (now 164th Street). The area was developed around this time by the Rickert-Finlay Company who started buying land just north of the station. Designated after the former name of Northern Boulevard, the station was originally at ground level, and in 1915, as part of the Long Island Rail Road's safety program, the tracks were elevated above the boulevard, and the grade was lowered considerably.

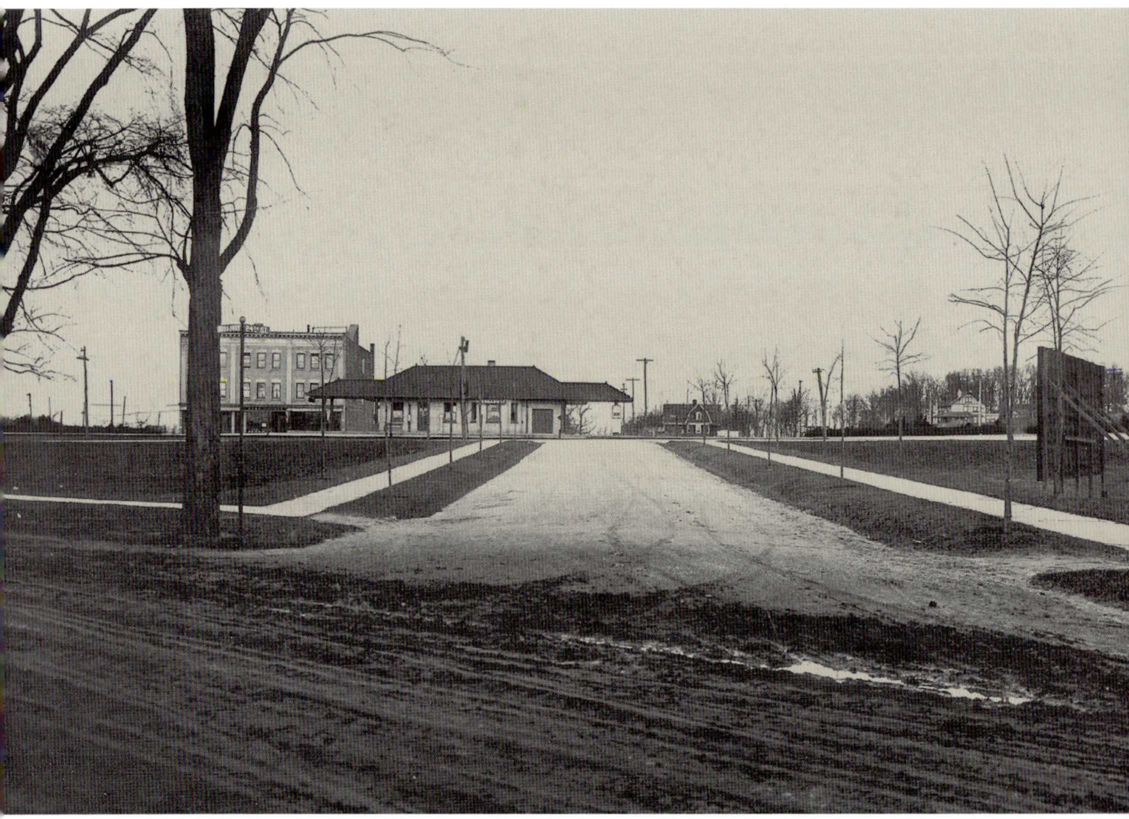

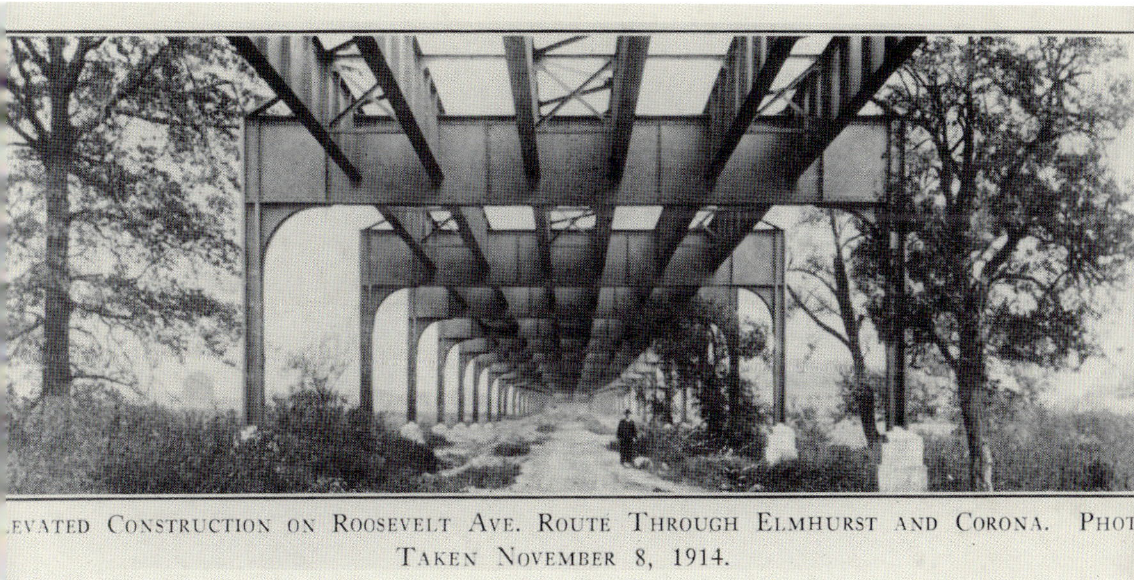

Shown here on November 8, 1914, is the elevated Flushing line of the Interborough Rapid Transit, or IRT, looking toward Corona. A lone man stands in the middle of an unpaved Roosevelt Avenue surrounded by vast open meadows. The Board of Estimate approved the avenue's construction on October 19, 1911. By 1913, the road was being cut through and would travel from Greenpoint Avenue to Flushing Creek. It opened for traffic in 1919. Skulls and bones were unearthed by contractors during its construction. (Courtesy of the LaGuardia and Wagner Archives.)

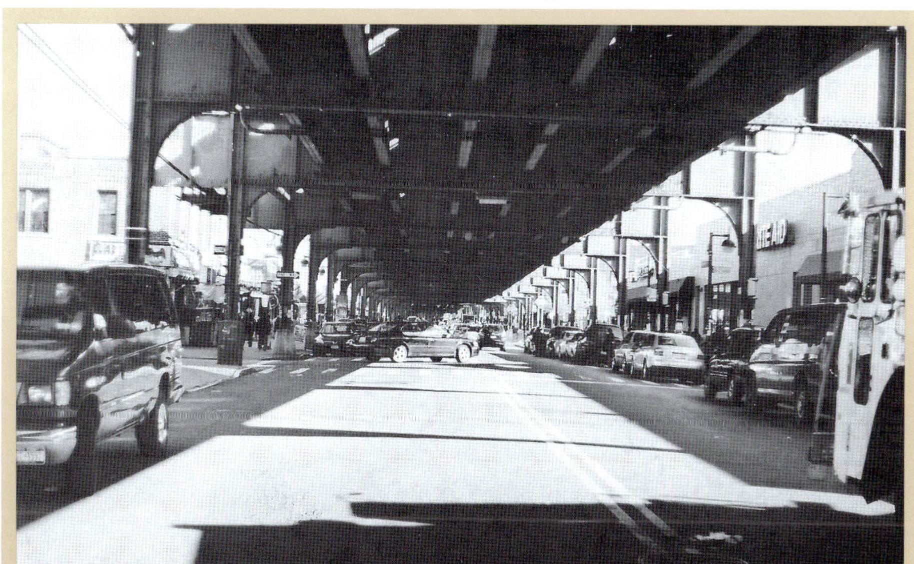

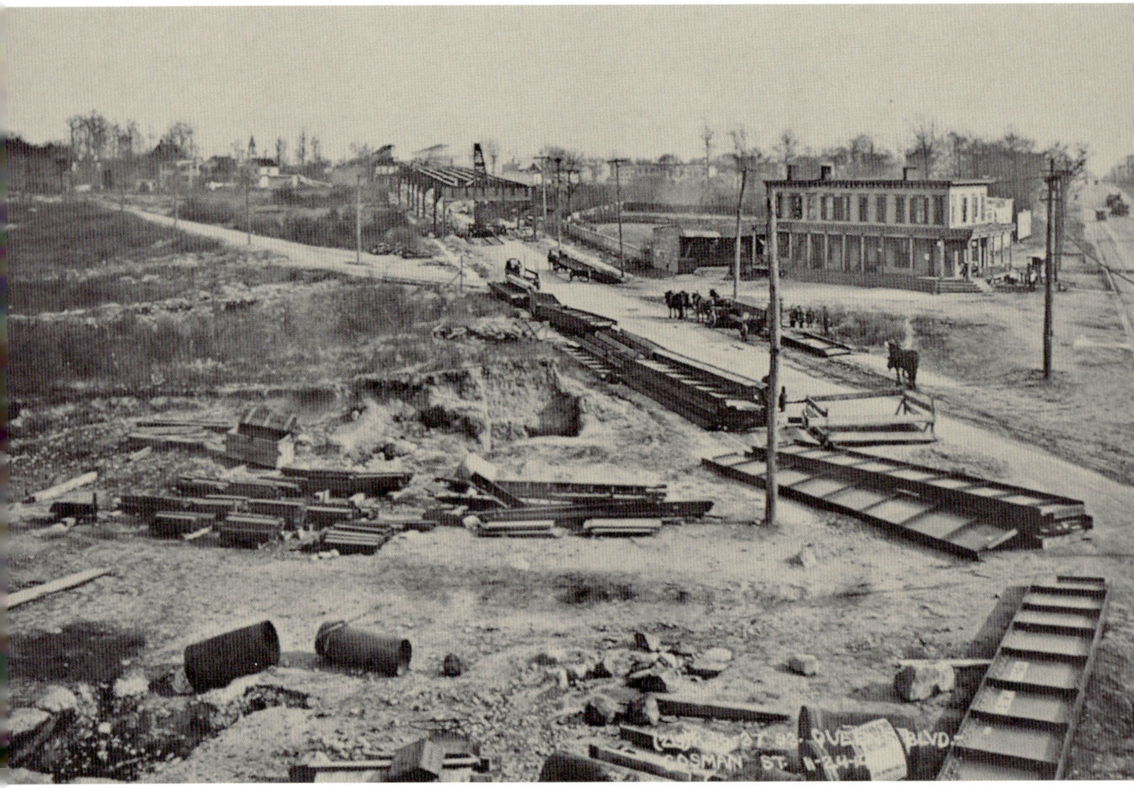

The elevated IRT steel trestle makes its way west toward Gosman Street and Queens Boulevard on the approach to the Bliss Street (Forty-sixth Street) station in this photograph taken on November 24, 1914. The building of the trestle attracted large numbers of people who came out to see the laborers raise the first pillar and set it in place on March 23, 1914, at 104th Street and Roosevelt Avenue. On April 21, 1917, the IRT opened 11 stations between Corona and Woodside. It would be another decade before the No. 7 train reached Flushing.

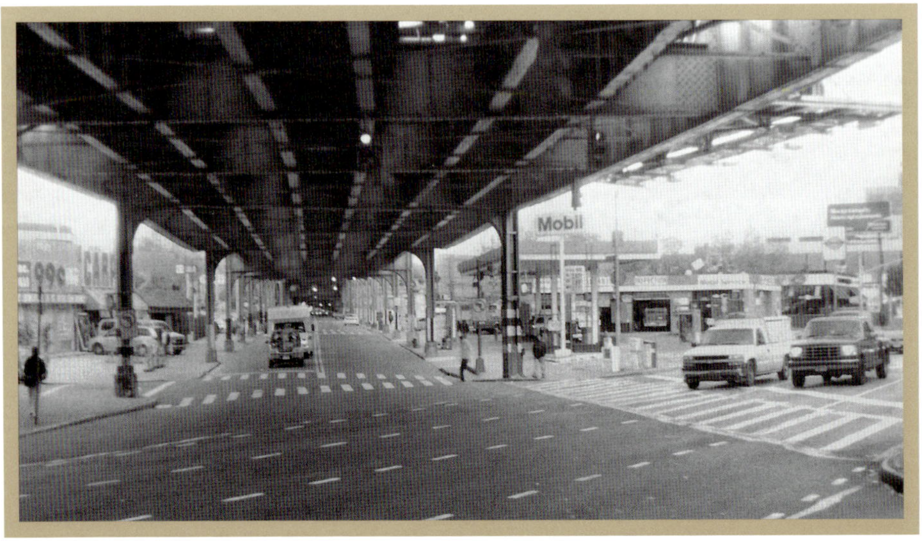

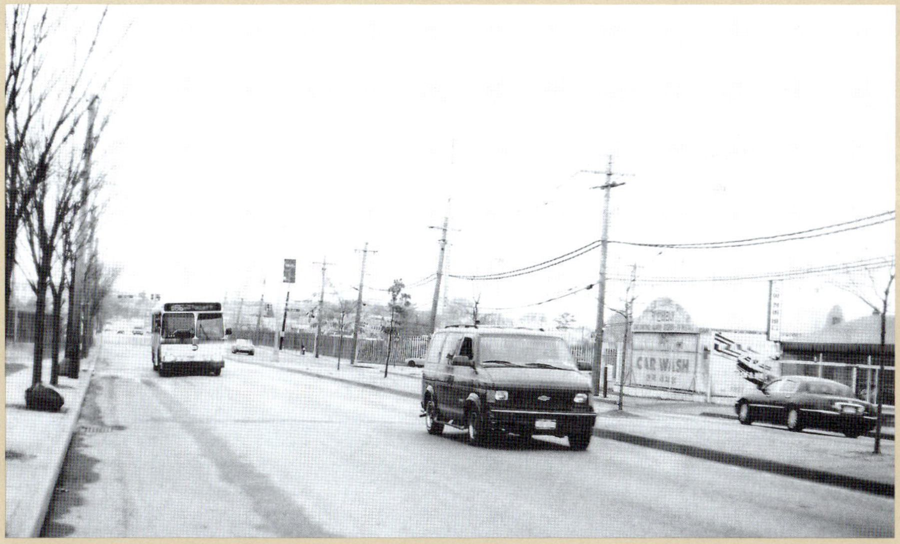

Another form of rail travel in Flushing was the trolley. The New York and Queens County Railway was the largest independent trolley system to operate in Queens. A Jamaica-bound trolley travels south along the College Point Causeway (now Boulevard) around 1930. It would turn east at Northern Boulevard and travel to Main Street where it turned south. It cruised along, picking up passengers before merging onto Kissena Boulevard and heading toward Parsons Boulevard. It would then cut through Kissena Park.

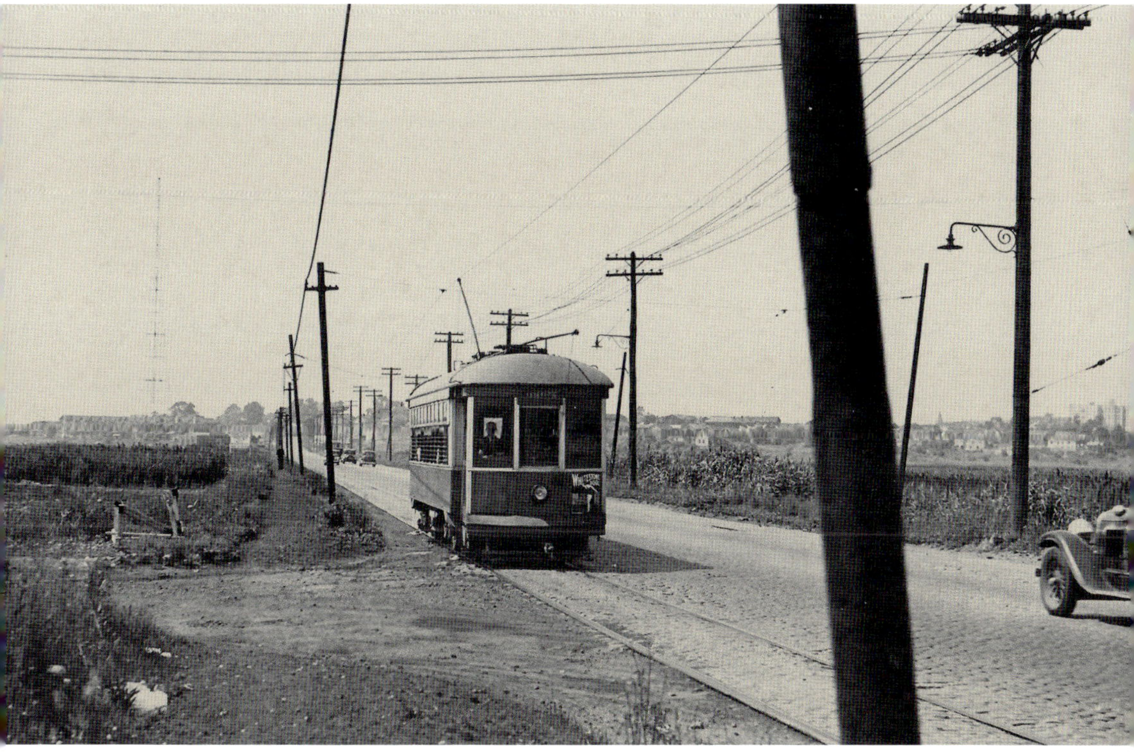

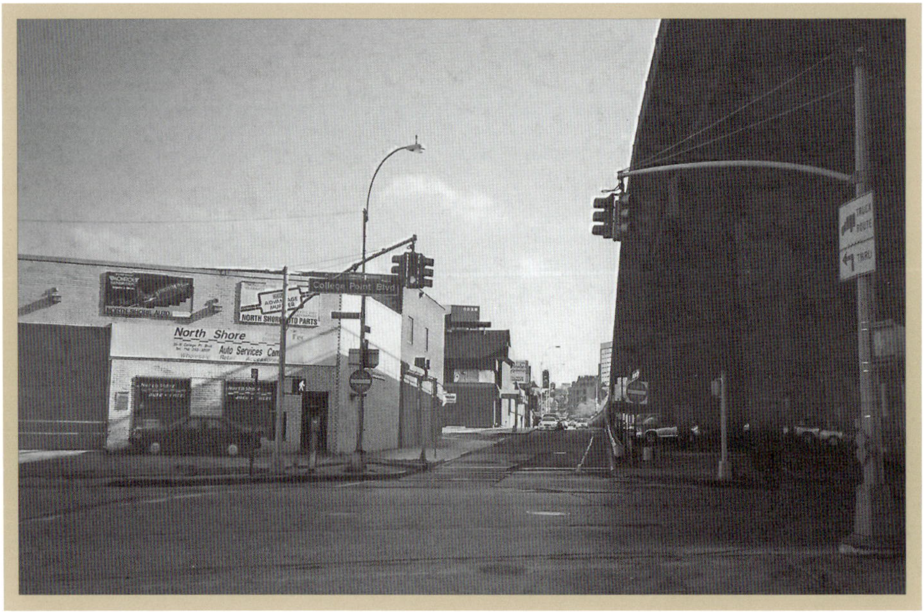

The conductor hops aboard a trolley known as an open car, as it gets ready to depart on its journey through Flushing for Jamaica, on the Jamaica-Flushing line at the northeast corner of College Point Boulevard and Northern Boulevard. The final stop was at 160th Street, just south of Fulton Street (Jamaica Avenue). The New York and Queens County Railway lasted until October 1939, when busses took over the lines. Most of the right-of-ways were destroyed to build automobile highways like the Grand Central Parkway. (Courtesy of Brian Merlis/Brooklynpix.com.)

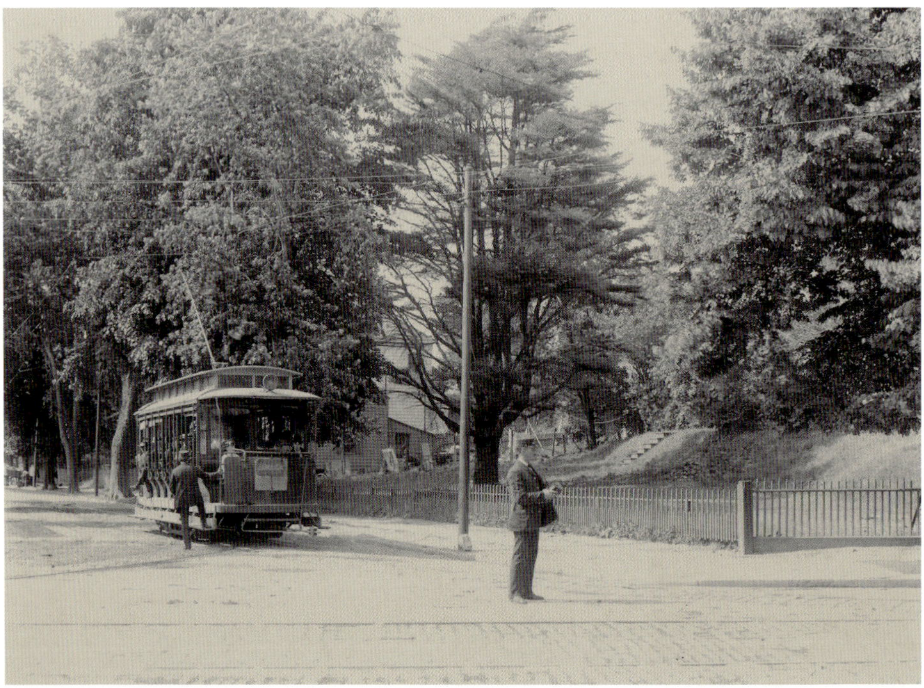

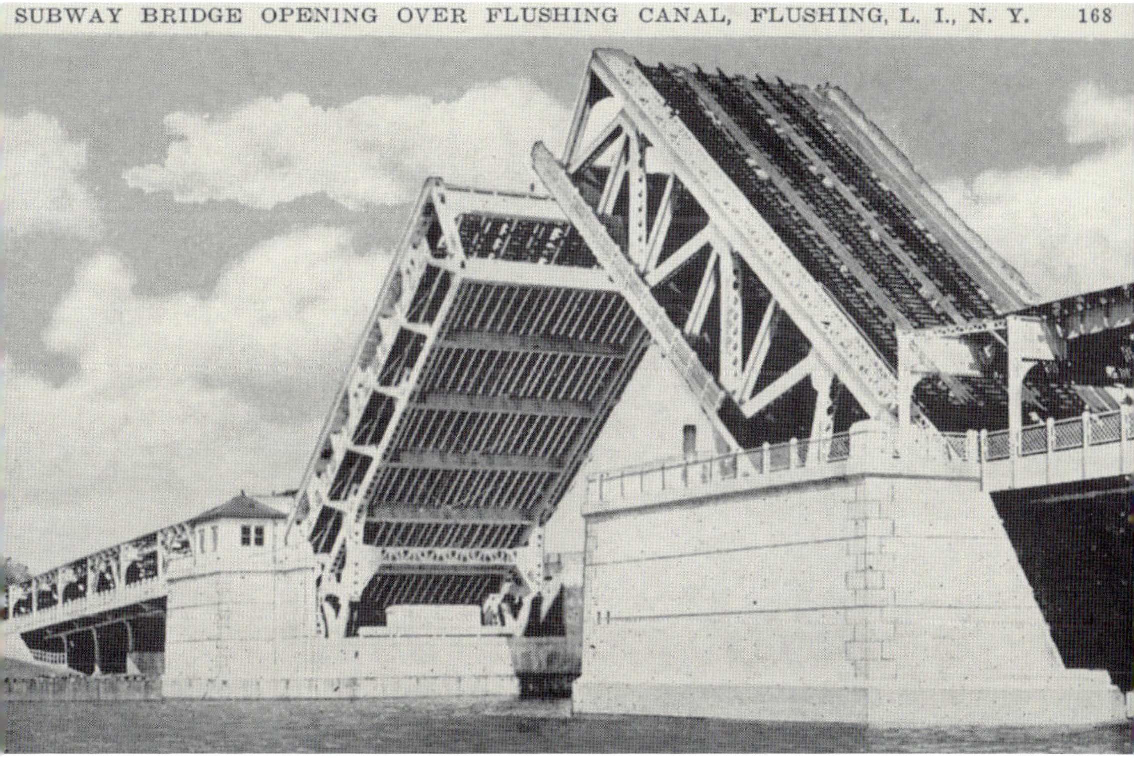

On January 21, 1928, the IRT No. 7 train arrived in Flushing with service to Times Square, which had opened the previous year. During that same month, construction on the Roosevelt Avenue Subway Bridge over Flushing Creek was completed at a cost of $2.6 million. Known as a bascule trunnion lift bridge, it was the largest in the world at the time. Four motors hoisted the draw weighing 4 million pounds in 45 seconds to allow vessels to pass. Today the bridge is fixed in the closed position while the Van Wyck Expressway, built over the creek, passes beneath.

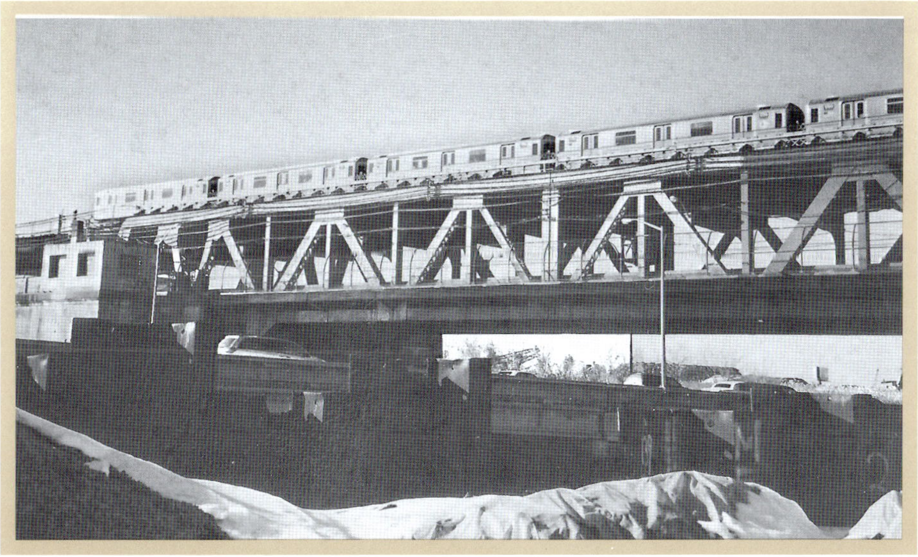

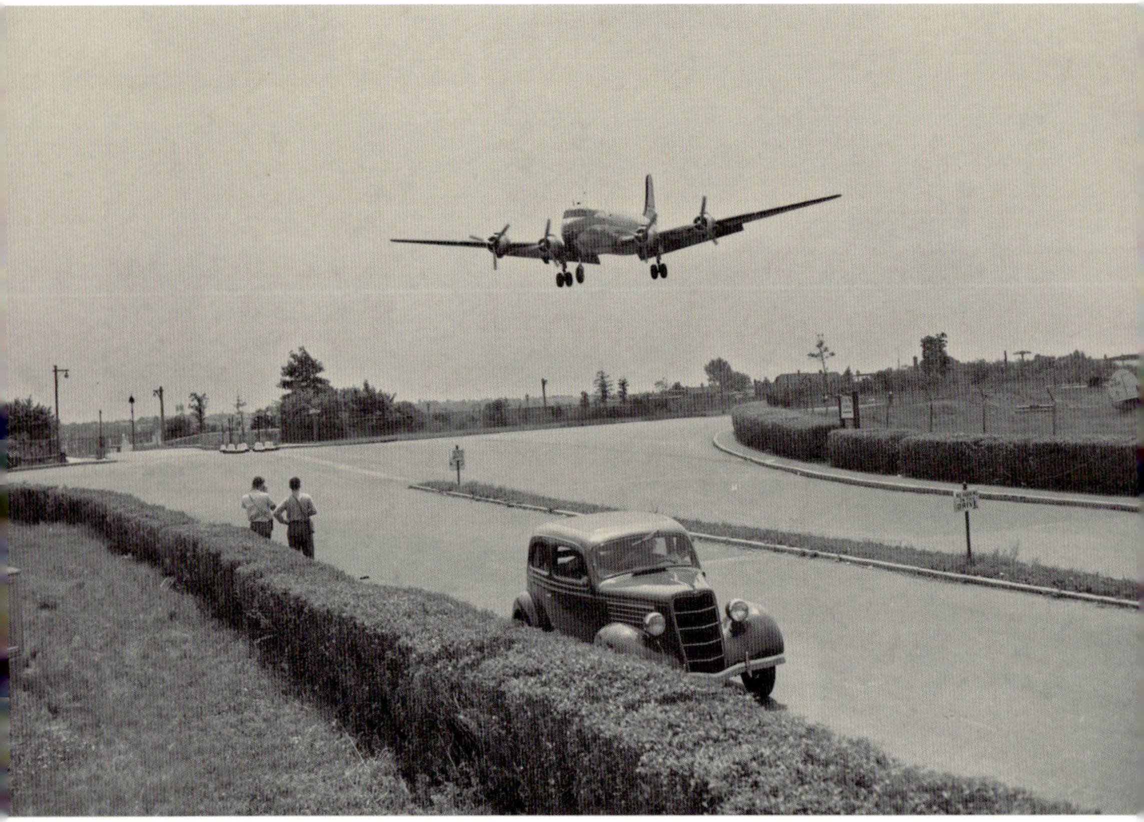

The New York Municipal Airport at North Beach was built on a 432-acre tract near the East River between Bowery and Flushing Bays. It was constructed for a cost of $22 million, of which the Works Progress Administration put up 70 percent. Eastern, United, and American Airlines serviced the new airfield, one of several in the area. There was also Flushing Airport and Holmes Airport. Opened in 1939, it was renamed LaGuardia Airport after Mayor Fiorello LaGuardia. (Courtesy of the Cradle of Aviation Museum.)

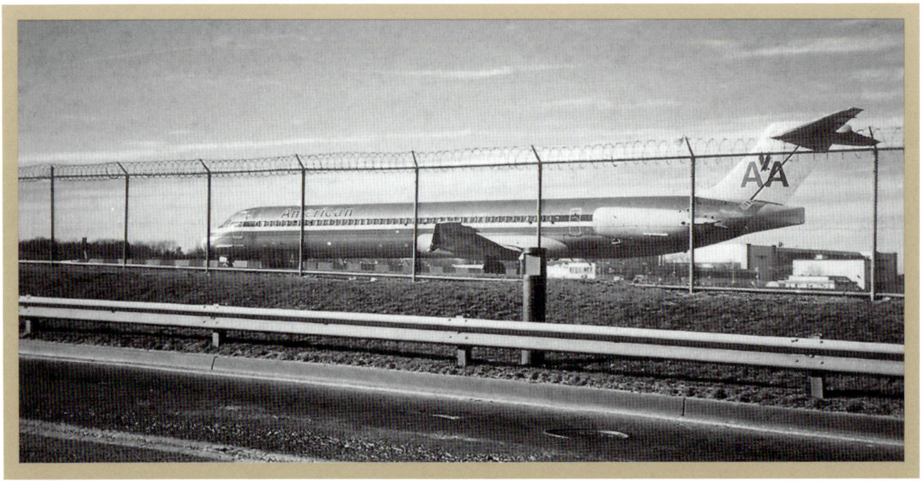

CHAPTER 4

Flushing Meadows

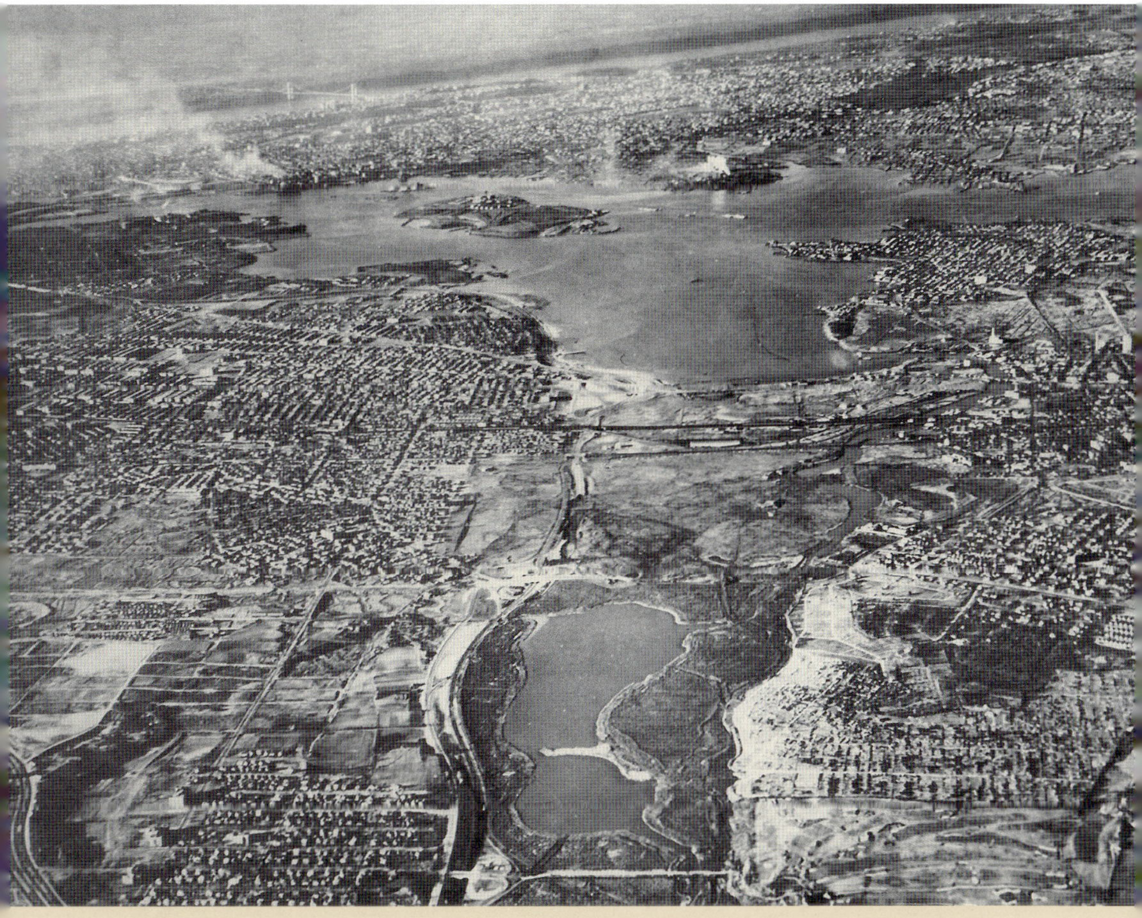

In his 1925 novel *The Great Gatsby,* author F. Scott Fitzgerald described the 1,200-acre Flushing Meadows as a, "Valley of ashes where a fantastic farm of ashes grows like wheat into ridges and hills and grotesque gardens." This description resulted from the work of John A. "Fishhooks" McCarthy and his Brooklyn Ash Removal Company, which unloaded 110 railroad carloads of garbage into the meadows each day. The meadows were rehabilitated when Parks Department commissioner Robert Moses brought the 1939–1940 and 1964–1965 New York World's Fairs to the area. (Courtesy of Fairchild Aerial Surveys.)

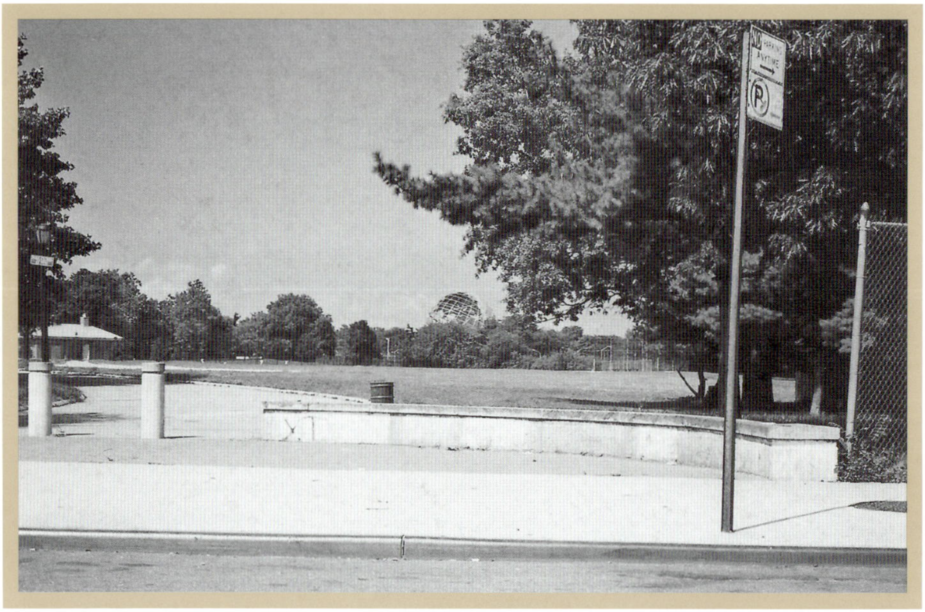

The corner of Colonial Avenue and Corona Avenue was the site of "Mt. Corona," a 200-foot mound of ash and garbage dumped by the Brooklyn Ash Removal Company. People living in Flushing and Corona were greatly affected by these conditions. At night the garbage would be incinerated causing an eerie glow to come from the meadows. The area was also overcome with the stench of rotting garbage and rats in the summertime. The current state of the meadows is a miracle of modern engineering, without any evidence of how it used to be.

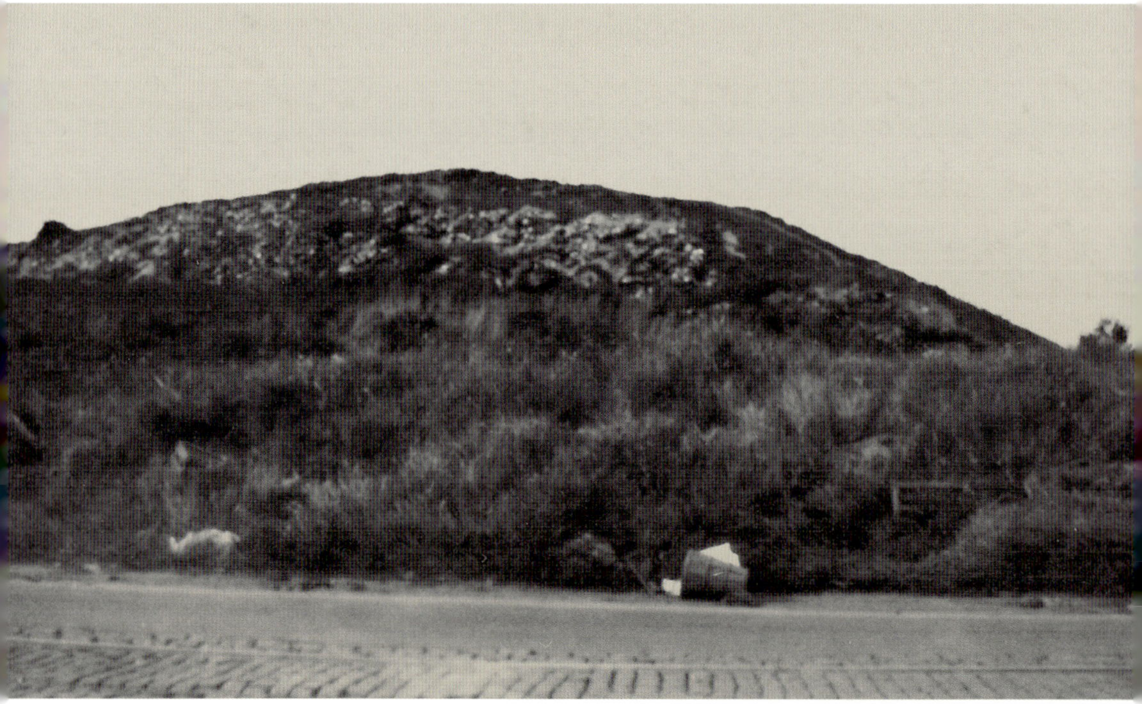

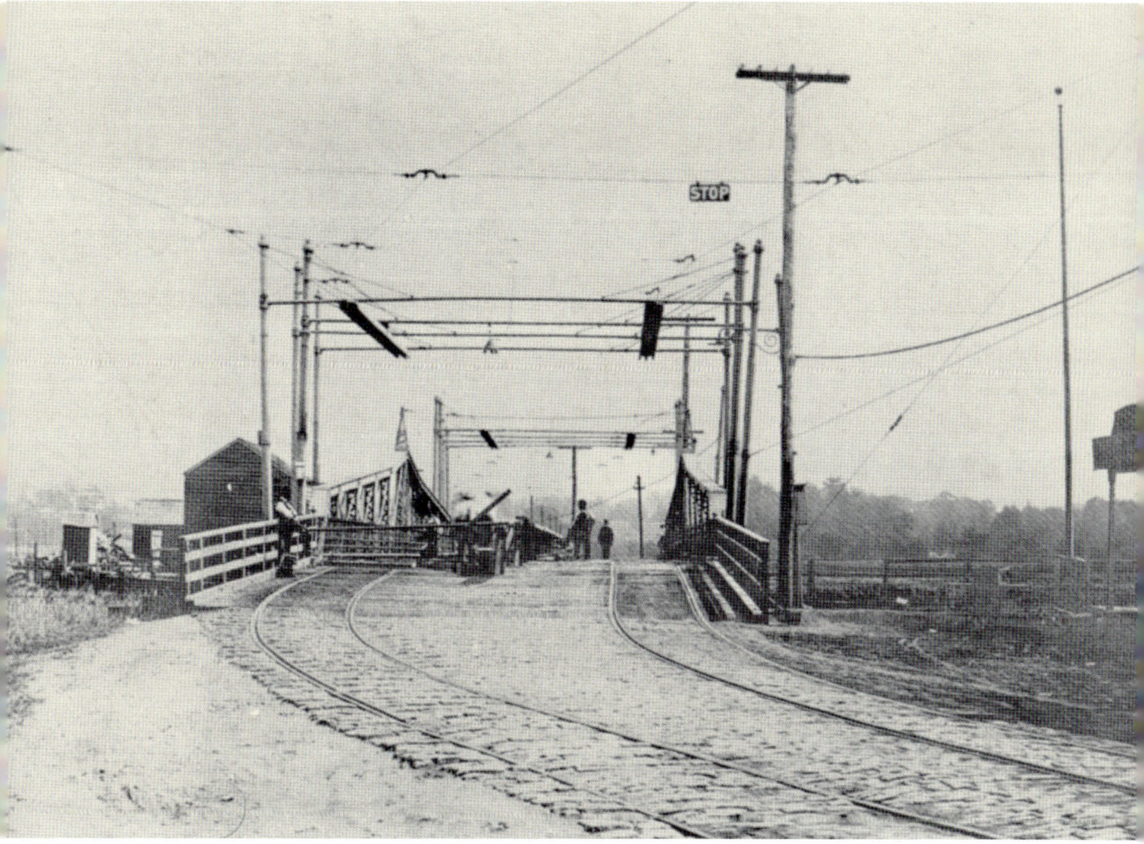

Strong's Causeway, the only road through the vast sea of mud and grass, spanned Flushing Creek at the southern end of the meadows. The bridge was named after the Strong family who lived in the area for more than 200 years. The first bridge was built in 1801 by the North Hempstead Turnpike Company and was only 15 feet wide. The causeway is shown in 1905 with George Mager's Spring Hill Clubhouse and Hotel on the right. Today this point is the Long Island Expressway near exit 22A.

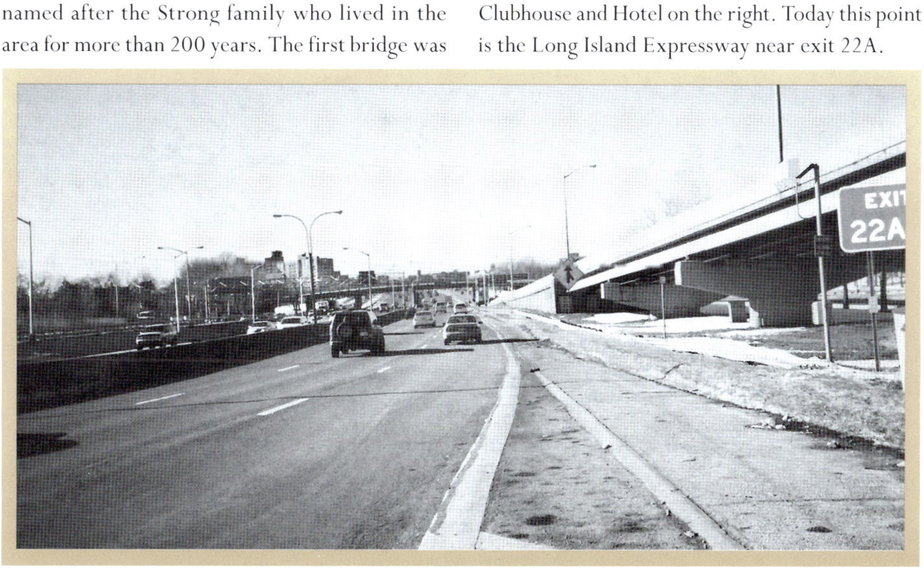

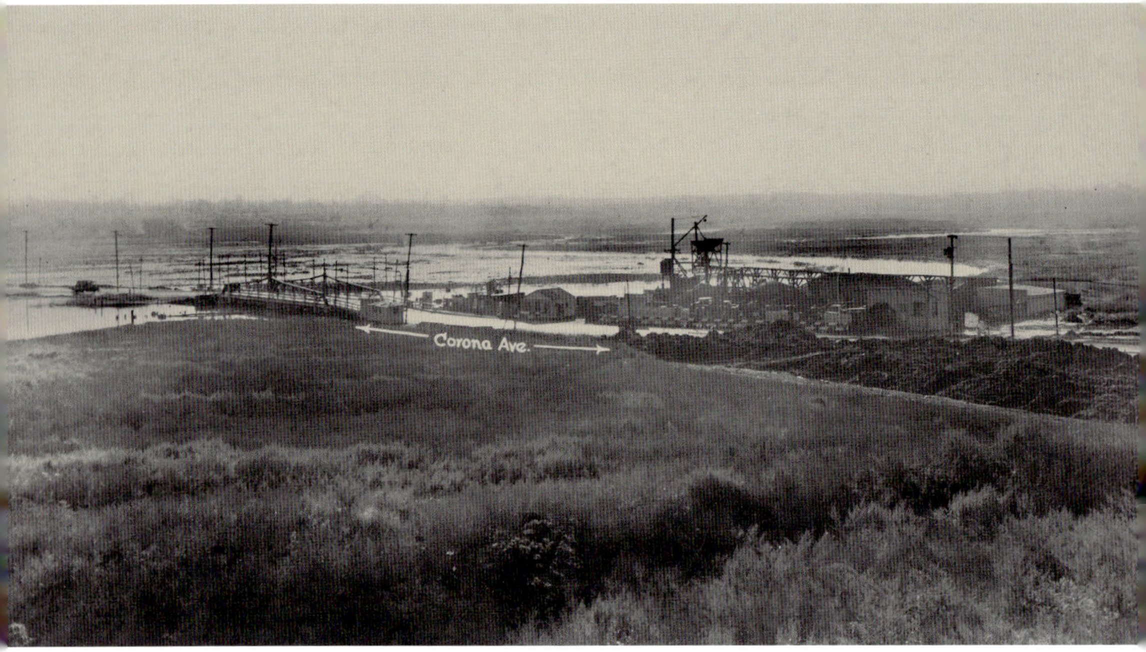

Another angle of Strong's Causeway looks south on November 9, 1935. In the wintertime, the swing bridge would flood, and trolley service would be held up for hours with stranded passengers aboard. This sixth and final version of the bridge opened on September 1, 1896, and was designed by the Berlin Bridge Company. It was 135 feet long and 30 feet wide. In 1939, it was removed for the Horace Harding Expressway, which became the Long Island Expressway in the 1940s. (Courtesy of the Queens Borough Public Library, Long Island Division, Borough President of Queens Photographs.)

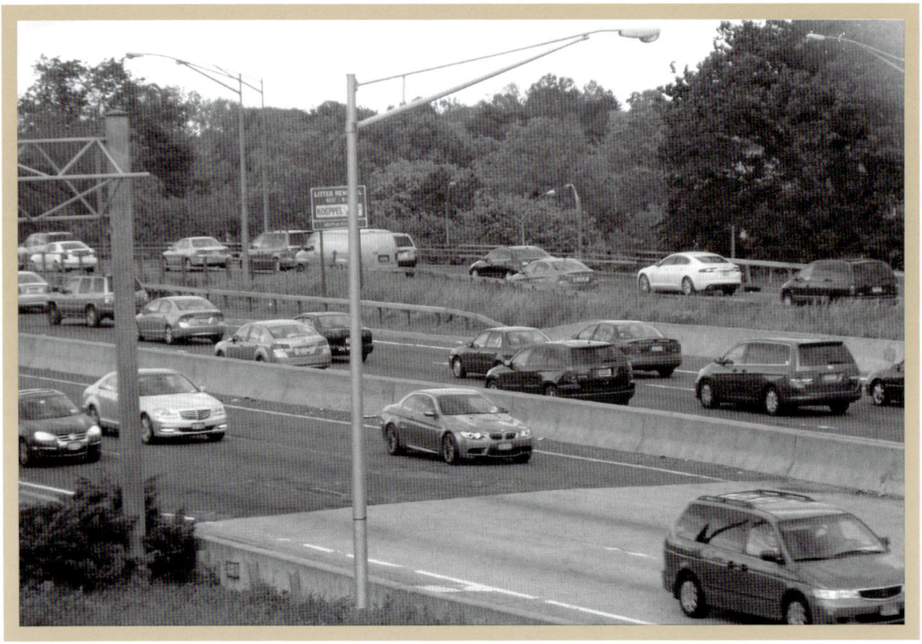

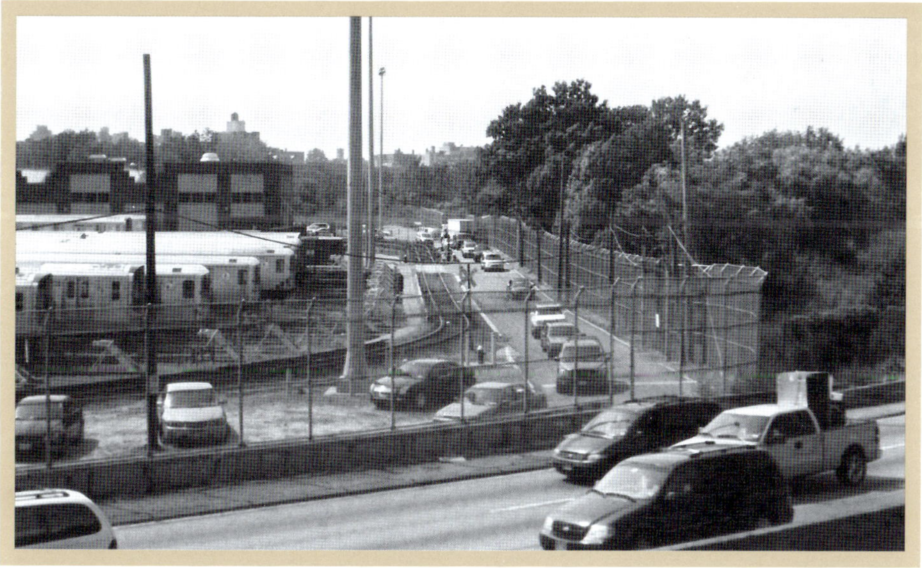

The Independent Subway System, or ISS, opened for operation in August 1933. Seen here is the special shuttle line that took people to a special station that was located along today's Van Wyck Expressway, just north of Jewel Avenue for the 1939–1940 New York World's Fair. The Grand Central Parkway is under construction on the left. Today the tracks of the Jamaica Yard stop abruptly at the Van Wyck Expressway, which travels over the former line's right-of-way.

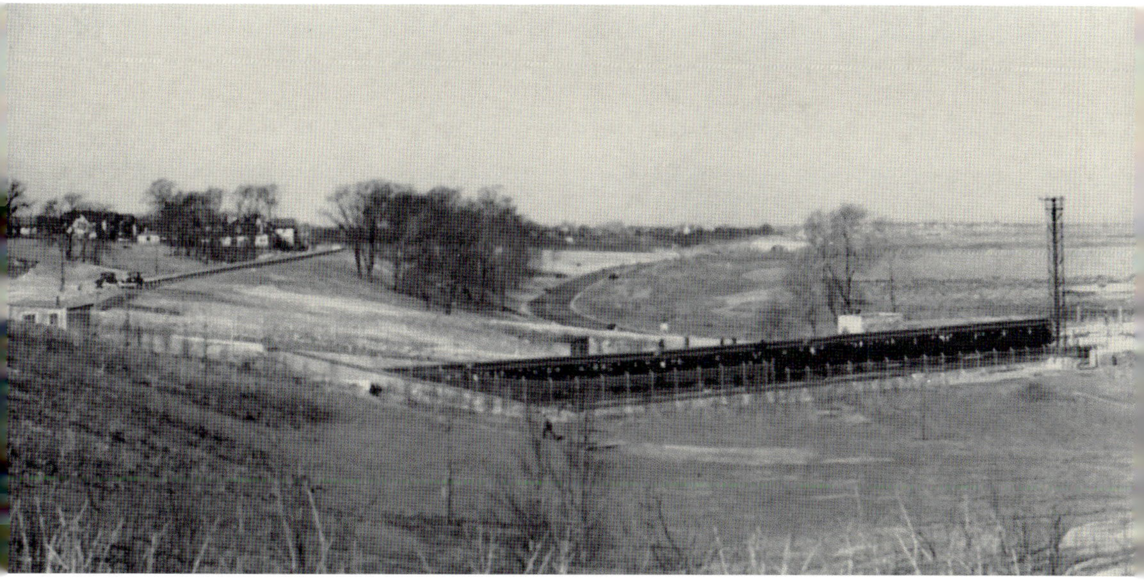

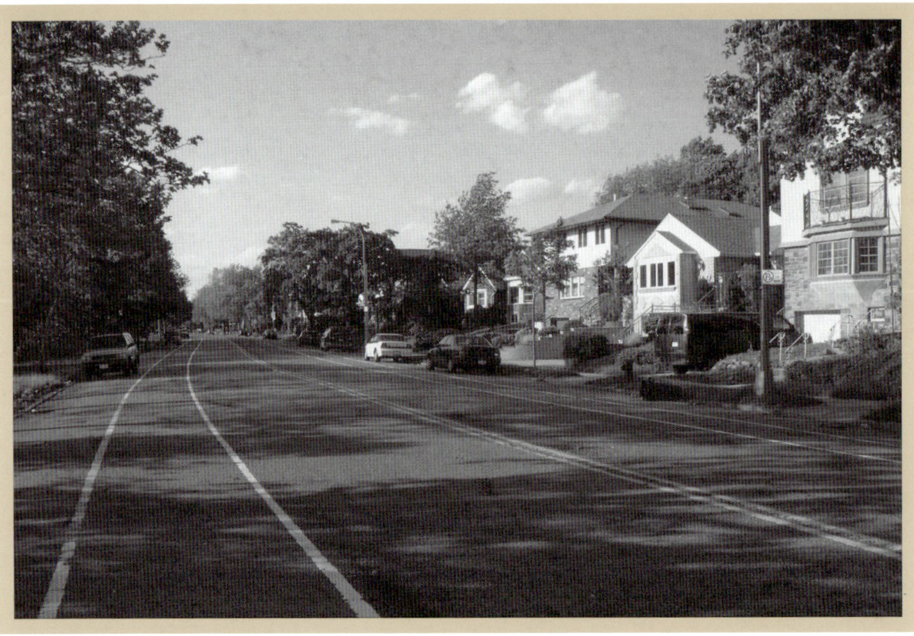

Seen here is the Queens Valley Golf Club looking north up Park Drive East, from Union Turnpike, in 1940. Union Turnpike was originally laid out as a thoroughfare stretching from Myrtle Avenue in Glendale to Marcus Avenue in North New Hyde Park in Nassau County. Initially designed as a toll road, and heavily used prior to the construction of Grand Central Parkway in the 1930s, it traveled through relatively undeveloped areas, serving as a border between the towns of Flushing and Jamaica.

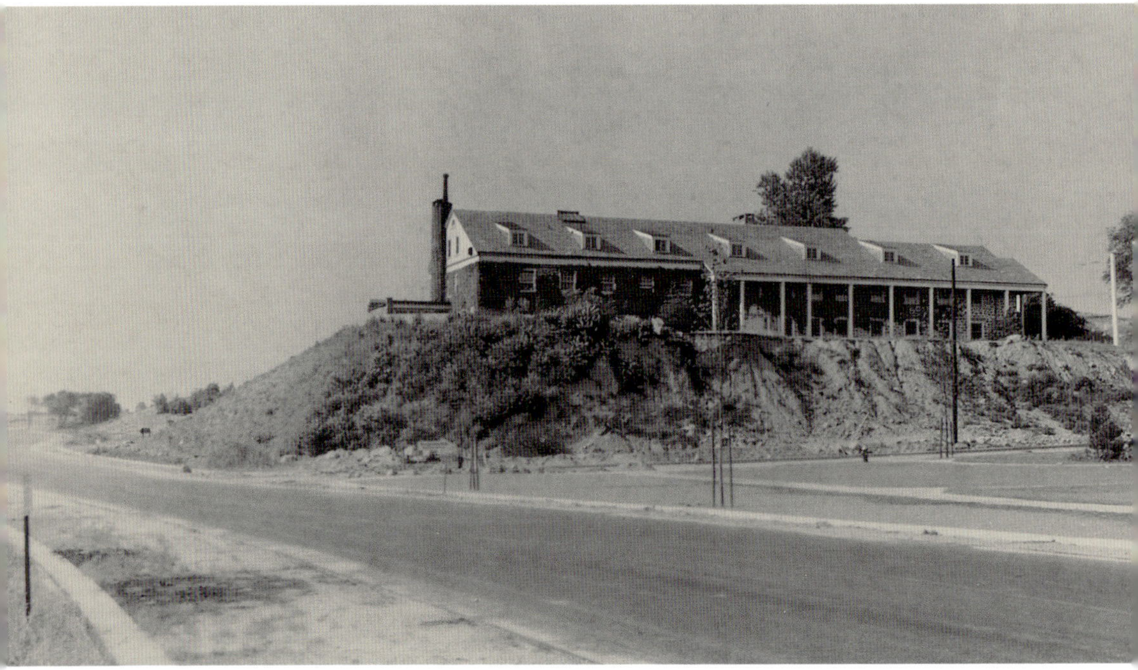

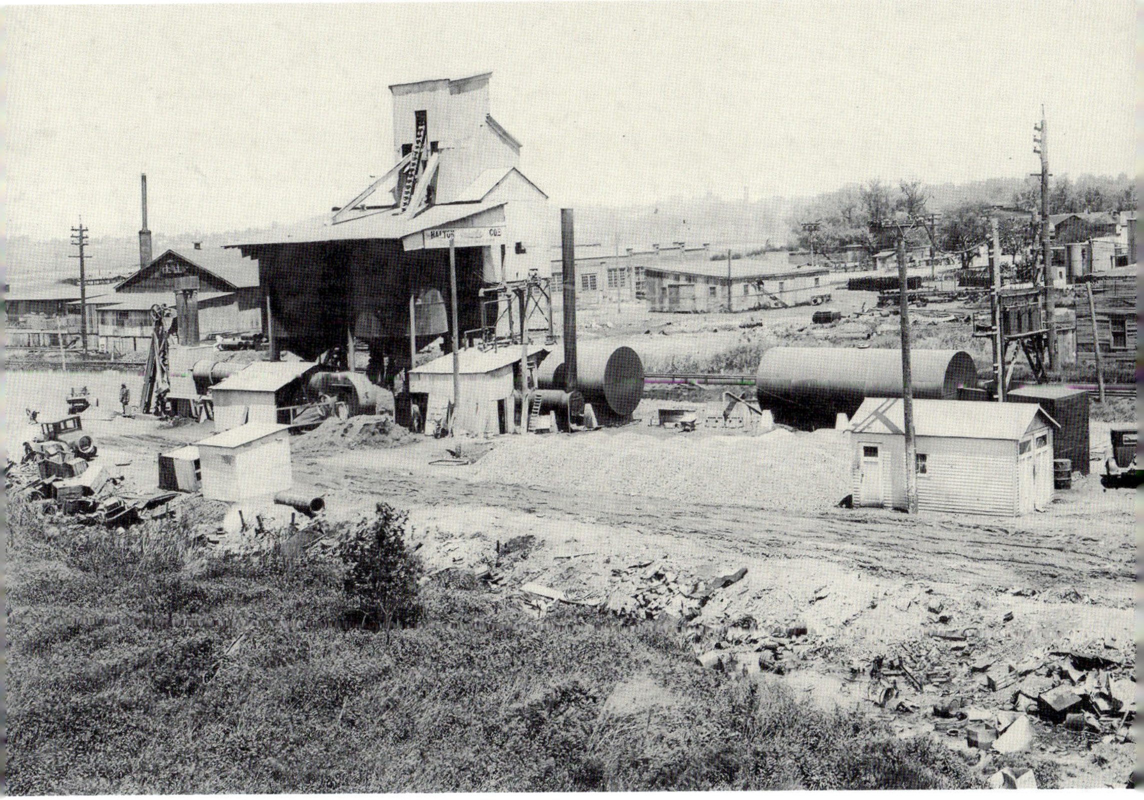

The Halton Amiesite Company Plant opened in 1913 and was located on the northern edge of the meadows. Amiesite was a type of asphalt used to pave streets. The first form of street paving was created by the Flushing and Jamaica Plank Road Company in 1852, which involved covering dirt roads with long, thin pieces of lumber. However, due to inclement weather and bad drainage, the wood began to rot, and the roads were soon removed. Today it is the site of the Casey Stengel MTA Bus Depot.

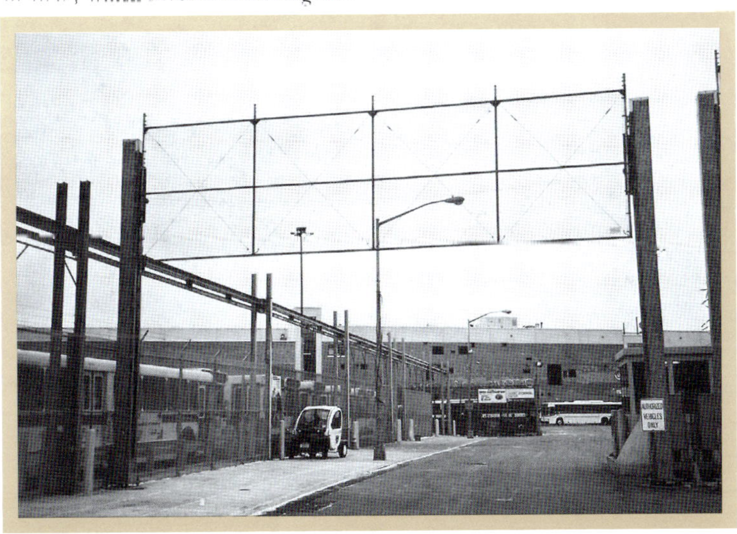

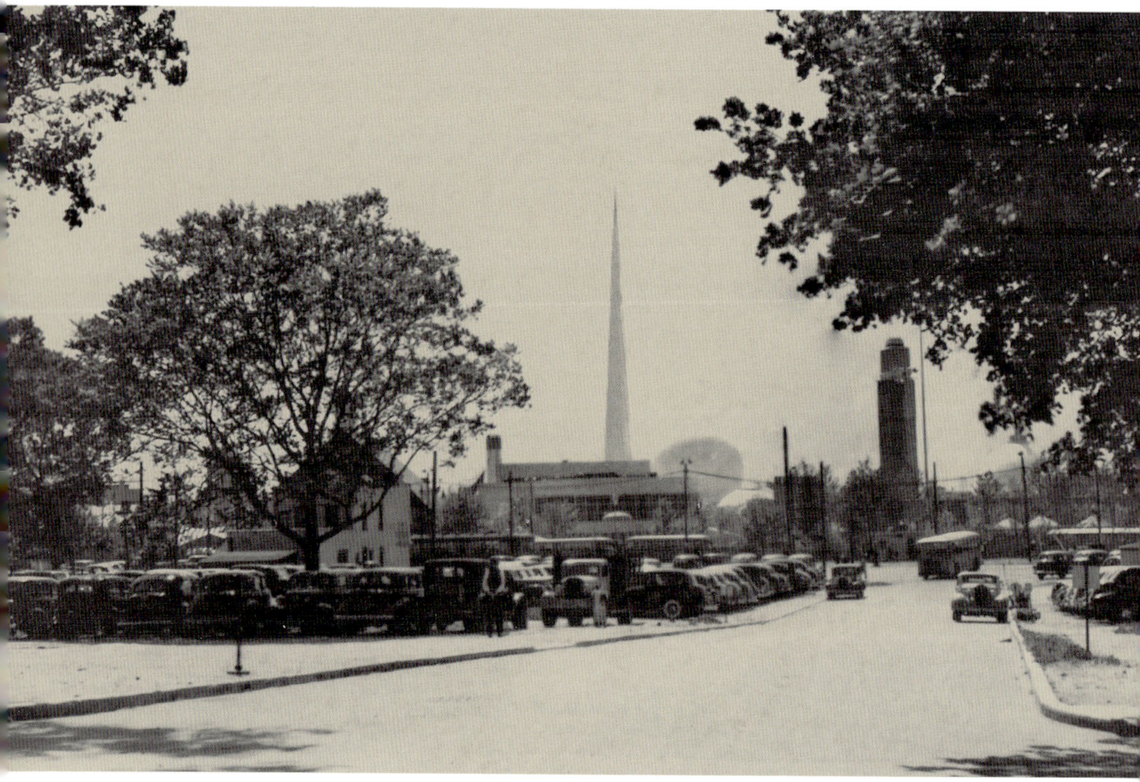

Flushing Meadows was saved from ecological destruction when it was chosen by Robert Moses as the site for the 1939–1940 New York World's Fair. Here the Trylon and Perisphere can be seen in the distance just beyond the Fifty-seventh Road approach to the fairgrounds just north of College Point Boulevard. The view is now obscured by the Van Wyck Expressway, which was opened on October 14, 1950. This was also the site of the old Ireland Mills during the Civil War period.

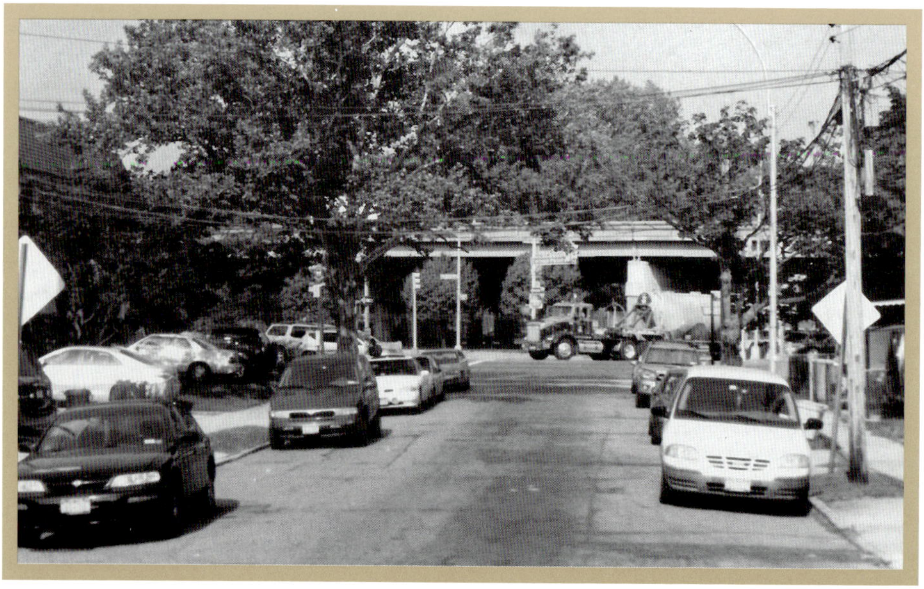

CHAPTER 5

Flushing in the Modern Age

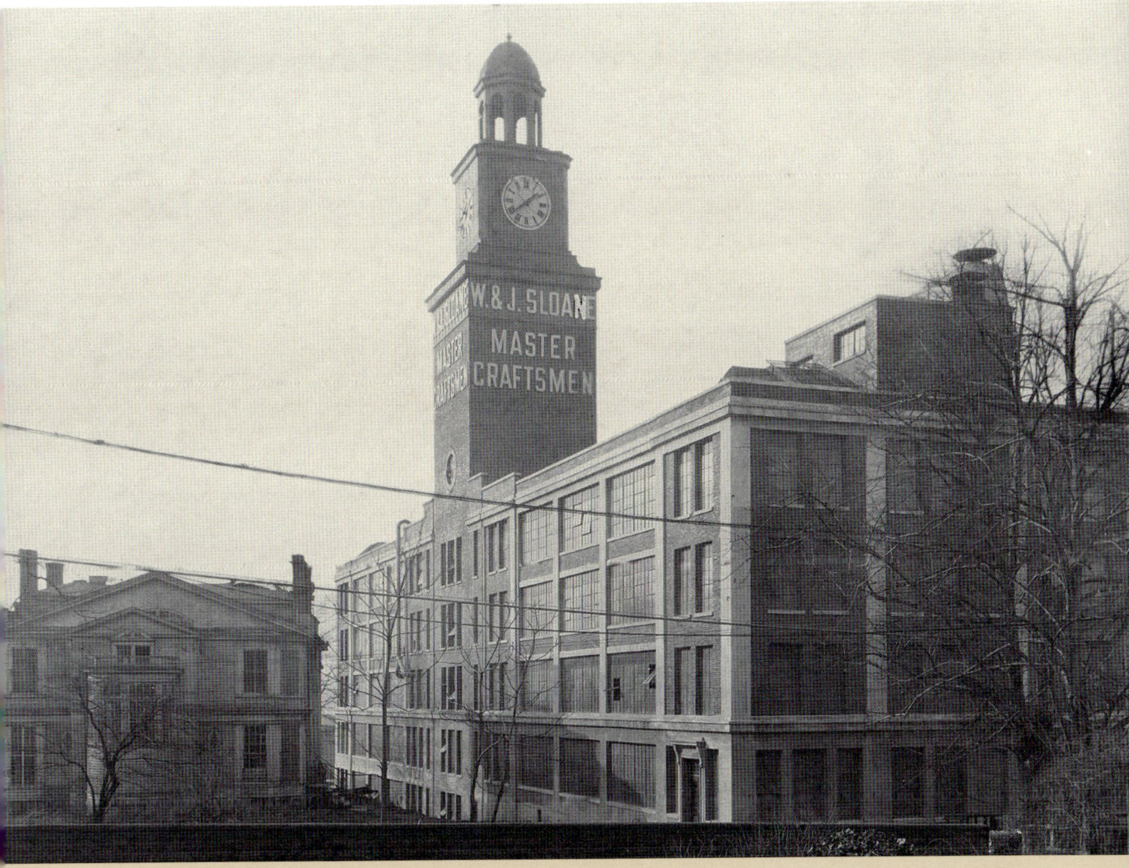

In a letter dated September 26, 1886, Mary Lawrence Bogert wrote to her husband about the changes occurring in Flushing: "There is a rumor of a horse railroad to College Point and also talk of electric lights too. Oh! Flushing is changing dear!" These words were written from Willow Bank, as shown here in its final days, standing in the shadow of the W. and J. Sloane furniture factory in 1926. This lasting image is a symbol of Flushing's transformation from tranquil village to an urban and industrial landscape. (Courtesy of the Queens Borough Public Library, Long Island Division, Eugene L. Armbruster Photographs.)

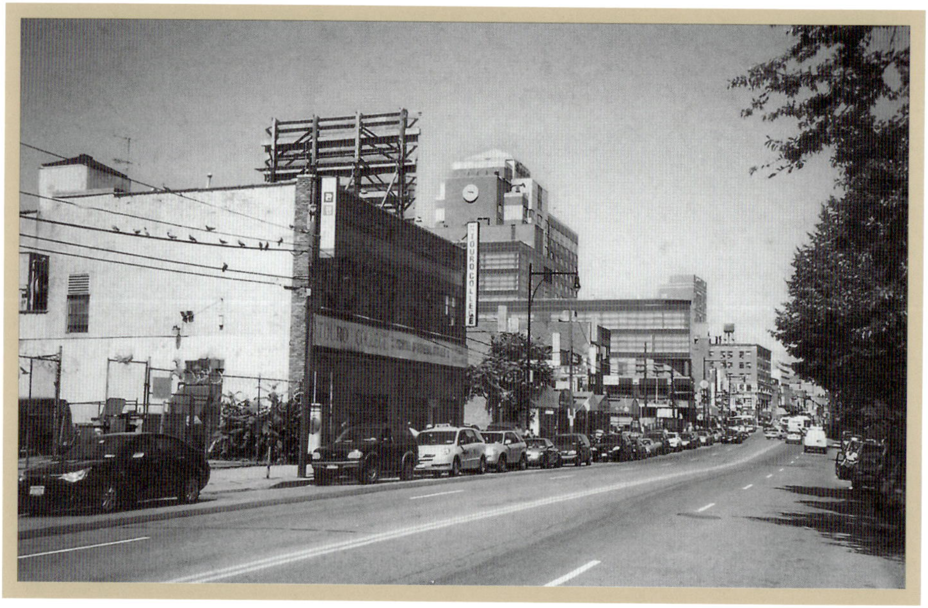

Amity Street was renamed Roosevelt Avenue in 1922 after Theodore Roosevelt. In 1928, the Interborough Rapid Transit (IRT) extended its No. 7 train service to downtown Flushing. The train traveled across Queens along the elevated line above Roosevelt Avenue before it descended below ground at College Point Boulevard. As a result, unstable property like the 19th-century-era wooden homes on the north side of the street, had to be destroyed because they proved to be too structurally unsound to accommodate the vibrations of the subway.

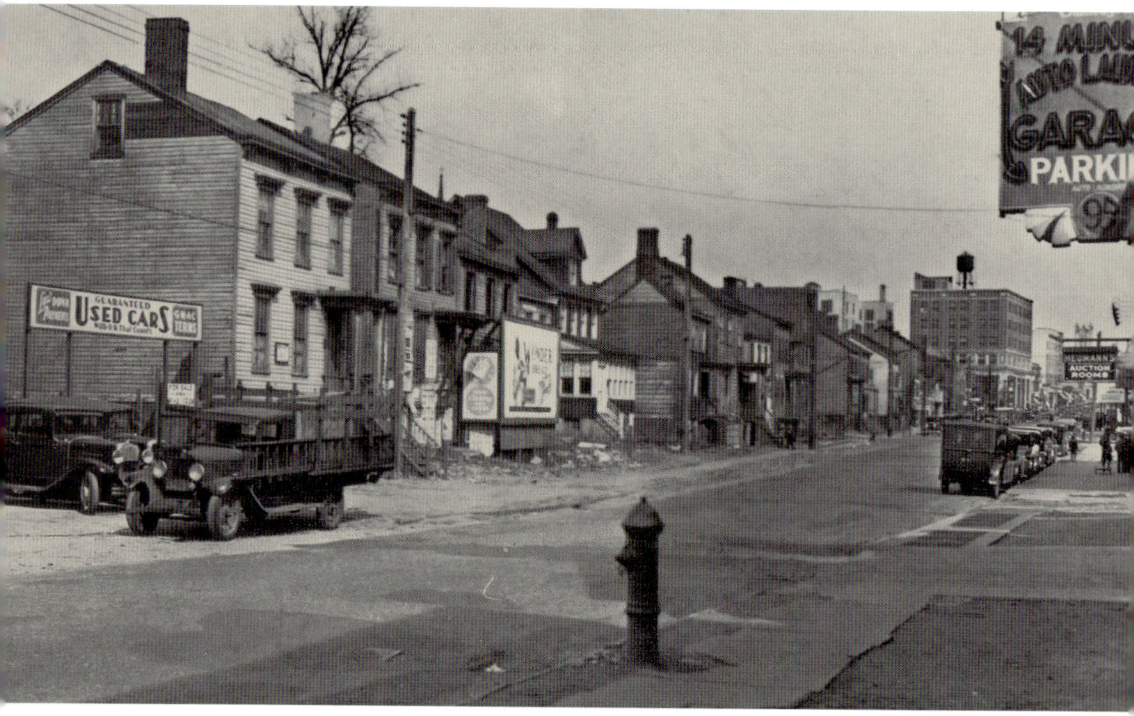

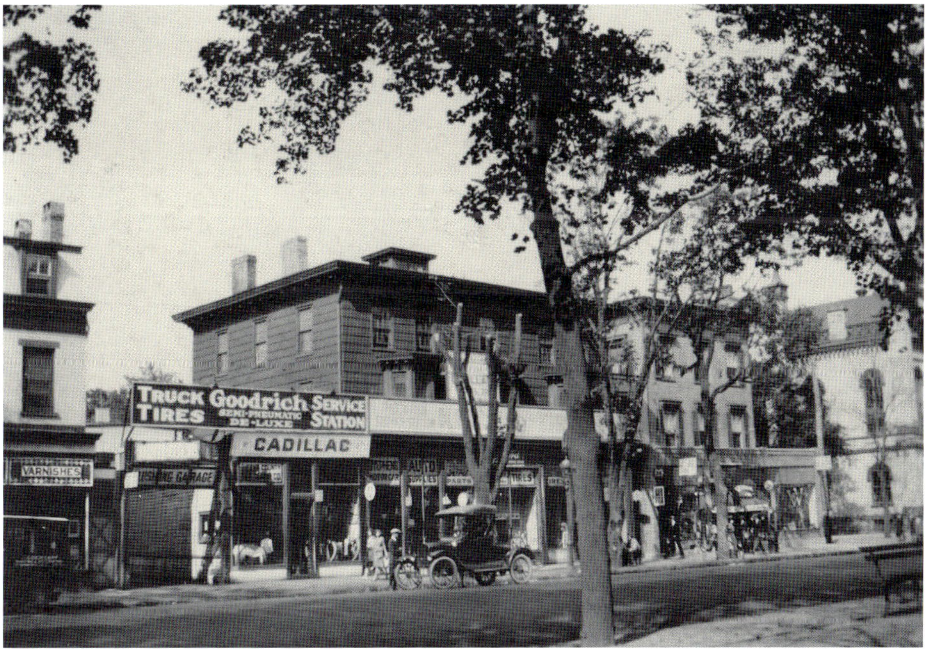

In 1934, the automobile had well surpassed the horse as the most standard means of travel when this photograph was taken. The shingled building being used as a car dealership was formerly known as Farrington Hall, owned by Nick Gilroy, and was located second from the northwest corner of Linden Place and Northern Boulevard. The building to the right in 1873 was known as the Monument Hotel because of its proximity to the Civil War Soldiers Monument in the adjacent square. A Mobile gas station now stands in its place. (Courtesy of the Queens Borough Public Library, Long Island Division, Eugene L. Armbruster Photographs.)

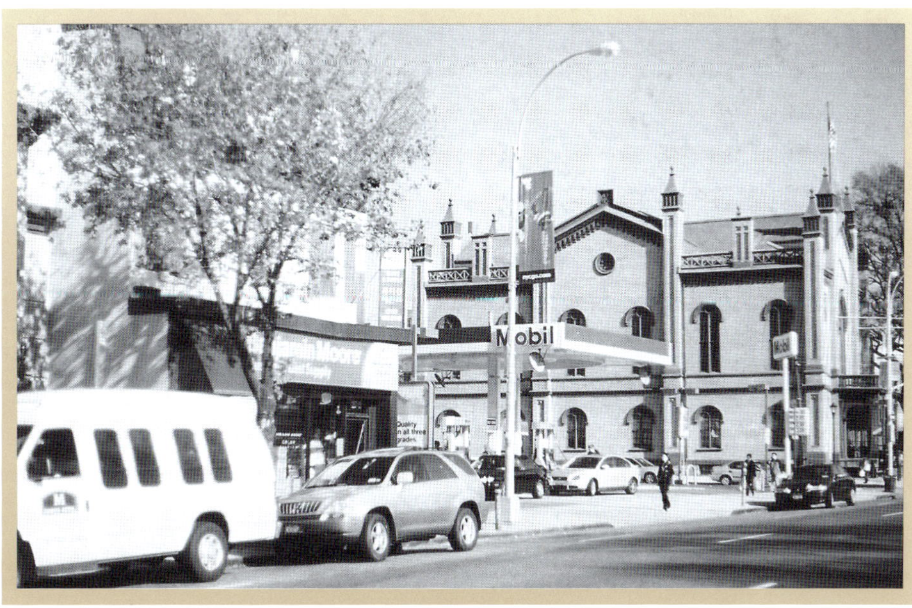

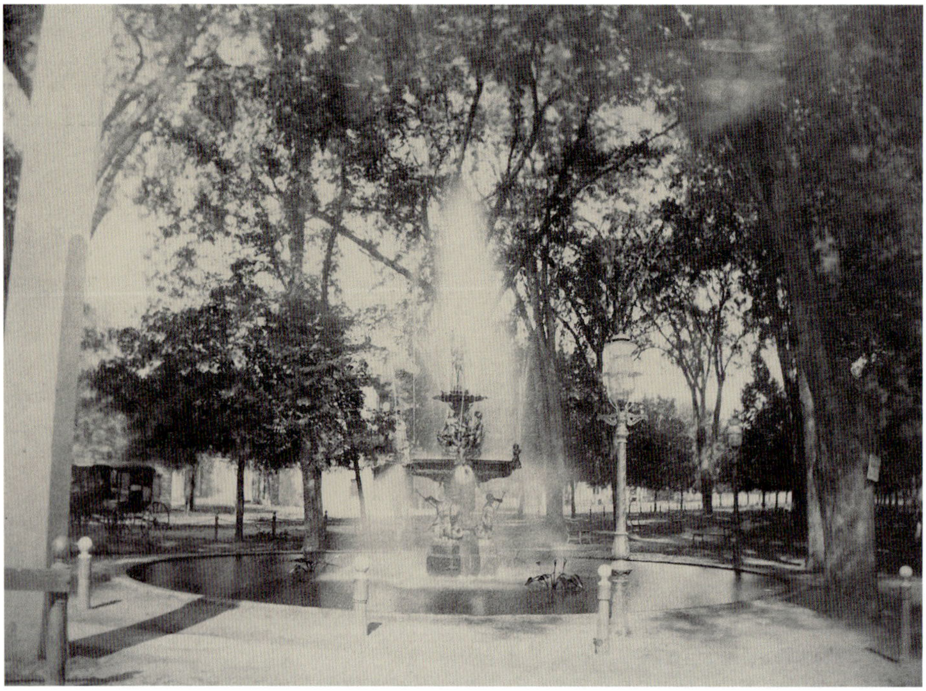

The grand Flushing Esplanade was located along Northern Boulevard terminating at the Main Street intersection. At its head was the beautiful King Neptune Fountain erected in 1874. Four mermaids and Neptune himself dominated the top, while 14 flower urns adorned the rim of the basin. Each spring, the urns were filled with fresh geraniums and petunias. Sadly it was removed in 1947. The square was named after Daniel Carter Beard who founded the Boy Scouts of America. (Courtesy of the Brooklyn Historical Society.)

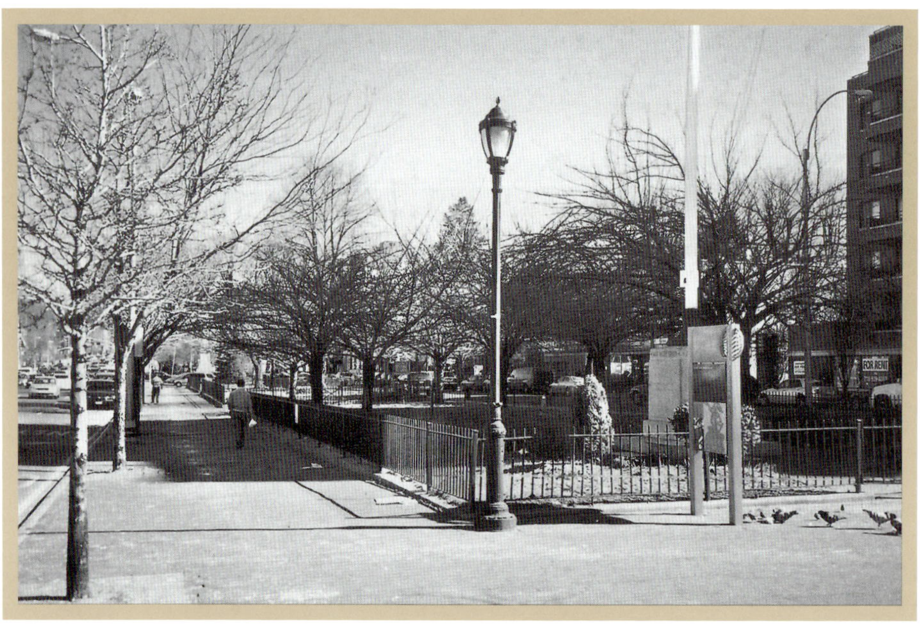

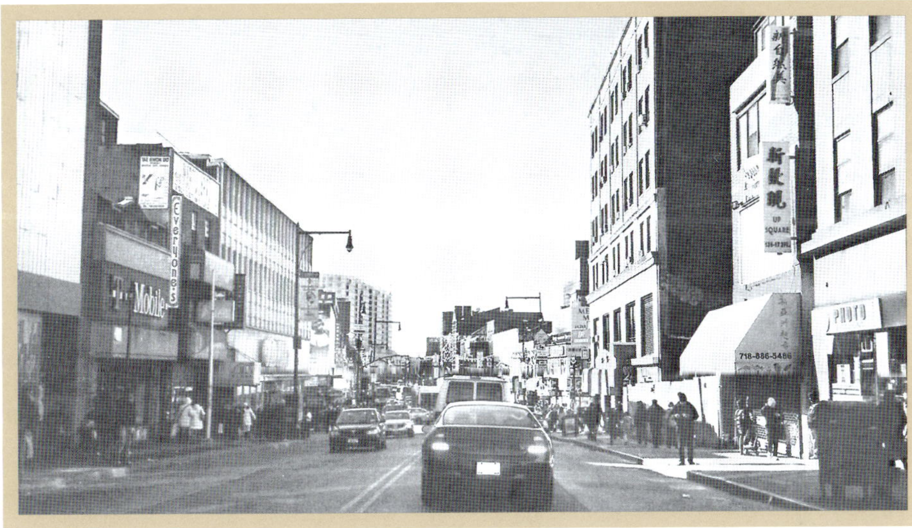

Roosevelt Avenue, looking west at Main Street on September 26, 1939, shows a more modern and metropolitan version of Flushing. The coming of the New York World's Fair and IRT brought about new changes to the area's geography and demographics. New parkways, wider roads, and a convenient subway brought bigger populations and new businesses to the area. The Bank of the Manhattan Company is on the right, and the Plaza Business School on the southwest corner of Main Street is to the left.

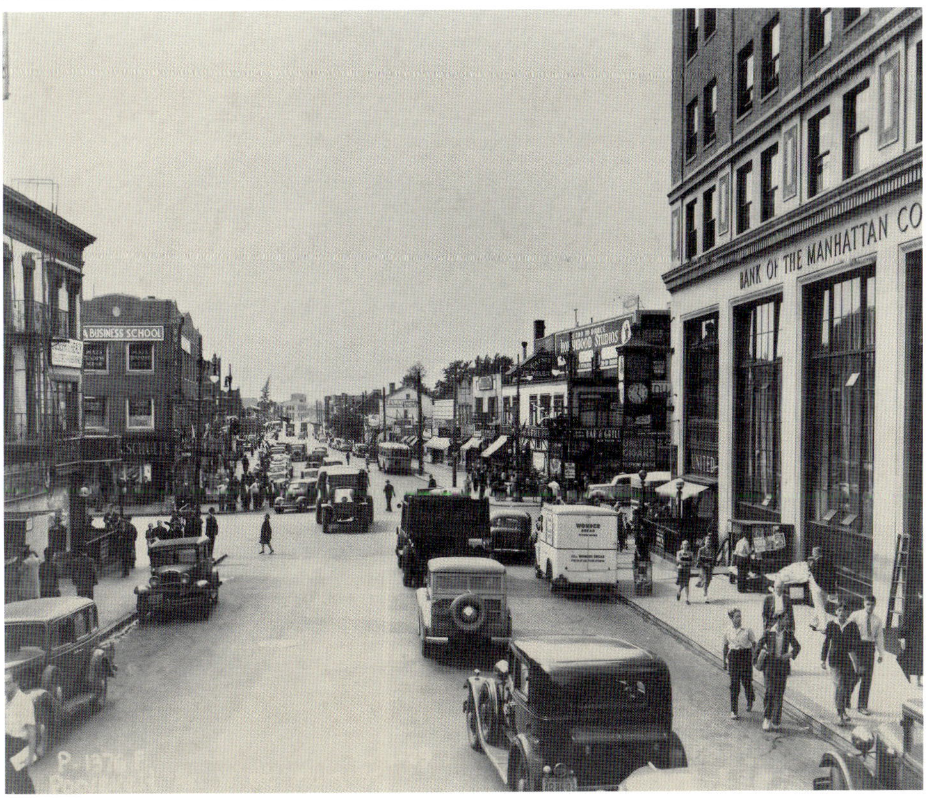

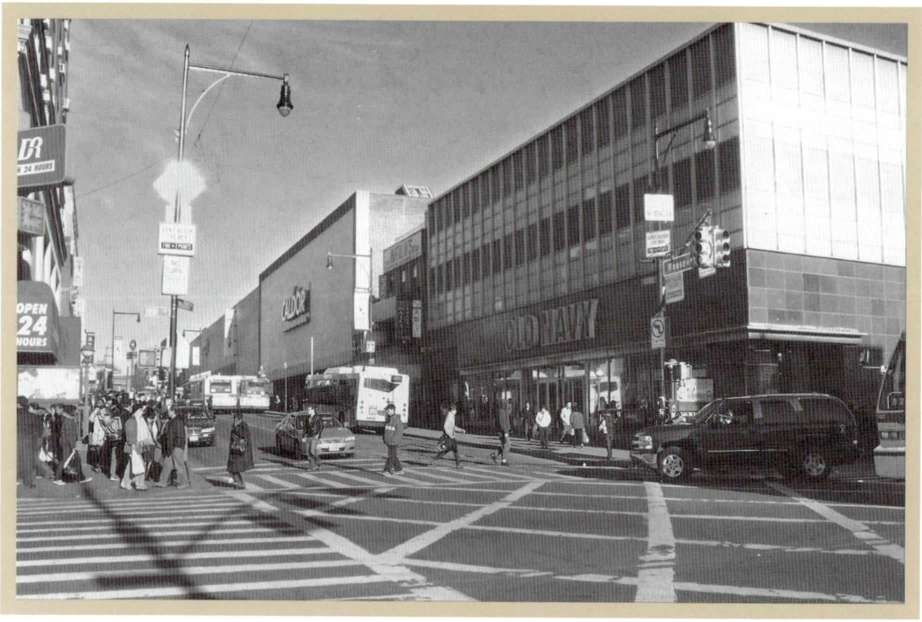

In 1926, one of the last relics of old Flushing finally succumbed to the changing times. The Flushing Institute and the hill upon which it stood for more than 100 years were finally destroyed. This was done to make room for buildings made of concrete and steel that would prove more stable with the rumbling subway beneath. Before the property was condemned, an auction was held to sell off personal property. Among the articles sold were the town's first bicycle and the first shower bath ever installed in Flushing. (Courtesy of the Milstein Division of U.S. History, Local History and Genealogy, the New York Public Library, Astor, Lenox, and Tilden Foundations.)

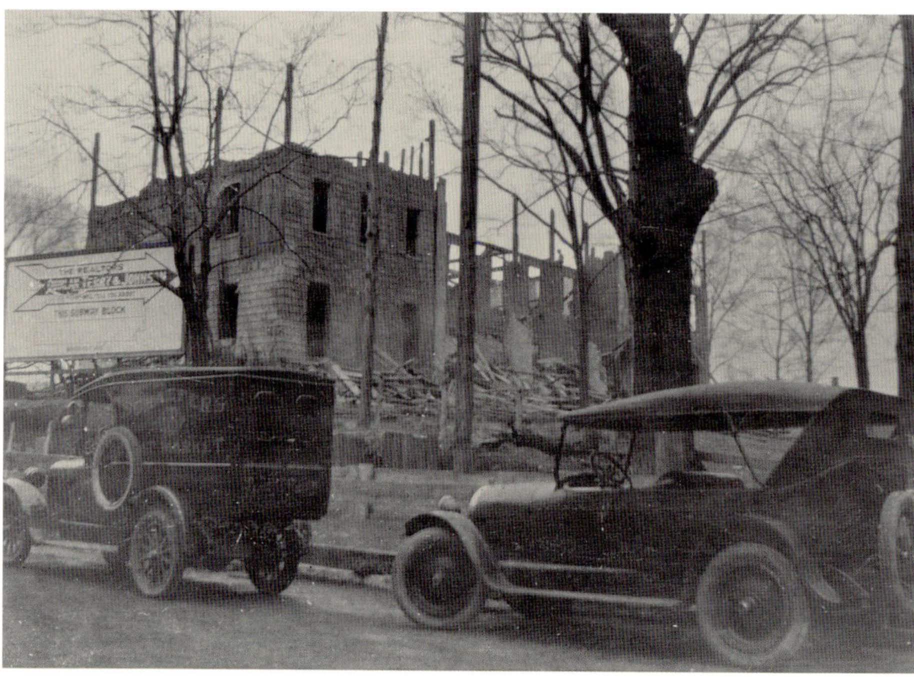

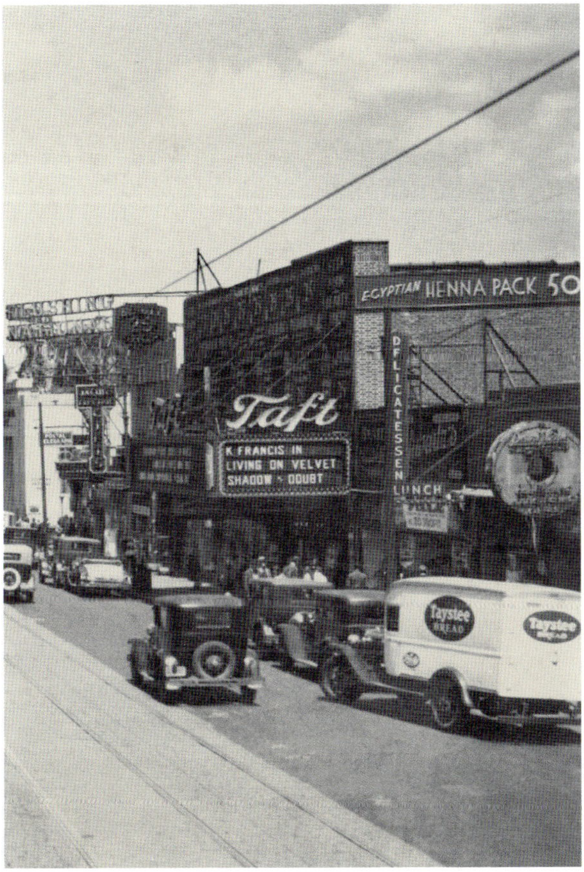

The Flushing Theatre opened at 37-11 Main Street during World War I. It had 600 seats, and in 1920, it was remodeled to accommodate 1,200. On December 31, 1931, it was renamed the Taft Theatre, advertising itself as "New and Magnificent - Featuring the Best Talking Pictures in a Refined Atmosphere at the Lowest Prices." The Taft, which was in competition with the RKO Keith's and Prospect Theatres, would screen the same movies a few weeks after. In 1959, it was destroyed to make way for a W. T. Grant Variety store. Today it is the Hong Kong Plaza flea market.

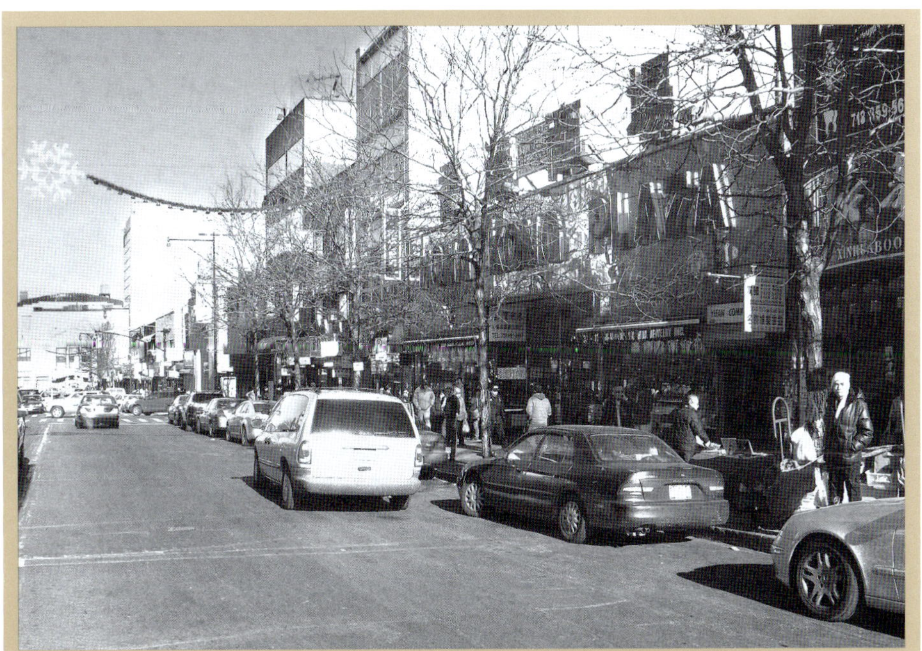

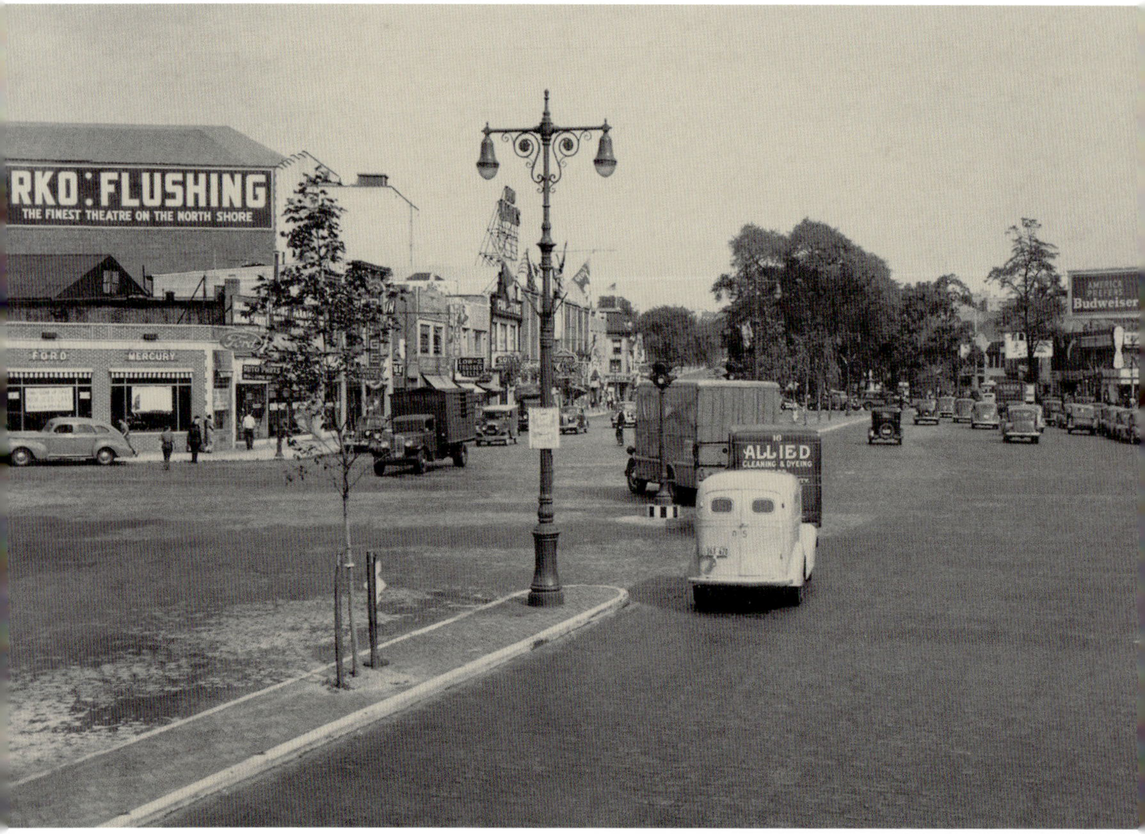

Northern Boulevard was widened from 1937 to 1938 from two to six lanes in anticipation of the 1939–1940 New York World's Fair. More than 100 dwellings and businesses were destroyed in the process, especially near the former Bridge Street section. On the left is the RKO Keith's Flushing whose vibrant advertisement claims it as "The Finest Theatre on the North Shore." Today the ghost advertisement is still visible on the side of the now-abandoned building whose fate is currently being determined.

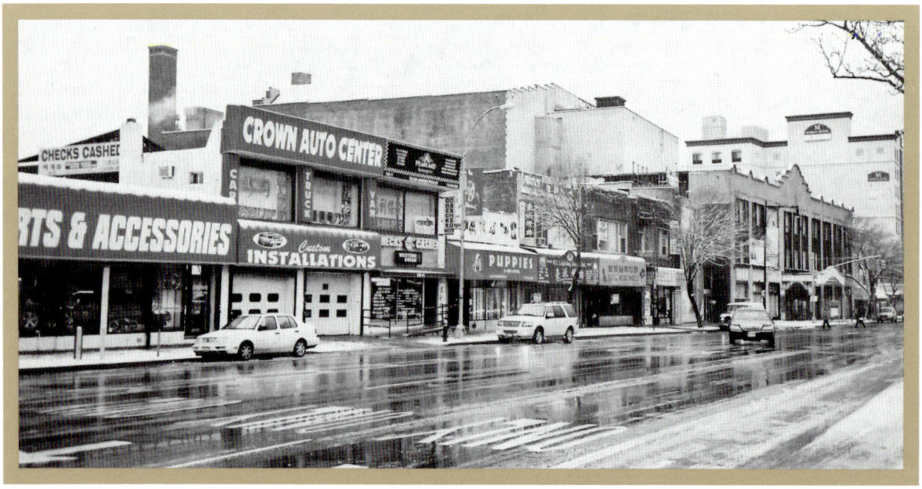

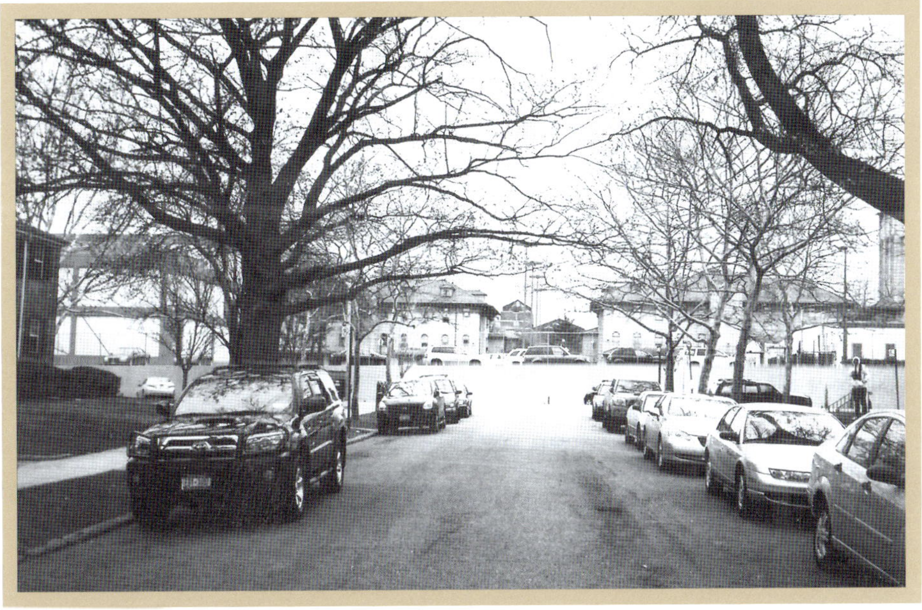

Queens College opened in October 1937. It was originally home to a school for delinquent boys. After it was closed, Mayor Fiorello LaGuardia decided to turn the campus into the first official college of the borough. Pictured here in 1947, the campus was constructed across from the Pomonok Golf Course and also among several farms such as this scallion farm. Six of the original Spanish-style buildings still stand. Jefferson Hall was constructed in 1900. The 77-acre campus is located at 65-30 Kissena Boulevard.

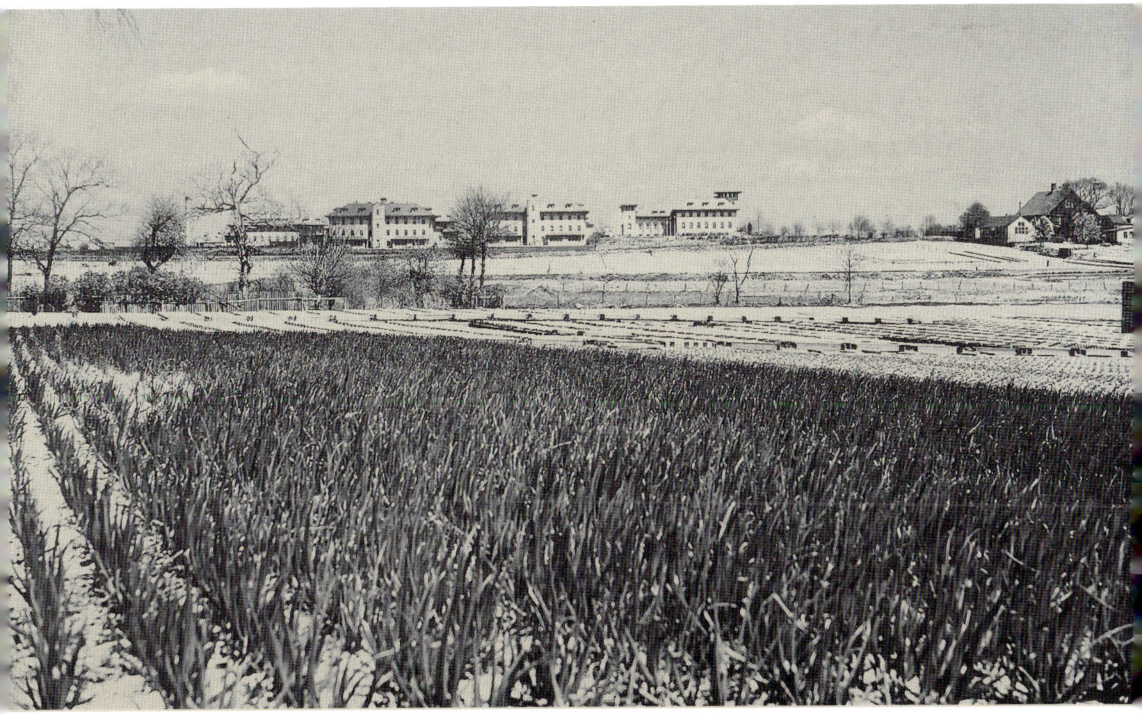

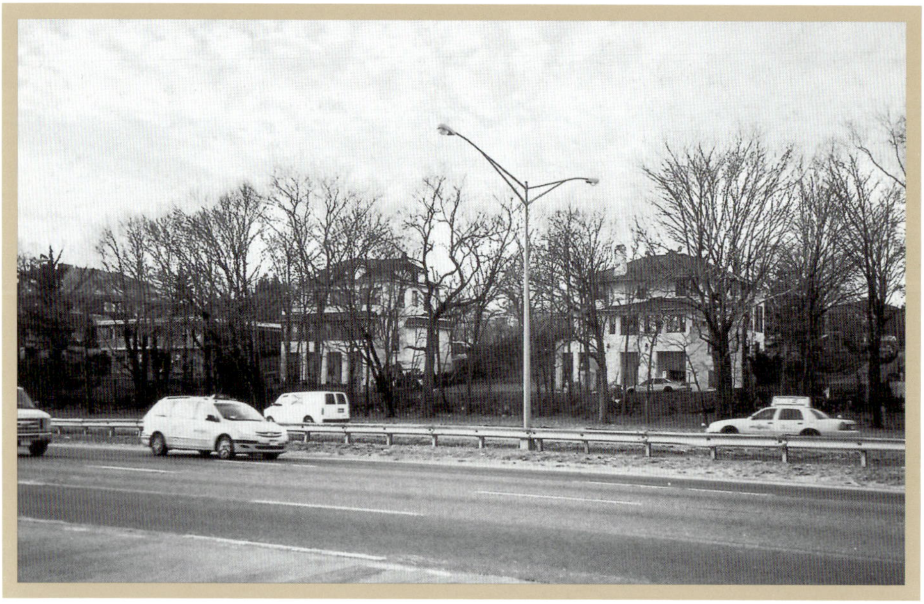

The modernization of Flushing and its environs is exemplified no more dramatically than in this panoramic view showing homes along the shoreline of Flushing Bay taken on May 1, 1934. Robert Moses originally considered condemning these homes along Ditmars Boulevard, but this proved too expensive. Moses found another solution. With help from the Public Works Administration, he brought in sand from Rockaway Beach to support the six-lane Grand Central Parkway. Today the steps behind these homes still descend to the private beach, which has long since gone.

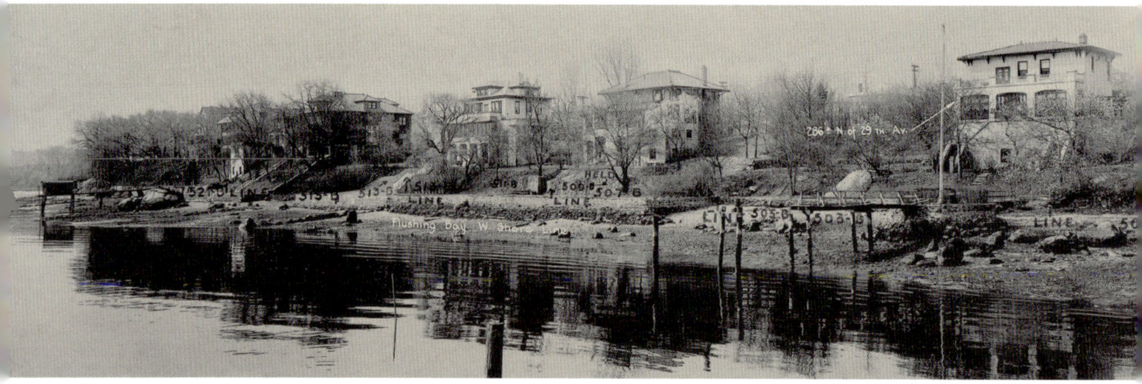

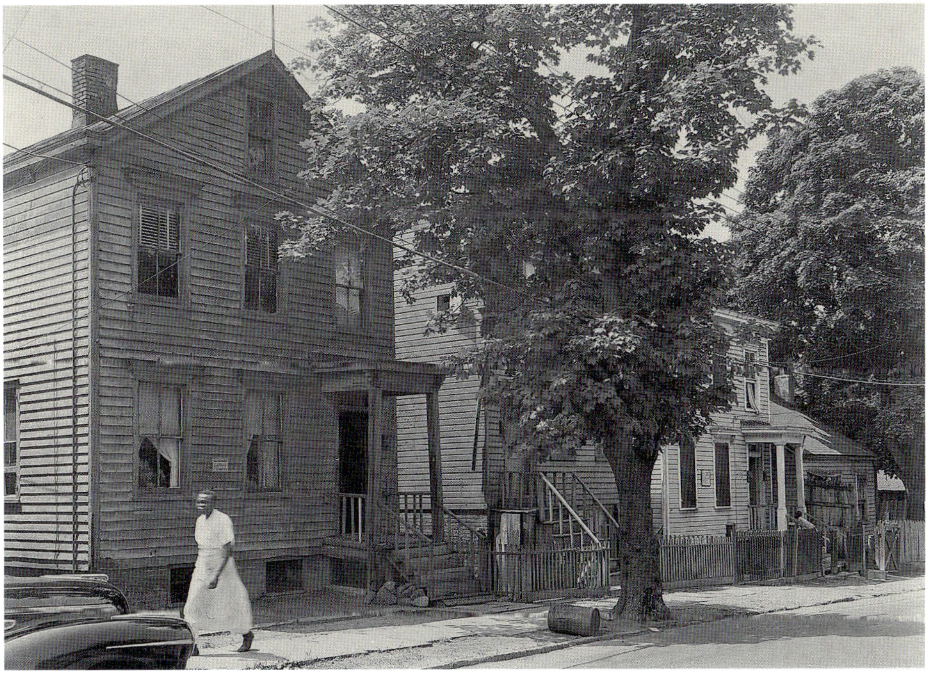

This view looks down Fortieth Road toward College Point Boulevard on June 25, 1948. These houses—located in a part of town nicknamed "Black Dublin" because of its heavy African and Irish American population—were soon cleared away to build the 6-acre James Allan Bland Houses. These were named after the African American composer who was born in Flushing on October 22, 1854. Called the "World's Greatest Minstrel Man," Bland composed classics such as "Carry Me Back to Old Virginia." (Courtesy of the LaGuardia and Wagner Archives.)

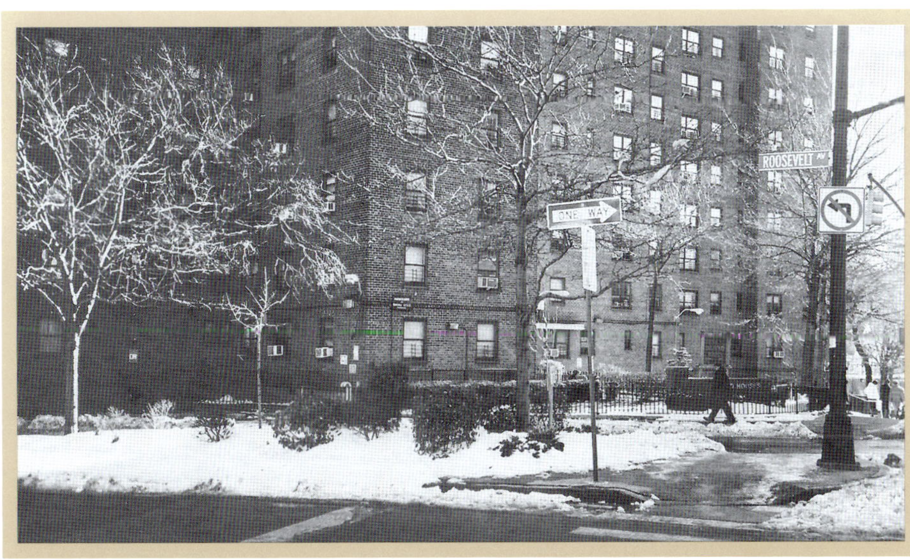

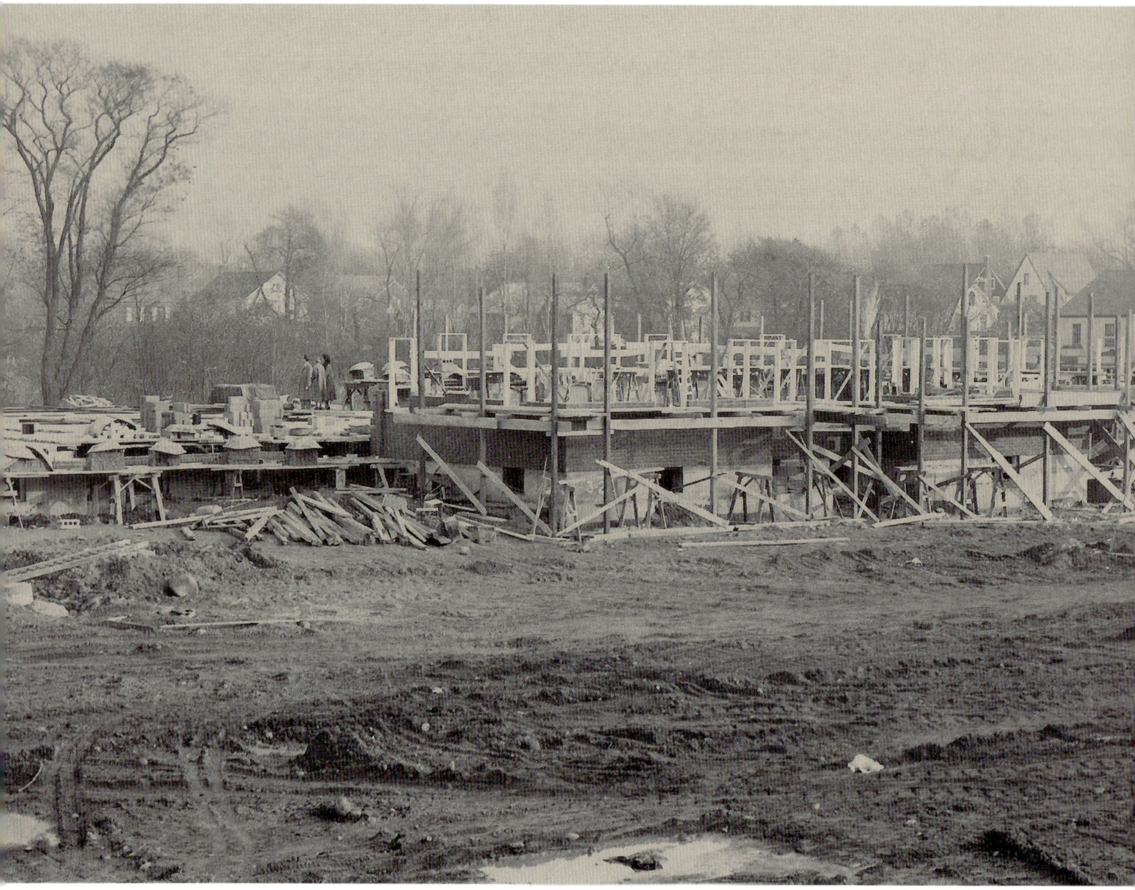

Mitchell-Linden Gardens was developed, just north of Flushing village, on an estate owned by Ernest Mitchell, which he called Linden Hill. Architects envisioned a cooperative project that would provide middle-income housing to veterans of World War II and Korea. Under Section 213 of the Federal Housing Act of 1950 and at a cost of $15 million, the project was enacted, providing homes for about 1,400 residents.

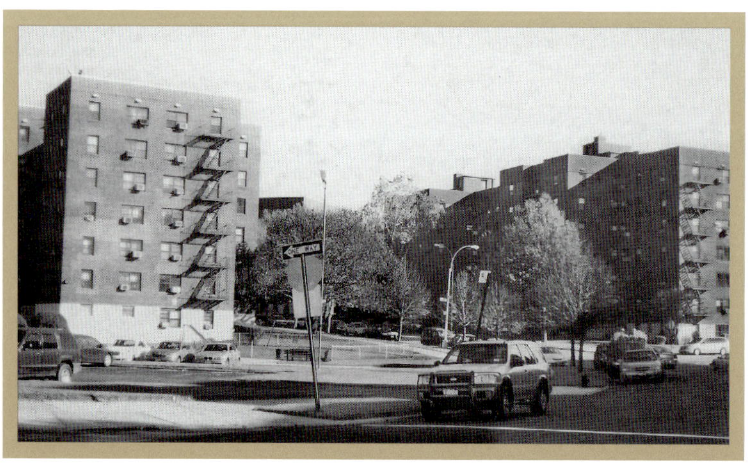

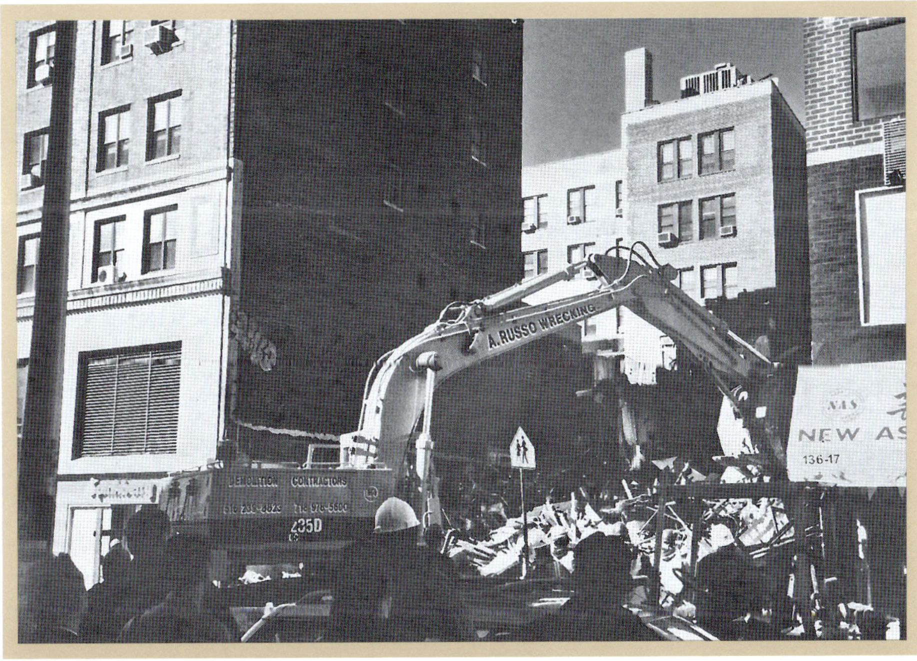

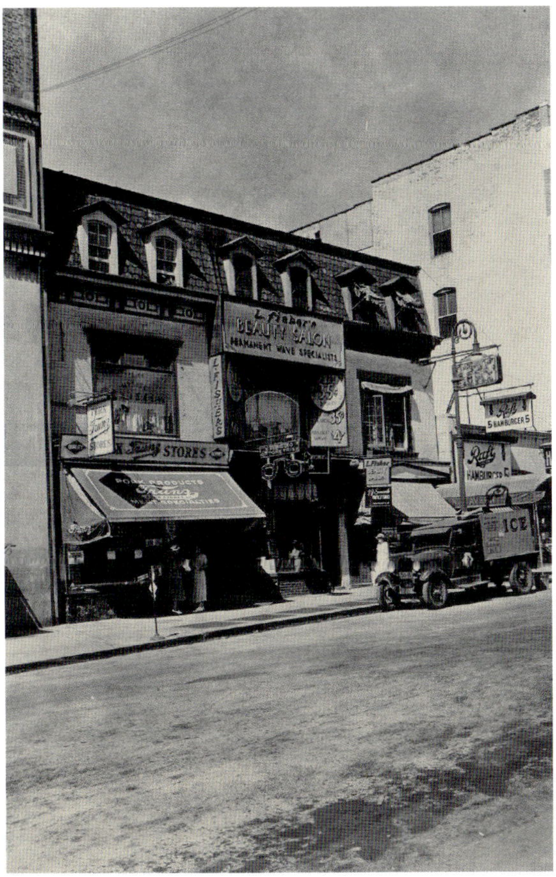

This three-story structure was located on the north side of Roosevelt Avenue just east of Main Street. It housed several businesses such as the Mystic Tea Room, L. Fisher's Beauty Salon, and Truns Pork Store. One-third of the structure was demolished in the 1930s. The remaining two-thirds lasted for decades as one of the only buildings original to the entire super block. It too was torn down in 2009. Another piece of history, gone from the Flushing that used to be. (Courtesy of the New York Public Library.)

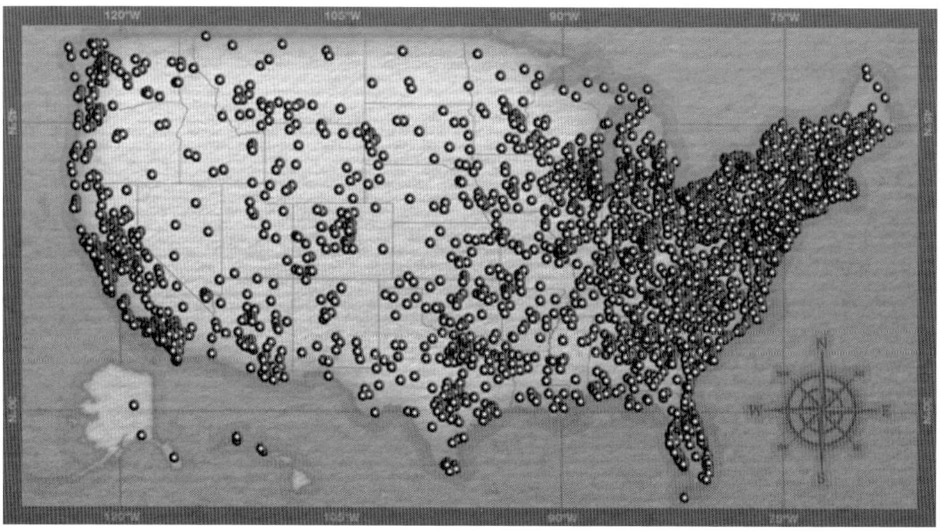